ISLAM AND GENDER JUSTICE

ISLAM AND GENDER JUSTICE
Questions at the Interface

V.A. Mohamad Ashrof

Publications
KALPAZ PUBLICATIONS
DELHI-110052

Islam and Gender Justice : Questions at the Interface

Rs. 875

ISBN: 81-7835-456-X

Published in 2005 in India by
Kalpaz Publications,
C-30, Satyawati Nagar, Delhi-110052
E-mail : Kalpaz@hotmail.com

Laser Typesetting at : Master Computers, Delhi
Printed at : Salasar Imaging System, Delhi

Contents

Foreword

Dr. Zeenat Shaukat Ali

The new book, "Islam and Gender Justice: Questions at the Interface" is a welcome edition to the existing literature on gender equations within the parameters of Islam. Mr. V.A. Mohamad Ashrof has made a serious attempt to reconstruct Islamic theology from an egalitarian perspective. It is particularly interesting since such diligence and pains have been made by the masculine to regard the feminine with equity and fairness.

The book boldly searches for an alternative interpretation, based on the concept of justice in Islam without evading important issues. It is a bold and serious attempt towards determining the status of woman in Islam in a bid to recapture the spirit of Qur'anic revelation. The arguments are systematically and cogently developed and there is a paradigm shift is from inherited frameworks. Pertinent Qur'anic verses and authentic Hadith relating to multi-dimensional issues on the subject of gender are analyzed hermeneutically as well as linguistically. The implications of the thesis are both interesting and impactful in contributing towards developing a theoretical basis for a Qur'anic theology on gender justice. It dispels much misunderstandings and stereotypes about the status of woman in Islam and the religion of Islam per se.

Earlier there have been men who have defended the rights of Muslim women. Some important names are Ahmad

Faris al-Shidyaq (1855); Rifa'ah Rafi al-Tahtawi (1801–1871); Muhammad 'Abduh (1849-1905), a founder of the Salafiyah (Islamic reforms) movement; Qasim Amin (1899) initiated much discussion; Lutfi al-Sayyid, publisher of Al-Jaridah, Turkish counterparts included Namik Kernal and Ahmed Mithat.

Among contemporary scholars Dr. Rafiq Zakaria is a distinguished, esteemed and well-known scholar. He has written several important books on Islam as well as those relating to national and international issues.

In almost all Muslim countries and communities there has been a history of resistance to the imposition of a uniform, identical authoritarian vision of society. Both women and men scholars have consistently challenged traditional patriarchal monopolies over the interpretation of Islam and questioned why the rights granted to women by the Qur'an, which is the epitome of human rights, have been diluted and watered down. Where democratic expression has been permitted to develop, the people in Muslim countries and communities have rejected the narrow understandings, while even in undemocratic countries women and progressive men have forced the opening of debate and had a measure of success in protecting the spaces for alternative voices.

A peaceful struggle or a jihad for gender equation is gradually emerging within the world of Islam. It seeks greater complementarity between the sexes, and is based on the Qur'an and authentic Hadith. It is a struggle for gender parity in Muslim society in the name of divine justice; it is a struggle to obfuscate a long standing gender rule that has paralyzed Muslim women, preventing them from being Muslim leaders in various fields of activities. In other words, a struggle for gender justice, which women scholars undertake and calls into question the very legitimacy of patriarchal leadership alienating women. In changing the paradigm of how we talk about gender in Islam, the contributions of these women and men to force a change in the way in which we speak about Islam and Islamic leadership in general is invaluable.

Some contemporary names are Amina Muhsin Wudud, Fatima Mernissi, Amira Sonbo, Riffat Hasan, Shatifa Al-Khateeb, Hibba Abugideiri, Dunya Maumoon, the late Annemarie Schimmel, Sachiko Murato among others.

In discussing gender relations within the parameters of Islam, it is necessary to understand that the issues raised by the modern concern with the politics of gender cannot be addressed through simple legalistic, sociological, western inspired objections. Such an approach is not sound since it speaks little of the deeper reasons for the Islamic gender-related worldview. The answer lies in the deeper intellectual cosmological traditions of Islam that have been concerned with exploring the masculine-feminine relations in its larger picture of the macrocosm (al-alam al kabir) and the microcosm (al-alam al saghir).

In other words, it is inquiries into some basic questions, which form fundamental concerns within the Islamic traditions. For instance, an investigation is required into questions such as: What is a human being? Once that is established, we can ask why there are two basic kinds of human being, male and female, and how the two interrelate. At this point, we have the right to ask if the mode of their interrelationship in any given situation is a correct one. And most importantly, we have to ask about the normative principles in terms of which we can judge the correctness of the relationship. (The Tao of Islam, Sachiko Murato Introduction, New York 1992).

With reference to such questions the Qur'an clearly states: "And of everything We created a pair" (51:49). Or again, "God Himself created the pair, male and female" (53:45). This goes on to show that all things in the universe are paired with other things. Several of the pairs mentioned in the Qur'an take on special importance as the fundamental principles of creation. These include the Pen (al-qalam) and the Tablet (al-lawh), which are specifically Islamic symbols as well as, and heaven and earth among others.

Careful reading of the Qur'an and the authentic Hadith demonstrate that Islam's basic view of masculine and feminine or man and women, postulate a complementarity of functions. Neither can be complete without the other. In Islamic cosmological thinking, the universe is perceived as an equilibrium built on harmonious relationships between the pairs that make up all things. The qualities of centrality, all comprehensiveness, vicegerency are inherent in both masculine and feminine. There is no established form of hierarchy. For instance, Adam was created without a father or a mother and Jesus—the spirit and word of God and one of the perfect human beings was created from Mary without an intermediary. This goes on to show how we understand relationships between the masculine and the feminine depend upon our perspectives and what we regard as our essence.

In reality, human beings are only two sides of a mirror therefore Islamic views on feminine can in no way be separated from Islamic views of the masculine. A well-known authentic Hadith speaks of women being the twin halves of men. It is a strange paradox that one has to distinguish between the Qur'anic worldview in relation to women with its ideals and the problems that arise from breaking those ideals. It is the spiritual intellectual approach within Islam that can re-establish its ideals.

Again, if the question was asked: What does gender signify in the worldview of Islam? How are male and female related to the structure of the natural world? What are the theological roots of gender distinctions? Does God have the attributes primarily of father, or mother, or both, or neither? (Murato, 1992)

The intellectual tradition answers that Allah has a 'Jalal' (Powerful side) and a 'Jamal' side (Compassionate and Gracious side) and these two together manifest in Him the

'Kamal' or perfection. How then can one deny that both the masculine and feminine sides in life be equally important, as without their co-operation no new life can exist on earth? "Not in vain did Rumi see mothers everywhere: Virtually everything in the cosmos is a mother giving birth to something higher than itself—whether it is the flint stone that gives birth to the spark, which in turn producers fire when it meets congenial matter, or the earth, that fertilized by the sky, produces plants as the result of *heiros gamos* the sacred marriage. Rumi even described women, in the first chapter of 'Mathnavi' as someone whom one would be tempted to call creator." (My soul is a Woman Annemarie Schimmel, New York 1990)

The word 'nafs' or soul in Arabic is feminine in gender and is a crucial and transcendent part in all humans. The poet al-Mutanabbi to honour the woman saint Rabia wrote the significant verse:

"If all women were like the one we have mentioned, then women would be preferred to men,

For the feminine gender is no shame for the sun nor is the masculine gender an honour for the crescent moon!"

Again it is interesting to note in relation to the feminine that the word womb is a branch (shajara) of the All-merciful. The Arabic word for womb (rahim) derives from the same root as the words mercy (rahma) and All-merciful (rahman). The mother's womb is the locus of God's life-giving mercy. Ibn al-Arabi sees one of the meanings of the hadith in the relationship between man and woman, since, the womb is a related term of the All-merciful.

Shifting the dimension to the intellectual approach leaves little room for misogynistic readings where one recognizes with little surprise the active roles of the feminine in all kinds of activities, be it political activism, economic empowerment, scientific endeavour or spirituality.

Therefore, we find that early Islamic history is filled with women who undertook various forms of political activism. The first martyr in Islam was a woman, Sumaya Zawgat Yasir. Sumaya was tortured and killed in the early period of Islam because of her belief in Prophet Muhammad and the message he brought.

A woman who also received praise from the Prophet was a woman traveller. Asma bint Umais travelled by sea and immigrated to Abyssinia when the Muslims were being persecuted in Makkah. It is significant to note in that Asma bint Umais and her travels in search of religious freedom appeared to be common knowledge and was noteworthy enough to receive praise from the Prophet. (Abdelhalim abu Shaqa, Emancipation of Women at the Time of the Prophet, 1990, Vol. 2 p. 37 (citing Bukhari 13:245 and Muslim, The Book of Pilgrimage, 4:101)).

Women like men fought in battles to defend Islam. Umm Imara defended the Prophet during the Battle of Uhud after the Muslim suffered losses. Umar ibn al-Khattab said "I heard the Prophet (PBUH) saying 'On the day of Uhud, I never looked right or left without seeing Umm Imara fighting to defend me." (Abdelhalim abu Shaqa, Emancipation of Women at the Time of the Prophet, 1990, Vol. 2 p. 53 (citing Ibn Sad, Tabaqat).

Another famous female warrior was Nasiba bint Kaab who fought with the Prophet in the Battle of Uhud (625 A.D./ 3 A.H.) and later on with Caliph Abu Bakr in the Ridda war (632 A.D./10 A.H.). She was known as such a courageous and dedicated warrior that Abu Bakr himself attended her reception upon her return to Medina. (M.H. Sherif, The Muslim Women Between the Truth of Sharia and the Fallacy of Falsification, Dar al-Marifa al-Jamiyiya, 1987, p. 78 (citing Ibn Sad, Tabakat 4:302-304).

Umm Salama, wife of the Prophet, was instrumental in advising the Prophet during the crisis at Hudaybiya in 628 A.D. (6 A.H.). Her advice prevented disunity among the Muslims after the Treaty of Hudaybiya and her opinion prevailed over that of many men, including Umar ibn al-

Khattab. (Muhammad al-Ghazali, Fiqh al-Sira, Alim al-Marifa, p. 363).

Umm Salama was also an inquisitive student of Islam. She asked the Prophet why only men were mentioned in the Quran and in response God revealed the following verse: "Verily, for all men and women who have surrendered themselves unto God, and all believing men and believing women, and all truly devout men and truly devout women, and all men and women who are true to their word, and all men and women who are patient in adversity, and all men and women who humble themselves before God, and all men and women who give charity, and all self-denying men and self-denying women, and all men and women who are mindful of their chastity, and all men and women who remember God unceasingly: for all of them has God readied forgiveness of sins and a mighty reward." (Quran 33:35). (Fatima Mernissi, The Veil and the Male Elite, Addison-Wesley Publishing Co., 1987, p. 118 (citing al-Tabari, Tafsir, Vol. 22, p. 10).

Umm Hani bint Abi Talib offered refuge to two non-Muslim men who sought protection after the opening of Mecca. After she offered them refuge she went to the Prophet and told him what she had done. He said to her, "We offer refuge to whomever you offered and we guarantee their safety". Thus, in essence, Umm Hani bint Abi Talib performed a significant political function, one often reserved only for the ruler, when she granted political asylum to these men. (M.H. Sherif, The Muslim Women Between the Truth of Sharia and the Fallacy of Falsification, Dar al-Marifa al-Jamiyiya, 1987, p. 71-72. (citing Sirat Ibn Hisham, 4:39-40).

Hazrat Aisha, wife of Prophet Muhammad, was a also politically active and influential leader. In the year 658 A.D. (36 A.H.) she played a major role in the armed resistance against Hazrat Imam Ali, the fourth successor after the passing away of Prophet Muhammad. Hazrat Aisha was the only woman on the battlefield, and led thousands of men into the Battle of the Camel or Jaml. (Fatima Mernissi, The Forgotten Queens of Islam, University of Minnesota Press, 1993, p. 66).

In addition, all the previous biographies of distinguished women, especially in the Prophet's household, show that women behaved autonomously in early Islam. The women about whom most data are available are Hazrat Khadijah, the Prophet's first wife, Fatimah, his youngest daughter; Zaynab his granddaughter; Sukaynah, his great-granddaughter; and 'A'ishah bint Talhah. Several ladies–artists, poets, cultural patrons, soldiers often challenged the wisdom of men, insisted upon equality with their husbands, and took initiatives sometimes directly counter to patriarchal authority.

One could go on and enumerate the women who played great roles both in the history and mystical thought and practice of Islam as is evident from biographies. Most of the spiritual leaders received their first religious inspiration from their pious mothers for did not the Prophet not state that "Paradise lies at the feet of the mothers"? The question to be asked is why is the feminine side to Islamic life is usually overlooked?

Unfortunately the role of the feminine has been discussed in the inherited perspective. The remark of the German Indologist, Moriz Winternitz, "that women have always been the best friend of religion, but religion generally has not been a friend of women" is frequently quoted when it comes to the study of women's position in Islam. Unfortunately critics look at the surface without making an effort towards making a deeper study. They judge the status of women from the misunderstood and misrepresented concept of polygyny, divorce, or seclusion of women from public life among other aspects.

Medieval Western comments, according to which women have little status and few rights in Islam, are constantly explored and exploited by some Orientalist scholars and even more by the general public. Very few scholars have tried to look deeper and investigate to discover structures that would surprise those who have been brought up with the negative attitude towards Islam. It must be submitted that some such views, to an extent have unfortunately been augmented by the Islamic world supporting the convictions of the critics and the impression that women, in a militant, fundamentalist society where terrorism emanates, are an oppressed group without any rights, not able to voice their opinions or to have a say in their own religious affairs.

On the other hand many Islamic movements in the modern world seem unwilling or unable to grasp or explore the nuanced appreciation of masculine and feminine provided by the intellectual tradition.

"Presently in human society, negative femininity and negative masculinity dominate the scene. And this is nothing new, since these negative gender traits mark the fundamental tendency of human beings since the time of Adam. That, at least, is the Islamic view. It explains why God has had to send "124,000 prophets" to human beings. People constantly surrender to their lower appetites and passively fall back into forgetfulness (ghafla) and ignorance. Then they make use of their controlling power as vicegerents, to shape the world in terms of their own egos. History is the story of the descent into negative masculinity and negative femininity" (Murato, Postscript, 1992).

The entire gambit of issues relating to the masculine and feminine including those that rule their persons and lives like economic empowerment, legal empowerment, spiritual empowerment have to be reconstructed in the egalitarian spirit of the Qur'an and to create an intrinsically a holographic interpretation where the masculine and feminine can be characterized by interconnectedness, harmony and justice. "And among His Signs is this that He

---

(Dr. Zeenat Shaukat Ali, Professor, Islamic Studies, St. Xaviers College, Mumbai).

created for you mates from among yourselves, that you may dwell in tranquility with them and He has put love and mercy between your hearts." (30:21)

Mr. V.A. Mohamad Ashrof has examined several important issues in his book. There are many interesting chapters in his book. For instance "Was Eve Created from the Rib of Adam?"; "Gender Equity does not Mean Negation of Gender Difference"; "Is God a Male?"; "Who is an Ideal Muslim Woman?"; Beyond the Patriarchal Interpretation". I commend the book of "Islam and Gender Justice: Questions At the Interface" whole-heartedly to readers has it will draw them closer to the primary sources of Islam, the Qur'an and authentic Hadith.

Preface

Muslims today number over a billion people and live in varying conditions of political, social, and cultural situations. It is therefore reasonable to assume that Muslim women will have different types of concerns depending on where they live and in what conditions. At the same time, however, it is agonizingly clear that in spite of the diversity of Muslim cultures and societies, women have to endure similar forms of gender inequality and bias. These range from cultural and psychological attitudes that ignore chauvinism or violence towards women, to laws that refuse to recognize them as legal and moral agents at par with men, to the restriction or denial of political-economic rights and resources to them relative to men. What is more, inequity, and even oppression, is often justified by recourse to sacred knowledge or, more accurately, knowledge claiming to be derived from religion, including Islamic Scripture, the Qur'an.

The general conception is that though in a number of its verses the Qur'an sanctions and provides for the spiritual, perhaps even for the moral, equality of men and women, in its social conceptualizations and cultural constructions of men and women, the Qur'an is predominantly, indeed all too authoritatively, patriarchal and hierarchical between the sexes and clearly introduces and lays down inequalities between the male and female that calculatedly, systematically, and effectively make men and women in Islam unequal in their social (familial), economic, political, psychological, and cultural lives. Some feminists argue that the problem lies in the nature of religion itself, especially in the worship of God as against goddesses. They make this claim on the ground that societies that worshipped goddess cults were egalitarian. Truthfully, however, such societies were also misogynistic and men, not women, were the real locus of power in them. Consider the ancient Greeks who, in spite of strong female goddesses in their pantheon, believed that women were just lesser men who lacked the ability to reason. On this basis, they excluded women from public and political life and the rights extended to men. For those committed to progressive values it has also come to mean a principle of holism that permeates all of creation and a struggle to repair the wholeness of creation destroyed by racism, environmental mismanagement, economic exploitation and sexism. A belief in the unity of God can only become meaningful if we display a concern for the way in which manifestations of it are being damaged. Sexism and the discrimination against women fly in the face of the holism of *Tawhid*, which is in direct contrast to the misogynist worldview where man replaces God for a woman and where a male-female relationship is expected to mirror that between males and God. Unfortunately, sexual discrimination, inequity and oppression have been, and remain, universal although they do take different forms in different societies at different moments in history. Therefore, the problem does not lie with religion, but with how we choose to interpret it. Every religion is open to both oppressive and liberatory, reactionary or progressive interpretations; therefore, if only repressive readings become predominant in a given society, we need to question why. Liberation for a woman does not mean being like a male, or taking up male tasks, but rather being herself and fulfilling the destiny God created for her. It is no use simply proclaiming that Islam provides adequate rights to women and does not do anything to stop the flagrant violation of women's rights in the name of Islam. It is time to look to the woman as an equal human being, not just as a bearer and raiser of children, a cook, a home-cleaner, or a dishes and dirty-laundry washer etc.

According to psychologists, deep stereotypes take longer to disappear than superficial ones, because they are based on gut instinct and unexamined emotional reactions. For this reason, the West has clung to stereotypes long associated with Islam. As descendants of the philosophers of the Age of Reason, we should know each other better. But religion based hostilities have always had great vitality, just like traditional attitudes toward the role of women. Under Qur'anic law a woman has legal status as a person and can perform religious duties similar to those of a man. She has the right to preach, to accept or refuse a marriage offer, to administer economic enterprises and, most importantly, to inherit property. Economic rights like inheritance were not granted to women in England until the Married Women's Property Act in the mid-19th century. In Europe, it was not until the turn of the century (13 centuries later) that French women became legally able to sell property without the permission of their husbands. In many nations, sons would inherit the name; wealth and position of the family and daughters could only hope to marry rich persons. In many western or eastern countries, women could not choose their husbands, and, widows were expected to mourn for their husbands until the end of their lives (still practiced in some countries). Until 1970, in some states in America, daughters still did not automatically inherit, particularly if valuable assets like farmland were at stake. Unless the father specifically designated his daughter as heir, and if there were no brothers, the land passed to the nearest male relative. Muslim women have had better rights since 632 C.E. Even after the British Parliament approved the first Married Women's Property Act in 1882, women continued to be denied property in their own right, independent of their husband's-a right that was granted to Muslim women in the 7th century, in the time of the Prophet Muhammad. The Prophet, recognizing that women were deprived of their rights (such as the right to property and the power to dissolve the marriage through *Khula'*-that is, by giving up some of her property to her husband) had completed the women's revolution in the 7th century.

The family life and raising children require the joint-effort of both man and woman. Since the woman has her rights and obligations in obtaining education according to the guidance of Islam, it is good for her personality and for the society, just as it may be good for the family itself to support the woman's right to work, and as long as this right is beneficial for all parties, it should be secured. According to many Muslim theologians, women have the right to education, to religious instruction, to honor and respect, to vote, and to employment. They claim that there are, however, restrictions imposed by the religion for the welfare and stability of society as a whole. To them a woman can be neither a political leader nor a judge; she must strive her best to limit her arena, and her 'natural' and 'sacred task' is to keep the household smoothly functioning and to raise and instruct her children to be good Muslims. Consequently, they continue, men, for their part, must shoulder the burden of providing for the family in material ways. However, as the process of modernization spreads around the world, Muslim women have asked various unpopular questions concerning the interaction between Islam and women's rights. The result has been the construction of various feminist traditions within the Muslim world. Muslim feminists derive their mandate not from the Qur'an but from the conviction that Islam is a patriarchal and misogynist religion that "professes models of hierarchical relationships and sexual inequality and puts a sacred stamp onto female subservience."[1] These are the words of the noted Moroccan feminist and sociologist, Fatima Mernissi. She denies that Islam is compatible with democracy and human rights. According to her, integrating the advantages of pre-Islamic polytheism as well as those of the Western civilization should reform Islam. Muslim feminists almost universally consider Islam oppressive because they view God "Himself" as being misogynistic. This is mainly because Muslim feminists consistently confuse the

Qur'an with its patriarchal, misreading. Those who read Islam as a misogynistic religion confuse the Qur'an with a specific reading of it, ignoring that all texts, including the Qur'an; can be read in multiple modes, including egalitarian ones. Moreover, patriarchal readings of Islam collapse the Qur'an with its exegesis. Thus, Islam and Muslims are confused on the one hand, and texts, cultures, and histories are collapsed on the other. Muslim / Islamic feminist's purpose is to critique the methods by which Muslims generate patriarchal readings of the Qur'an and to recover the egalitarian aspects of Qur'anic epistemology.

If people constantly were confronted with only one type of reading of sacred texts (or, of history or any other subject), they would find it hard to imagine alternatives. It would be hypocritical to deny that the Qur'an and other Islamic sources offer possibilities of alternative interpretation. Clearly, the contemporary puritans exploit these possibilities. But the text does not command such restrictive and intolerant readings. Historically, Islamic civilization has displayed a remarkable ability to recognize possibilities of tolerance, and to act upon these possibilities. Islamic civilization produced a moral and humanistic tradition that preserved Greek philosophy, and generated much science, art, and socially benevolent thought. Unfortunately, however, the modern puritans are scattering and wasting this inspiring moral tradition. They are increasingly shutting off the possibilities for a tolerant interpretation of the Islamic tradition. There is a verse in the Qur'an that counsels, exhorts, and admonishes Muslims that God changes the conditions only of those who endeavor to change their own condition (13:11), just as it teaches that moral individuality and agency lie in using intelligence ('aql') and Knowledge ('ilm'), to understand and practice religion (20:114, 7:171). Armed with this certainty, we should be unafraid of any challenges; but the burden is upon human beings to make the right decisions and the right choices.

The revelation of the Qur'an established women's equal status and equal rights (30:33). The Prophet treated women as equals and was very responsive to their thoughts and needs. However, there was a tendency toward "ignorance" in the society where Islam was revealed, and it crept back in after the Prophet's death and brought back some of the negative things that Islam had reformed, including misogyny. Eventually the misogynist attitude left over from "ignorance" gained a foothold in Islamic law and took away some of women's rights and lowered their status. The conservatives positioned the text mono-interpretatively; and it is interpreted once forever. The meaning of text to them is identical and permanent with text. Yet, text is a cultural product; God's word recorded in the form of a text, produced by the reasons and events called as 'asbâbun nuzûl'. One of the prominent qualities of the Qur'an is that its laws and decrees take a generalized form, which must be necessarily subjected to interpretation before they could be implemented. This in effect displays the considerable degree of flexibility and universality of the Religion. The Qur'an therefore becomes a dynamic progenitor moving ahead of time and society. The interpreter or Jurist must nevertheless be a "trustee of God" (2:30), who can maintain the norms of justice and truth while considering the conditions of time and place in his rulings. In fact, the concept of the "trustee of God" alludes to the fact that a certain level of moral and spiritual justification and affluence is necessary, to ensure that the interpreter is not, like others, at the service of his/her egocentric needs and desires but envisages the world at a more elevated level of contemplation. The Jurist therefore becomes entrusted with the responsibility of safeguarding the integrity of the Religion and ensuring its wholesome application in a manner, which would guarantee the advancement and betterment of that society. This responsibility becomes particularly demanding when we consider the endless interaction of customs, tradition and thought with religion; infiltrating its ranks during centuries of turbulent social and political developments.

One major problem, related to orthodox interpretation, is the incapability of contemporary Muslim 'ulema' to relate Islam with universal humanitarian issues like poverty, discrimination, exploitation, marginalization, corruption etc. Yet one important the *raison d'etre* of the emergence of the Prophethood of Muhammad is mankind's liberation from all types of exploitation (7:157). His concept of 'Tawhid' (the Oneness of God) always related to the social transformation of the exploitative order towards a fairer one. When Islam is not related to this crucial idea of social transformation, it is tantamount to a betrayal of the spirit of its own mission. Needless to say, the Muslim world is far from emerging out of the patriarchal values and the traditional 'ulema' are immersed neck-deep in these values. Any deviation from them is denounced as unpardonable heresy. As in other monotheistic religions, the classical 'fiqh' texts-that is, texts of early Islamic legal jurisprudence-ignored gender equality as it was presented in the Qur'an and introduced interpretations in line with the patriarchal social order. Thus, one can find several logical contradictions in the classical 'fiqh' texts since they reflect two dissenting voices: an egalitarian voice inspired by the revelation ('wahy'), and a patriarchal voice incorporating the social order and social, cultural and political pragmatisms of the time and place where Islam was trying to ensure its survival. An analysis of discourses based on the Qur'an and the early literature of Islamic legal jurisprudence leads to contradictory conclusions about the construction of women's sexuality in Islam. The Prophet instructed that women have the right to own property, to choose their own partners, and have equal rights to education. In accordance with prevailing culture, however, these rights became metamorphosed into the duties of women to take care of children and remain in the house.

Every expression of the law must be subject to the requirements of justice and compassion. Because the law, wherever it is originated from, is always approached and interpreted by historical human beings, it must be interpreted in terms of the ever approximating and developing notions of justice and compassion, the pivotal values that makes them truly Islamic (Qur'an 5:8, 4:135). Some flawed traditions, along with mistranslations, ingrained patriarchy into Qur'anic interpretation, in spite of obvious Qur'anic injunctions to the contrary are some of the major reasons of continuing patriarchy in the Muslim world. Patriarchal structures of Arab culture, in the form of loosely camouflaged traditions ascribed to the Prophet, left woman intellectually crippled, while the male jurists prepared the text of the laws for her sinister dominion by male members of the society.

Muslim misogynists often seek refuge in the concept of the dignity of women as means to support an ideology that regards women as minors who have to be eternally protected from themselves and from the naturally predatory behavior of males. The divergences between theoretical statements about the rights and status of women in Islam and the actual implementation or application of these rights within the present-day state policies, in the legal arena, by providing opportunities for education or work, etc.-are to be specifically addressed. I am not seeking a woman-centered hermeneutics or a repudiation of a 14 century-long tradition; rather my aim is just to point out some obvious historical biases and imbalances. In trying to be reformist or critical, one has to avoid the Orientalist tone and standpoint that historically represented Muslim woman as across the board the eternally downtrodden oppressed female, her inferior position taken as a symbol for an inferior culture and religion.

There is a "striking difference between what can be safely inferred from the Qur'an itself and what has frequently been read into it."[2] Religious texts don't interpret themselves, people do and people don't read and interpret texts in an epistemological or methodological vacuum. They always bring their own insights and knowledge and biases into the interpretive process. We should therefore be able to question both the meanings generated from the Qur'an as well as the methods used to generate those meanings instead of treating the method itself as sacred and indisputable. Ultimately, the Qur'an, or any other Holy text, speaks through its reader. This ability of human beings to interpret texts is both a blessing as well as a burden. It is a blessing because it provides us with the flexibility to adapt texts to changing circumstances. It is a burden because the reader must take responsibility for the normative values he or she brings to the text. And those possibilities are exploited, developed and ultimately determined by the reader's efforts-good faith efforts, we hope-at making sense of the text's complexities. Consequently, the meaning of the text is often only as moral as its reader. If the reader is intolerant, hateful, or oppressive, so will be the interpretation of the text.

As a practicing Muslim I firmly believe that Islam will last till the Day of Judgment, which means that it must always address itself to changing social realities. A static vision of Islam will fail to reflect the mercy, what is in Arabic called the 'rahma', of God. Now, that is the sort of Islam that is unfortunately so deep-rooted in most of our societies. Many Muslims are so obsessed with the finer points of 'fiqh', about the details of rituals about washing and veiling, as if this is what Islam is all about, that they forget that the oppression of women is itself a gross affront to God's mercy. Progressive Muslims have long argued that it is not the religion but patriarchal interpretation and implementation of the Qur'an that have kept women oppressed. For them, the way to reform is the reexamination and reinterpretation of religious texts. Qur'anic verses have been used to limit women's public and private role, even to justify violence toward Muslim women, even though their original meaning and context defy such interpretations. Shari'ah, which represents the moral and ethical values of Islam, from which Islamic law can be distilled, is aimed at establishing a just society. But how can Islam be credible as a force for social justice, how can it proclaim itself as egalitarian, when Islamic law has come to enshrine gender injustice, which explicitly denies women real, and tangible equality. How do we explain this seeming contradiction at the heart of Islam? Is this a reflection of divine will? Or could it be that masculinist ideology with its own interpretive tilt has become institutionalized into the very heart of Islam and has found ways to subvert divine will, with its core message of justice, equality and compassion?

What is commonly paraded in the Muslim world, as "Islam" is sometimes only the pre-Islamic ignorance and culture that enabled men to justify the burying of girls alive. The Qur'an not only prohibits the action of physically burying them alive, but also dispels the myths that demonize and vilify the female gender so that burying girls alive seems a reasonable thing to do. The people of Arabia buried them because they believed that women are promiscuous and that this promiscuity would bring shame to the family. This practice was prohibited during the lifetime of the Prophet, yet the Arabs later resumed killing women as "honor killing." Today in "honor killings", physical abuse and psychological torture we also see other forms of "killing" women in more subtle, culturally accepted and 'legal' ways. The objective in every case is to prevent society from being affected by the feminine qualities of womanhood, cast as evil by Arabs in much the same way and perhaps for the same reasons as the Christians and Jews blamed women for the sin of Adam, thereby condemning woman to a history of shame and humiliation as punishment for the sin that God forgave. It does not make you a "radical feminist" to decry honor killings and volunteer for peaceful campaigns to educate and change laws. Raising your voice against Female Genital Mutilation does not mean you want to "undermine Islam." To the contrary, working against these injustices in the way of Allah is a manifestation of the desire to uplift Islam and the Muslim people. The Qur'an informs us that both Adam and his spouse disobeyed God, and that both shared the penalty and the mercy of God, through which they both found forgiveness. Despite this, Arab societies and many that have been "Arabicized" have perpetuated the ignorance and woman-hatred of pre-Islamic Arabia by various means, including the denial of women's right to share in the establishment and development of Muslim society. Other ways have included denying women equivalent opportunities in education, biased opportunities in the workplace, and reasonable and religiously permissible access to other human beings and other resources. Denying Muslim women political participation (such as in Saudi Arabia and Kuwait) will ultimately result in the further erosion of various freedoms, and the right of political participation for both men and women in the Muslim world. It will enable the "culture" of the masses to dictate the objectives of Muslim government and the rights of the people by opinion rather than Islamic law, and will reduce Islam in Muslim society from an authoritative resource to a relic of the past.

It is clear that cultural practices run deep and mould individuals and societies. One cannot really understand the impact Islam had on the Arabs without first understanding their pre-Islamic customs. The Qur'an is in the language of those receiving the message, both literally in Arabic, and figuratively, in the cultural "language" that one behaves through. That may account for the reason why some may argue that certain sexist attitudes are encouraged in the Qur'an; yet in a deeper, more holistic reading, one that considers and respects the historical context, it encourages a liberating equality of women. In religious patriarchies, the ideological source of women's oppression are misogynistic and patriarchal interpretations of sacred texts which allege that God has established men as rulers over women. In secular patriarchies knowledge of disciplines like biology and psychology have been used to argue that men and women are not just biologically different, but also unequal. A close look at the Qur'anic text reveals that all these beliefs about women being half of men are not Islamic. These are a result of Arab traditions prevalent at the time of the advent of Islam somehow fusing into the teachings of Qur'an. Because interpreting the text has remained an exclusively male domain, it is highly likely that early Islam interpreters saw all these questions in the light of an Arab culture, which were tilted heavily against women.

We need to recognize that the problem lies not in Divine Speech but in our failure to read it in a just and ethical manner. The crisis today is not of Islam, as enemies pronounce it to be; rather, it is a crisis of Muslims who have thwarted Islam's democratic promise and its inherently just and egalitarian worldview because of what they have wrought with their own hands and minds. Since the problem is of our own making, we must also be the ones to unmake it. Muslims must realize that women's experiences are part of what it means to be human. Throughout Muslim history, however, men have dominated the construction of Islamic thought yielding certain perspectives on the notion of the divine. It is manifestly apparent that the results of male domination over the very meanings of God and text have been a major determinant of women's inferior status within Muslim histories and cultures. Women have been silenced, shunned, mutilated, and even killed in following these primarily androcentric interpretations and applications.

Interpreters are people who carry the inescapable baggage and cordiality of the human condition. Indeed, each and every generation of Muslims since the time of Prophet Muhammad, carrying its peculiar synthesis of the human condition, has produced its own commentaries of the Qur'an. The present generation of Muslims, like the many preceding ones, faces the option of reproducing meaning intended for earlier generations or of critically and selectively appropriating traditional understandings to re-interpret the Qur'an as a part of the task of reconstructing society. The Qur'an does not prescribe one timeless and unchanging social structure for men and women, affirming that the Scripture holds greater possibilities for guiding human society to a more fulfilling and productive mutual collaboration between men and women than as yet attained by Muslims or non-Muslims. The challenge for every generation of believers is to discover their own moment of revelation and their own being guided by the principle of progressive revelation.

Every human individual, female or male, Muslim or non-Muslim, rich or poor, northerner or southerner, has exactly the same intrinsic worth. The essential value of human life is God-given, and is in no way connected to culture, geography, or privilege. The true measure of a human being's worth is a person's character. All members of the human race have this same intrinsic worth because each of us has the breath of God breathed into our being: 'wa nafakhtu fihi minruhi' (see Qur'an 15:29 and 38:72). I feels that the concerns of the privileged or the dominant classes are not the primary subject of Islam; its focus is on those who have become "objects of exploitation by governments, socio-economic institutions and unequal relationships", in the words of the Qur'an; those who had been marginalized (11:27, 26:70, 22:5) or downtrodden in the earth ('mustad'afun fi'l-ard' as mentioned in 4:97, and 8:26). The declaration describes the 'downtrodden in the earth' as those individuals and groups who, for no willful reason of their own, find themselves pushed to the edges of society to live in conditions of social, political and economic oppression. My work, basically, is also motivated by the Qur'anic call for serving as 'witnesses for God in justice' (42:15). In our 'jihad' (striving) to end oppression, we must be mindful of the Islamic teachings of mutual cooperation and respect of the two genders. The Qur'an states: 'And [as for] the believers, both men and women, they are protectors of one another: they [all] enjoin the doing of what is right and forbid the doing of what is wrong, and are constant in prayer, and render the purifying dues, and pay heed unto God and the Apostle. It is they upon whom God will bestow grace: verily, God is almighty, wise' (9:71). It further proclaims: "O you who believe, stand firmly for justice, as witnesses for God, even if it means testifying against yourselves, or your parents, or you kin, and whether it is against the rich or poor, for God prevails upon all. Follow not the lusts of your hearts, lest you swerve, and if you distort justice or decline to do justice, verily God knows what you do" (5:8). Women in the West remain sex objects as much as ever, as every beauty contest will demonstrate. Conservative Muslims usually accuse the West for the spreading of the highly distorted impression of woman in Islam without introspectively analyzing their own stand on critical ontological issues. Of course, the anti-Muslim hate-mongers of the West might have their own biases and agendas in misrepresenting the status of woman in Islam. However, this doesn't justify their own internal inconsistencies and contradictions related to gender questions. The idea that Muslims must stand up for justice even against their own self-interests is predicated on the notion that human beings are capable of achieving a high level of moral agency. As agents, Muslims are expected to achieve a level of moral conscientiousness, which they will bring to their relationship with God. In regards to every ethical obligation, the Qur'anic text assumes that readers will bring a pre-existing, innate moral sense to the text. Hence, the text will morally enrich the reader, but only if the reader will morally enrich the text. The meaning of the religious text is not fixed simply by the literal meaning of its words, but depends, too, on the moral construction given to it by the reader. So if the reader approaches the text without moral commitments, it will almost inevitably yield nothing but discrete, legalistic, technical insights.

In his 1928 lectures on Islamic thought, delivered at the University of Madras in India and subsequently published under the title of 'The Reconstruction of Religious Thought in Islam', Muhammad Iqbal (1876-1938) lamented the closure of the door of Ijtihad, because for him it was precisely "the principle of movement in the structure of Islam," which is also the title of what I think is the most important chapter in his book. Iqbal wrote: 'What then is the principle of movement in the structure of Islam? This is known as 'Ijtihad'. The word literally means to exert with a view to form an individual judgment on a legal question. The idea, I believe, has its origin in a well-known verse of the Qur'an-'And to those who exert we show our path'. We find it more definitely adumbrated in a tradition of the Holy Prophet. When Ma'ad was appointed ruler of Yemen, the Prophet is reported to have asked him as to how he would decide matters coming up before him. 'I will judge matters according to the Book of God,' said Ma'ad. 'But if the Book of God contains nothing to guide you?' 'Then I will act on the precedents of the Prophet of God.' 'But if the precedents fail?' 'Then I will exert to form my own judgment'[3] 'Ijtihad' is a learning (knowing) process and has an important, progressive and civil role in the life of an individual and the society altogether with the state. It also participates in developing the civil life and opening the legislative prospects before it. Without the process of 'Ijtihad', many human activities are difficult to develop in the sphere of an Islamic life. It is time to re-open the gates of 'Ijtihad' not just in the interests of women's rights but also in the interests of justice for all. The biggest disservice that Muslims do to Islam and Prophet Muhammad is through their uncritical approach to Islamic sources. Islamic religious sciences, which languish in the middle ages, confuse memorization with understanding and literalism with faith. This posture towards religious sources has led them to allow false narratives and often-bizarre interpretations to become cardinal elements of belief. We must be against 'taqlid', the blind imitation of jurisprudential precedent of the schools of 'fiqh'. Moreover, I feel that a purely legalistic approach to Islam represents a misreading of the actual intent of the Qur'an. To reduce Islam simply to 'fiqh' or 'shari'ah' is a major blunder. Instead, what I talk about is moving from 'shari'ah', in the sense of laws, to the underlying aims and ethical impulses of the 'shari'ah'. This suggests that in order to attain the aims of the 'shari'ah' today, in some respects, other than in ritual or strictly religious matters, one might need to devise new means. Conservatives in particular condemn new readings of sacred texts and religion because of their fear that such readings will undermine the legitimacy of interpretations inherited from the past, most of which are anti-women. In the name of tradition and religious purity, they obstruct the development of religious knowledge, forcing a sort of stasis upon it. Empowering women to participate in the structural development of government, as well as in implications and applications on social roles in relevant cultures, means women's full rights in terms of policy and development, and women's full rights to self determine their role in the family and the society at large. On the practical level this means that women must also be empowered to participate in all levels of Muslim governance and culture. We should not advocate exclusivist movements; to the contrary, enlightened women and men need to work together towards shared ends. For an enlightened understanding of the text of the Qur'an, we have to learn to read it in such a way as to be able to recover its radically egalitarian message.

Muslims need to stop people who abuse the religion of God and His messenger, Muhammad. They need to oppose those who would brutalize women in the name of Qur'an and Sunnah. They need have jealousy for their religion, so that those who would abuse and misuse it realize that they will have no success and no headway under their vigilance. It is time to wake up to reality. While Muslims often like to boast about the large size of 'ummah', the fact is that they are losing more hearts and minds everyday, due in large part to their silence about human rights abuses, especially those directed towards women. These people will continue to turn to the secular philosophies promoted by those who do take the time to speak out on their behalf: the feminists, socialists, and secularists. Prophet Muhammad was mocked and assaulted because of his strong and courageous stance on the status of women. He came with a message that lifted women up and gave them dignity. Fourteen hundred years later, we have descended back into the dark pit of 'Jahiliya', and Muslim women around the world find themselves cast into the same slavery that the Prophet was sent to liberate them from. In order to bring about a change in the status of women, we need to bring about a change in men's attitudes towards women as well as tradition and religion. Personally I am a believing and practicing Muslim who wishes to reconstruct Islamic theology on an egalitarian perspective. This book is a serious attempt at a reevaluation of the gender questions related to Islam with some major reformatory aims. In the theological exploration, I have employed the holistic hermeneutics for my inference and deduction. The book boldly searches an alternative interpretation, based on justice, rather than evading from the real point at issue where there is an apparent conflict between gender equity and Qur'anic Weltanschauung (at least in the arena of interpretation). I am of the firm opinion that asking new questions and questioning accepted interpretations is part of our evolving knowledge of Islam. This book is a humble contribution towards that end. It also attempts to achieve a paradigm shift in re-interpreting gender equity vis-à-vis the Qur'an. I do not claim any originality either in the sphere of arguments or hermeneutics; rather I am heavily depended upon so many authors whose work I have freely used. I'm especially indebted to scholars such as Amina Wadud, Asma Barlas, Fatima Mernissi, Azizah al-Hibri, Riffat Hassan, Feisal Abdul Rauf, Ernest Gellner, Armando Salvatore, Farid

Esack, Shaykh Tâhâ Jâbir al-'Alwânî, Huda al-Khattab, Chandra Muzaffar, Jamal A. Badawi, Abou El Fadl Khaled, Ali Shari'ati, Ziauddin Sardar, Barbara Freyer Stowasser, Fathi Osman, Abdul Aziz Sachedina, Judith E. Tucker, Murad Wilfred Hoffman, Karen Armstrong, Muhammad Asad, Mahnaz Afkhami, Sachiko Murata, Judith E. Tucker, Abdul Hakim Murad, Sheikh Muhammad al-Ghazzali, John L. Esposito, Annemarie Schimmel, Hassan Turabi, Yusuf al-Qarzawi and Leila Ahmed, among others, for having done brilliant work in the sphere of Islamic studies, and whose reading has helped me much. I express my deep felt gratitude for the affection and appreciation shown by Dr. Rafiq Zakaria (Mumbai), Dr. Yoginder Sikand (Bangalore), Dr. A.K Ramakrishnan (Kottayam), Dr. Syed Hamid (New Delhi), Dr. Zafarul Islam Khan (New Delhi), Prof. K.M. Bahauddin (Kochi), Dr N.A. Karim (Trivandrum), Mr. Biju Abdul Qadir (Bangalore), Mr. C.S. Ibrahim Kutty (Panaikulam), Mr. N.M. Hussain (Kalamassery), and Dr. K.K. Usman (Aluva). My thanks are beyond words to Dr Zeenath Shoukat Ali who has found time, despite her hectic work schedule, to crown my book with a prestigious and brilliant 'Foreword'.

End Notes

1. Fatima Mernissi, *Women's Rebellion and Islamic Memory*, Zed Books: London, 1996, pp. 13-14.
2. Neal Robinson, *Discovering the Qur'an*, SCM Press: London, 1996, p. 29.
3. Muhammad Iqbal, *The Reconstruction of Religious Thought in Islam*, Sh. Muhammad Ashraf: Lahore, 1968. p. 2.

1

Gender Questions in Islam: An Introduction

One often wonders why is it seemingly that all religions of the world treat women secondarily and denies them some basic rights all humans should have. This phenomenon is present nearly in all religions, and progressive men and women of all religions try to explain and correct this unfortunate situation. There are some obvious reasons for this male bias in religion. It must be admitted that Christian, Jewish, and Muslim scholars have neglected the wisdom of their respective revelations concerning the equality of the sexes. Qur'anic commentators and jurists in particular seem to have ignored the broader intellectual aspects of a woman's testimony. In addition, some seem to have allowed themselves to completely overlook the basic Qur'anic principle of gender equality, even though this teaching is mentioned in literally hundreds of Qur'anic verses. Instead, they have engrossed themselves in studies emphasizing biological and psychological differences, thereby attempting to derive evidence from divine revelation to support the attitudes and customs of their pre-Islamic heritage.

Muslim women, like other women, have been suffering for long for lack of empowerment in the male dominated society. Enlightened Muslim scholars want to liberate themselves from medieval interpretations of the Qur'an.

Tragically, some Muslim men actually use Islam to "justify" their abusive behavior. Focusing on rituals, considering themselves to be Islamically knowledgeable, and disregarding the spirit of Islam, they wrongly use the Qur'anic verse that says men are the protectors and maintainers of women to go on power trips, demand total obedience, and order their wives around. They disregard the Islamic requirement for the head of the household to consult with other members of the family when making decisions. The women's question needs to be tackled with new sensitivity and freshness of approach. Among the many respected leaders of the modern Islamist movement who follow this attitude are Hasan al-Turabi of Sudan, Rachid al-Ghanouchi of Tunisia, and Yusuf al-Qaradawi of Egypt.

Voice for Equity in Muslim Countries

In the first centuries of Islam, the religious practices of women and men were basically identical. Both received religious education, participated in daily prayer at the Mosques, and led in worship. Following the Prophet's death, and especially after the rightly guided Caliphs, however, women's status in both religious institutions and the broader Muslim culture declined dramatically. The decline is attributed to the consolidation of religious power into male hands which was supposedly necessitated by Islam's spread to areas which were more rigidly patriarchal than the Arabian peninsula. Despite the fact that in the recent centuries few Muslim women have had any opportunity to shape or even gain first hand knowledge of their tradition, the egalitarian core of Islam remains quite explicit within the Qur'an. So, in spite of the male-dominated accretions into the practice of Islam itself, Islam's primary sacred text remains uncorrupted. Indeed, much justification for women's subordination to men within Muslim culture is derived from the lesser authoritative Islamic religious sources. Thus while the Qur'an is theoretically the most authoritative Islamic text, in actual practice the Qur'an is read through the lenses of existing cultural assumptions about appropriate social relations and portions of less authoritative sacred texts which are more in line with patriarchal values. As a result, the view that women are inherently inferior to men is deeply imbedded in Muslim culture.

The Qur'an, however, consistently describes the creation of humanity by God in egalitarian terms. There is no indication that man is created prior to woman, or that woman is created from man's substance. Indeed, implicit in many of these Qur'anic passages is that God's original creation is sexually undifferentiated. Sexual differentiation into male and female takes place at a later time, thus downplaying the significance of the differences. In fact, a latter-day Muslim interpretation of human creation appears to be shaped more by Judaeo-Christian teachings and the creation accounts in Genesis than the Qur'an. Even though the Qur'an does not mention the name of the Arabic counterpart of Eve, in Qur'anic interpretations she is nevertheless blamed for the transgression and the subsequent 'fall' of humankind. However, in the Qur'an, the act of disobedience is portrayed as a collective act committed simultaneously by both the man and the woman. Furthermore, responsibility for the transgression is given neither to one of them alone, but is shared by both. Similarly, envisioning life outside of the Garden as a punishment is actually inconsistent with the Qur'anic account. For it insists that human being s presence outside of Paradise was originally intended by God since from the beginning God intended for Adam to be a vice-regent on earth (2:30). Women's full and equal humanity is attested to not only in creation, but also on the final judgment day. The Qur'an makes it clear that both men and women are called upon by God to uphold God's commandments, and that both men and women are accountable to God for their righteousness (3:195, 4:124, 9:71-72). Indeed the Qur'an goes beyond insisting that individual women and men are to be treated identically. Instead it insists that men and women recognize their interconnectedness and interdependence. It affirms that men and women in the *'umma'* are members and protectors of each other (3:195, 9:71).

In modern era, education is spreading fast in all countries including Muslim countries. Muslim women in almost all countries are going to universities in ever-larger numbers. These educated women become far more aware of their rights than illiterate women. In the domain of public life she is not allowed to make any original contribution to the promotion of the religious quality of life. Whenever she was allowed to work towards the material development of life that was likely to be in a context of exploitation or as unexciting work with little spiritual satisfaction or significance. It is not true to say that what the medieval theologians thought on this question is immutable and divine.

Cases of discrimination and violence against women in the name of Islam can be documented from worldwide. Experiences of formalization of *shari'ah* in Muslim countries like Saudi Arabia, Afghanistan, Sudan, and other gulf countries show that women are systematically marginalized, forced to veil themselves, may not go out without a guardian, or work in public places. In Iran after the Revolution of 1979, child marriage, which had been outlawed, made a come back and the legal age of a girl bride was reduced to 9! Almost in every Muslim country, women are made to become detainees in their husbands' homes. For accidental homicide, there is a law of 'diya' mentioned in the Qur'an (4:92). 'Diya' is the technical term for blood-money (for wounds, killing etc.), compensation paid by the perpetrator to the relatives of the victim (in unintentional cases). The value of the life of all people is equal in Islam (5:32, 25:68-69). Given that our primary frame of reference is the Qur'an, we find that its statement is general and does not privilege the man with any special status (4:92). There is not a single well-authenticated statement by the Prophet to establish that the blood money paid for the killing of a woman is half the sum paid for the killing of a man. However, shari'ah, as interpreted by the contemporary 'ulema', has wrongly and quite unjustly prescribed *'diya'*, as half for female victims than it is for male victims. Woman's humanity stemming from the same origin as that of the man, her blood is the same as his, he being from her and she from him and equal retaliation in kind being the rule common to both cases of homicide and hell and damnation being the other worldly punishment for the killing of either man or woman, so the rule of the verse (4:92) applies to the accidental homicide of either a man or a woman.

Thus there is hardly any country with sizeable Muslim population where women are not asserting themselves. Even in a conservative Sheikhdom like Kuwait women are demanding right to vote and right to hold political offices. A woman who is forbidden from driving a car in Saudi Arabia will cheerfully take the wheel when abroad, confident that her country's weird law has nothing to do with Islam. There is no legal basis found in any of the four schools of law which could be constructed as prohibiting women from driving, yet such a law exists in a State which declares that the Qur'an and the Hadith it the ultimate law. Afghan women educated before the Taliban rule know that banning girls from school is forbidden in Islam, which encourages all Muslims to seek knowledge from cradle to grave, from every source possible. One often hears a lot of how Islam is great for women in theory. In practice, there have been many systemic abuses against women in Muslim societies. The Taliban were the worst and most extreme example. When the Taliban decided to deny education to any girl over a certain age, it is the conservative Muslims, the ones who profess adherence to "Qur'an and Sunnah" that should have spoken the loudest against this. The longer we stay silent, the more people, both Muslim and non-Muslim, will begin to equate "Shari'ah" with the oppression of women. So there is an urgent need to re-establish women's rights, based the Qur'an and the Prophet's example, and dismantle the patriarchal rule that has plagued too many Muslim societies.

In Iran, on the other hand, they not only have voting rights but also can be, and are, elected to parliament and to high elective offices like vice president. Today in Iran, if divorce takes place for no fault on the part of women or on account of her misconduct, she can claim from her divorcing husband half the property acquired during the married years or its equivalent. Another important right, which the Iranian women have won, is of divorce on many counts. Countries such as Syria, Jordan, Morocco, Egypt and Iran, have adopted the ruling that a husband, who has agreed in his marriage contract not to take another wife during the marriage, is bound by that stipulation. The awareness about being able to do this is high in those countries and many couples do insert this stipulation into the marriage contract.

Dr. Zaki Badawi, head of the Muslim College, London, correctly observes: "Very few Muslim countries have given women their full rights, and both Islamic law and the message of Islam have been violated... The movement (fundamentalism) is pushing the doctrine that is anti-woman, anti-intellectual, anti-progress and anti-science." [1]

Anti-woman Laws in the Name of Islam

Women in Pakistan face all kinds of gross violence and abuse at the hands of the male perpetuators, family members and state agents. Multiple forms of violence include rape; domestic abuse as spousal murder, mutilation, burning and disfiguring faces by acid, beatings; ritual honor-killings and custodial abuse and torture. According to a report by Amnesty International released on June 15, 2000, several hundred women and girls die each year in so-called 'honor-killings' in Pakistan, in a backdrop to government inaction. She is killed like a bird in family feuds to create evidence of "illicit" connections and cover them under the garb of "grave and sudden provocation" to escape severe punishment.

Rape law in the United States had long reflected cultural patriarchal assumptions about female sexuality and consent. A frequent casualty in rape trials is the rape victim's reputation, as the court attempts to sort out the issue of consent. This problem is exacerbated in Pakistan because the convoluted placement of rape as part of the 'Zina Ordinance' encourages the use of a woman's unsuccessful claim of rape as some sort of default evidence of 'zina' (adultery). Thus, there is a strong tendency to suspect any charge of rape to be a "loose woman's" attempt to escape punishment for 'zina'. Female sexual stereotypes dangerously fuel these cases. Such biased and derogatory attitude against women by the Islamic courts in Pakistan reveal a basic cultural male bias in the perception of women and female sexuality. In two infamous cases in Nigeria, women involved in adultery cases were held to a lower burden of proof than the men who impregnated them. However, Islamic law does not distinguish between men and women when it comes to proving adultery or fornication. In Pakistan, it is not unusual for women to be jailed for fornication or adultery when they attempt to report and be treated for rape in hospitals. But there is nothing in Islamic law that says the victim of sexual violence should be treated as a criminal and jailed. God holds accountable those who transgress His boundaries, and having one standard for men and another for women in these matters is a transgression and injustice.

This bias also manifests itself in conclusions that a given sexual encounter must have been consensual if there is no physical evidence of resistance by the woman (another issue familiar to rape law reformers in the West). Many Pakistani judgments of rape have been converted into adultery ('zina') cases because of the absence of evidence of such resistance. This stereotypical concept of women supposes that if a woman does not struggle against a sexual assault, then she must be a sexually loose woman–justifying a conversion of the charge to 'zina'. This attitude unfairly generalizes human reaction to force and the threat of violence.

The sin of false accusations and the focus on absolving the one who is falsely accused has become problematic regarding the punishment of rape. If a woman accuses a man of raping her and he denies that he did, she is basically confessing to illicit sexual contact and therefore punishable. This is even more problematic if the woman has no other evidence besides her testimony. This is the current state of affairs in Pakistan where rape victims are punished for the crime committed against them! Based on some medieval interpretations, the woman is made to suffer for a crime committed by another because the focus is erroneously on the sexual act and not on rape as an act of violence. Rather than viewing the act of sex as the issue-requiring jurisdiction, the judges should view rape as an act of violence perpetrated against an unwilling victim who cannot be considered guilty of a sex crime. And, this generalization works to the detriment of women who have been subjected to a rapist's attack and survived only by submitting without physical resistance.

Ironically, this is exactly the type of speculation regarding women's sexual activity, which the Qur'an explicitly condemns in the very verses establishing the crime of '*zina*'. Judicial and societal speculation about women's sexual looseness clearly does not correspond with the Qur'anic admonition that "it is not for us to speak of". The intertwining of rape with *zina* in the Pakistani ordinance, however, encourages such speculation. Rather than constituting a separate violent crime against women, rape—under the title '*zina-bil-jabr*'–is perceived more as a woman's expected defense to a *zina* charge, and thus subject to judicial speculation.[2] As if anticipating the misogynistic tendency of society, the Qur'an first establishes that there is to be no speculation about a woman's sexual conduct. No one may cast any doubt upon the character of a woman except by formal charges, with very specific, secure evidence (i.e., four eyewitnesses to actual intercourse) that the woman is disrupting public decency with her behavior. If such direct proof does not materialize, then anyone engaging in such a charge is subject to physical punishment for slander. For even if the information is true, any witness who is not accompanied by another three will be punished for slander (24:11-17).

The 'Zina' Ordinance of Pakistan, however, adds a limitation on the admissibility of evidence that we have not yet addressed: the witnesses must all be men. That is, the standard of proof in the '*Zina* Ordinance' for 'zina' is either confession or testimony by "at least four Muslim adult male witnesses."[3] However, the Qur'anic '*zina*' verse setting forth the original four-witness requirement is not exclusive to men: "Those who defame chaste women and do not bring four witnesses ('*shuhada*') should be punished" (24:4). This verse refers to these four witnesses with the Arabic masculine plural, "shuhada" ("witnesses"), which grammatically includes both men and women, unless otherwise indicated.[4]

The inclusion of the word "male" in the 'Zina' Ordinance thus prompts the question: was this interpretation taken from Islamic law or is it a Pakistani cultural polish on the rule? Despite the Qur'anic use of the plural noun inclusive to both men and women, many Muslim jurists and scholars have traditionally limited the four witnesses in a 'zina' case to men.[5] The exclusivity of male testimony as an application of cultural male bias to the Islamic law of 'zina' is unfair. But the exclusion of female testimony becomes appalling when expanded to apply to 'zina-bil-jabr' as well. It is a clear travesty of justice to deny a victim of rape the right to testify to this violent attack merely because she is a woman. In applying the exclusively male evidence rule of traditional 'zina' law to the crime of 'zina-bil-jabr,' Pakistan has transformed what was merely an unfair antiquated male bias into a direct violation of the human rights of women. The direct contradiction to the Qur'anic injunctions to stand up firmly for justice is obvious (4 : 135, 5 : 8). Moreover, depriving women as an entire gender of the right to testify in a 'zina' case–where a woman's honor is generally at issue has serious societal ramifications. First, it prevents women from fulfilling the Islamic duty to bear witness to the truth, repeatedly emphasized in the Qur'an: "O you who believe, be custodians of justice (and) witnesses for God, even though against yourselves, or your parents or your relatives, and if you prevaricate or avoid (giving evidence), God is cognizant of all that you do" (4:135). But even more significant is the fact that the permanent rejection of testimony is itself a Qur'anic 'hadd' penalty. That is, in its verse prohibiting slander, the Qur'an establishes that deprivation of the right to testify is a severe punishment–one of the two consequences of falsely accusing a woman.

Significance of Critical Analysis

Men have dominated women in most cultures of the world most of the time. There are many manifestations of such dominance in the behaviors of men and women even today in the 21st century. It is not the domain of this discussion to explain why have men dominated women and what are the biological and historical causes and the anthropological evidence for that as this has already been discussed by investigators in those fields. Rather, the present study examines the effects of such dominance on religion, in particular, on Islam. In fact the status of women cries for help in many places of the world not just in Muslim countries or Muslim cultures governed by secular regimes but even in the secular West.

Muslims must be made aware of, and be on guard against, negative stereotypes of women and their effects on various communities. They must approach this issue objectively and without prejudice, recognizing that the same ignorance that has resulted in the repression and oppression of Muslim women, and the denial of women's rights in the Muslim world, is being imported into Western Muslim society through the proliferation of so-called 'Islamic' publications that degrade women. Some men and women, who claim to be scholars, frequent mosques and study-circles, where they spread vicious and false *ahadith* that degrade women. These false and non-Islamic teachings and the culture they promote threaten the rights of all Muslims, men and women. Muslims must now consider this important question of Muslim women's rights, and develop responses that reflect the sound principles of justice and equity in society that comprise Islam.

The reasons for the diminishing status of women in Muslim countries over several centuries are not fully clear. Many theories have been put forward to explain this phenomenon, but none address the revival of pre-Islamic ignorance that has come to prevail over the pure teachings of the Qur'an and *Sunnah* and that have caused Muslim woman to be excluded from the mainstream of society, her voice silenced and her inalienable rights ignored. The results manifest as poverty among women, abuse of women through unfair and un-Islamic laws and customs; emotional, spiritual, and material neglect of children, along with the refusal to educate women and enforcing strict codes of conduct on women that are not also attached to men. All this creates unbalanced, unjust and extreme interpretations of honor and chastity that are sometimes brutally enforced on women, but completely ignored when it comes to men, giving the erroneous impression that only women are bound by law to chastity and morality, while men can indulge in immorality to the extent that norms have been established in Muslim societies that suggest that such immorality is somehow being "manly," or a part of the male 'fitrah ' (nature). Even though we know, in theory, that the nature of a human being, our 'fitrah', is pure, whether male or female (Qur'an 95:4), we have somehow accepted that men are inclined toward immorality, so we should be tolerant of their sins, despite knowing from the teachings of Islam that immorality can and has brought entire civilizations to their knees.

Whether a woman is an orthodox practicing Muslim or Christian is not an indicator of her oppression or lack of rights. Other factors such as education and socio-economic status are powerful predictors (among others) of the quality of life for most women. Moreover, abuse that occurs to women at the hands of men such as rape, incest, domestic violence, sexual harassment, is not related to any religion and is prevalent in many societies. The common theme of such abuses is that men in position of authority and power abuse women. Thus, due to the fact that human society is patriarchal, the male dominance infiltrated religion as it did many other aspects of life and there are numerous behaviors that reflect this phenomenon (outside of religion). Further, in religious issues, this male dominance is so profound and so ingrained that Muslim scholars for example, interpret the Qur'an to disadvantage women even when the Scripture is strikingly clear and presents unequivocal argument to support women.

The thought and practice of Muslims have come lately to misrepresent most of the doctrinal and normative teachings of Islam on female affairs. The female is hardly ever religiously addressed except through the mediation of the male and as an addendum to him. In the fallen society of Muslims, women have little freedom to marry the person she likes, or to separate from a husband she loathes. Nor is she, as wife, entitled to full consultation and gracious companionship by her husband. In many cases she hardly enjoys an equal opportunity to earn and own property, or the full capacity to manage her property or to dispose thereof. All sorts of subterfuges are employed to deny her inheritance. Her role in private life has been reduced to that of a housewife chosen not for her personal merit, for she was denied the education or the opportunity to acquire merit, but for the merit of her men folk.

The divergences between theoretical statements about the rights and status of women in Islam and the actual implementation or application of these rights within present-day state policies, in the legal arena, through facilitating opportunities for education or work, etc.-are also to be addressed. If we look at the Muslim world, a civilization that has been all but cleansed of women's influence, we can appreciate how important women's freedom; inclusion and influence are to the social and cultural advancement of societies. In the contemporary Islamic movement, Muslims have placed great emphasis on the fact that Islam is indeed the original liberator of women. Yet few have been willing to recognize, let alone challenge, the erosion of Islamic rights and practices pertaining to women, the re-emergence of pre-Islamic attitudes and customs in the Muslim world, and the effects of these dark traditions on generations of Muslim women, their children and societies. Perhaps the greatest failing of many Islamic scholars has been their apparently deliberate failure to correct gross distortions of the faith, such as the idea that women's voices are prohibited because they are seductive, or that women are the property of husbands or other male family members.

Spirit of Religion Versus Cultural Influence

If we need to keep in mind the historical contexts of the Qur'anic revelation in order to understand its teachings, we also need to keep in mind the historical contexts of its interpretations in order to understand its conservative and patriarchal exegesis. The most definitive work, not only in Qur'anic exegesis but also in law and tradition, is considered by many Muslims to have been produced during the first few centuries of Muslim history, the Golden Age of Islam, which coincided with the Western Middle Ages. It was also a period where misogyny was widely prevalent. Naturally, misogynic interpretations were smoothly assimilated into Muslim theology by way of the commentaries ('tafsir') and the narratives detailing the life and praxis of the Prophet (*Ahadith*) It was a process of "textualization of misogyny" in Islam. These texts have come to eclipse the Qur'anic influence in most Muslim societies today, exemplifying the triumph not only of some texts over others in Muslim religious discourse but also of history, politics, and culture over the sacred text, and thus also of the cross-cultural, transnational, and nondenominational ideologies on women and gender in vogue in the Middle Ages over the teachings of the Qur'an. However, since we often do not distinguish between texts, cultures, and histories when studying Islam, we tend to ignore this inversion. As a result, we end up confusing the Qur'an with its interpretation, and confusing Islam with patriarchy and the practices of repressive Muslim states that have a history of using Islam for their own political ends.

History is replete with examples of traditional societies where women have typically been subject to more restrictions than men, exemplified by lack of opportunities (being able to work or vote) or immobility (needing permission from a male relative to travel or not being able to drive), etc. Although it is mistakenly argued Islam has played a strong role in restricting the freedom of women in Muslim societies, these restrictions are not inherent in the religion of Islam, but rather stem from cultural interpretations. Trying to incorporate 9th century Arab customs to 21st century populations is often inappropriate despite intentions to have a pure society. When looking to Islam for guidance, it's important to separate what is cultural from the essence of the religious prerogative. If an authoritative ruling from Saudi Arabia states that women cannot drive because it would increase possible contact to freely mix with men, who can lead to sins, this logic must be judged against Islam and history. It is a fact that the Qur'an emphasizes modesty for both men and women in order so that we conduct ourselves respectfully. It is also a fact that men and women in the time of the Prophet did interact, so the justification of this law on Islam is sham. It is unduly harsh and anti-Islamic. It should not serve as an example of how Islam restricts women, as much as it should serve an example of how illogical it is to cut off one's nose to spite one's face.

Further, the nature of the Arabic language must also be taken into account. For example, each word in Arabic is designated masculine or feminine and it does not follow that use of a male or a female noun necessarily restricts the application to the mentioned gender The question is commonly asked though: Why did not God simply and explicitly prescribe equality for women and men and prohibit all discriminatory practices? There are two answers possible to this query. The first is verses that have been traditionally interpreted as discriminatory are affected by subjective linguistic treatment and are descriptive rather than prescriptive. The second answer is that, again, we must consider the influence that the community at the time of the revelation had on the expression of the Message; how the objective was achieved in that context. Islam has a strong practical element. It must work for Muslims in their time and place. Therefore, restricting the right to polygyny with a long-term view to its prohibition achieved the objective of protecting the interests of women at the time in polygamous marriages and destitute women without social and economic support Further, the intellectual regeneration of Islamic scholarship is and must be coterminous with the reopening of the door of '*Ijtihad*', or if the argument is accepted that the door never actually closed, then letting more people pass through the door. We cannot afford any longer to be limited by the cultural constructs of seventh century Arabia.

The Thrust for Equity

While traditional jurists acknowledge the improved status of women with the advent of Islam, they do not acknowledge the full status of women; that is, full intellectual, physical, and moral capacity, in control of their own agency unchecked by any notion of a male guardian. Islam treats women as autonomous intellectual beings; traditional Islamic jurists do not. There is a serious need for constructive and bold humanism that would restate Islamic social ideals in order to back up this new legislation. There cannot be a claim to a "scientific" interpretive methodology, nor can there be a claim of objectivity. The Qur'an is universal, and therefore its interpretation cannot be limited to the expressions of the revelations in seventh-century Arabia. We must ascertain the Divine objective, and interpret according to contemporary circumstance and our contemporary appreciation of rights and responsibilities as individuals, and members of society.

The Qur'an only sets down principles. Indeed, they can and should be interpreted by each successive generation to fit circumstance and culture. But they often seem to have been progressively forgotten in favor of a traditional, androcentric Islam, based as much on self-interest as on myth, and on a partial and biased reading of what, nevertheless, remains potentially a radical document and tradition, precisely because of its egalitarian ethos. The same process of restrictive interpretation, of intellectual sclerosis, is sadly evident in much of the current debate about modernity, based once again on both a partial and partisan understanding of Islam's intellectual history, and a denial of much of its own past. Qur'an describes God's self as inherently just, and it asserts that God has decreed mercy upon His Self (6:12, 6:54). At the theological and philosophical level the constituents of justice have not been subject to close examination in Islamic doctrine; and part of the explanation for that limitation lies in a basic tension in understanding the nature of justice. Does the divine law define justice or does justice define the divine law? If it is the former then whatever one concludes is the divine law therein is justice. If it is the latter, then whatever justice demands is, in fact, the demand of the divine.

Already within the last ten to twenty years there has been a growing trend among researchers and scholars studying such issues. They are discussing and analyzing discourses and methodologies from within our indigenous tradition that can be developed or employed to articulate gender awareness. They also seek to apply the intelligent use of Islamic principles and fields of meaning for the acquisition of rights or for revising discourses that encourage gender consciousness. Examples of issues being debated that might have positive implications for Muslim women are: a return to a more direct examination of the Qur'anic text and message; exaggerated gender distinctions should be superseded by the Qur'anic egalitarian worldview and repeated emphasis on ethico-moral religious equality (i.e., regarding distinctions are strictly legal and functional and not inherent); the higher paradigm of egalitarian values should be made to prevail, thus focusing on the general 'just' intent and purpose of the Divine message; consideration of inner-Qur'anic references to view the overall picture of certain themes and issues; considering seriously the Qur'anic view on women's integration to the public sphere and the evolving problematic of the private-public dichotomy (i.e., how much of it is actually Qur'anic and how much is cultural and historical); studies on the formation of the legal tradition of Islam ('fiqh') incorporating non-Qur'anic cultural pre-suppositions (derived from the wider region of the pre-Islamic Middle East) etc.

As regards the question of gender, therefore, a dynamic reading of the Qur'an allows for the possibility of new meanings to be read into the text with the passage of time, which, in turn, makes for new gender-just understandings of the divine mandate. Far from suggesting any inadequacy of the Qur'an, this book argues that this itself provides conclusive proof of the Qur'an being God's word, for in this way it proves its continuing relevance in every age. The advocacy of a dynamic hermeneutics of the Qur'an naturally brings to the fore the question of 'taqlid', blind following of past jurisprudential precedent, and 'ijtihad', creative exercise of reason in understanding the sources of Islamic jurisprudence. This has a vital bearing on issues of jurisprudence involving women. Hierarchical authoritarian interpretations appear to have prevailed as jurists' own authoritarian perspectives colored meanings. In the majority of translations and interpretations the gender bias and misogyny are explicit and are, thus, unacceptable.

There are of course other significant areas of interest that are important to this discussion. What is important in any discussion concerning equality of rights for women in Islam is a consideration of the possibilities for different readings of the Qur'an. I would argue that a reading that furthers equality of rights is consistent with the Qur'anic worldview and therefore in order to achieve Islam's objectives, must be pursued in favor of a reading that compromises equality of rights for women.

Islamic traditions would dictate that women's progress be achieved in tandem with the wider struggle to benefit all members of the society. The good of the group or totality is always more crucial than the good of any one sector of the society. In fact, the society is seen as an organic whole in which the welfare of each member or organ is necessary for the health and well-being of every other part. Disadvantageous circumstances of women therefore should always be countered in conjunction with attempt to alleviate those factors that adversely affect men and other segments of the society. Muslim societies are called upon to take seriously the issue of the humane and equal treatment of women-respect for their common humanness-a theme that is reiterated throughout the Qur'an but is never allowed by interpreters and religious scholars to be a governing principle in constructing gender relations.

A deeper analysis has shown that oppressive interpretations of the Qur'an are influenced mostly by cultural practices and values, which regard women as inferior and subordinate to men. It is not Islam that oppress women, but human being with all their weaknesses who failed to understand God's intentions. Linguistically speaking, Islam has a very fundamental concern for peace, justice, and well-being. Each and every Muslim should inwardly internalize these values in the first place. The feeling of being secure and safe in the mind of every Muslim individual is a basic capital for transcending the same feeling to others, making them sensitized to society's needs and interests. This feeling generally grows along with the process of ritualism and ritual practices, which will strengthen one's commitment and vision on the equality of all human beings. Islam teaches that there is no hierarchical structure among Muslims and all are equal before God (49 : 13). The combination of spiritual and ritual practices will produce Muslims who have balanced personalities, inwardly and outwardly, vertically and horizontally.

The traditional Muslim Society, which is over-impressed by its historical decline, had developed a general preference for circumspection and cautiousness over the demands of positive pursuits. It has become unduly conservative for fear that freedom of thought would lead astray and divide the community; and that freedom of women would degenerate into licentious promiscuity-so much that the basic religious rights and duties of women have been forsaken and the fundamentals of equality and fairness in the structure of Muslim Society, as enshrined in the Qur'an, has been completely overlooked.

Historically most translations and interpretations of the Qur'an (exegeses) were written almost exclusively by men. In examining a historical narrative of gender from them, one should employ a particular mode of analysis, namely, anti-sexist hermeneutics. The aim is to critically evaluate and expose patriarchal structures, values and male-centered concerns. This approach focuses on the text as an ideological andocentric product. Specifically my pleading is to apply a critical egalitarian hermeneutic to the 'tafsir' texts. In so doing we will subject some of the formative gender discourses in traditional Islamic exegesis to ideological examination and critique.

The centrality of the Qur'an in a Muslim worldview has been well recorded. Muslims generally perceive it as the ultimate reference point, the distinguishing criterion (*'al-Furqan'*) for good and evil and as the transcendent authority that sets parameters and standards for human existence. Consequently it occupies center-stage in the Muslim religious imaginaries. It thus influences social structure, ideas of normative human relations and boundaries for appropriate behavior. Hence the Qur'an is not only a religious text but also a profoundly political text that shapes the understandings of Muslim societies. Due to this powerful position of the Qur'an in Muslim consciousness it is appropriate to examine its implications for gender relations. The Qur'an mediates itself into social and collective consciousness through human understanding. Therefore in analyzing the application of the Qur'an to society and gender relations it is necessary to examine the authoritative mediations of the Qur'an. Qur'anic understandings do not enter socio-cultural vacuums but are presented into already symbolically and culturally meaningful contexts. Hence Qur'anic readers and interpreters bring to the texts their own "prior-texts", their own worldviews and their own traditions of meaning informed by particular socio-historical positioning. Thus the creation of meaning of and from the Qur'an fundamentally involves the human interpretive ascription.

The purpose of this book is to examine the ideological assumptions embedded in the authoritative interpretations of the Qur'an. These exegetical studies are indicative of the structural complicity of religion in discourses of violence against women. Thus, for example, a verse, which in contemporary understanding can be seen to create a space for the violation of women, in a medieval context, may be arguing to limit the physical violation of women. There is thus a dynamic interplay between context and hermeneutics. The hermeneutical lenses of the classical exegetes have and continue to inform authoritative Islamic discourses. However it is necessary to challenge and critically engage their gender ideology and interpretations of the Qur'an in the contemporary Muslim world. It is vital to provide alternative constructions of women and men if we believe in the dynamism of Islam and the continuing relevance of the Qur'an to people in their full humanity.

Qur'anic Vision of Gender Justice

Biblically, Eve's first sin was not eating the forbidden fruit but stepping out from under Adam's authority to deal with the serpent herself and then to tempt Adam to sin by offering him the fruit. God's words of judgment bring her face to face with her insubordination and assure her that she will not prosper in it. In short, male tyranny over females stems from the 'fall' and the 'curse', but the godly and loving authority of husbands over wives and of male leaders in the Church stems from creation and is restored in redemption: "It was Adam who was first created, and then Eve" (1 Timothy 2:13). St. Paul uses the temporal order of creation as one ground of his argument against a woman's teaching or exercising authority over a man in Church (1 Timothy 2:12), indicating that the order of creation, through whatever hidden premises in Pauline logic, betokens male authority over females in terms of roles in the Church. Thus we have it on the authority of Scripture itself that Adam's being created first and Eve later (Genesis 2:7, 18, 22-24) implies that Adam properly had some sort of authority over Eve instilled at creation. Adam named both the animals (Genesis 2:19-20) and the woman (Genesis 2:23) whom God brought before him. In Biblical thought, to name something is to exercise authority over it. Similarly, Eve's resistance to Adam's authority is also rooted in the 'fall' (Genesis 3:16-17).

Men according to the Bible are the owners of women, just like an animal is owned. Exodus 20:17 states the famous tenth commandment lumps a wife together with his servants, animals and house. A man could sell his daughter as a slave (Exodus 21:7-11) or give her in marriage to whomsoever he chose. This subordination of women to men in the Bible, which shaped western thought on the issue, is made clear in Leviticus 12:1-8. The New Testament cites approvingly the fact that "Sarah obeyed Abraham, calling him lord" as exemplary for Christian wives (1 Peter 3:6), whom it exhorts, "be submissive to your own husbands. For in this way in former times the holy women also, who hoped in God, used to adorn themselves [with "chaste and respectful behavior"], being submissive to their own husbands" (1 Peter 3:1, 5).

Though non-Muslims in the West have seized the rhetorical high ground, charging Islam with holding degrading ideas about women and fostering the ill-treatment of women, it is a fact that Islam is the doctrine to deny the concept of woman as evil seductress, responsible for the original sin and fall of mankind. It was Islam that granted women rights of inheritance, the right to choice in marriage, and the right to full discretion in the disposal of her personal assets. It was Qur'an that first addressed the sexuality of the human being as a matter of dignity and not evil, assuring us that God rewards the conduct of human sexuality when conducted within the purifying bounds of divine law, and prohibited celibacy and the avoidance of women as an act of worship outside of the divine precepts that guide ritual worship. These principles apply to both men and women.

Islam is based on justice and equity. The Qur'an says, "Say: My Lord enjoins justice" (7:29). "And for every nation there is a messenger. So when their messenger comes, the matter is decided between them with justice, and they are not wronged" (10:47). "Certainly We sent out Our messengers with clear arguments, and sent down with them the Book and the Balance (of Right & Wrong), that people may stand forth in justice" (57:25). The justice mentioned in the verses above and in so many other verses in the Qur'an signifies "justice" in its broadest sense. So the Islamic treatment of the gender issue is essentially equitable and justifiable. Qur'anic worldview endorses equity, justice, harmony and compassion. In marriage there should be harmony (4:128), love, and mercy (30:21), and spouses should protect each other: "They are a raiment for you and you are a raiment for them" (2:187). Moreover, the Qur'an repeatedly warns against the use of injurious statements by a husband against his wife (58:2-4).

However, since the Qur'an was revealed in an existing patriarchy and has been interpreted by adherents of patriarchies ever since, Muslim women have a stake in challenging its patriarchal exegesis. It was not God who wronged them, but they wronged their own souls (30:9). Both genders are recipients of the "divine breath" since they are created with the same human and spiritual nature (*'nafsin-waahidah'*) (4:1, 15:29). Both genders are dignified and are trustees of God on earth (17:70, 2:30). Men and women have the same religious and moral duties and responsibilities. They both face the consequences of their deeds.[6] The general rule in social and political life is participation and collaboration of males and female in public affairs (9:71). As vicegerents of God on earth (2:30), it is our duty to be concerned about the whole world and about all of God's creatures.

According to the Qur'an, Eve was not restricted from the Tree in order to follow God's commands by default. She was tested, chose to disobey God, just like Adam, and went to the Tree on her own free will. She also paid the price. There is nothing wrong with making a wrong decision, for it is better to learn, repent and be stronger for it than never to be challenged at all and remain meek all our lives. As equal, independent creations of God, the ultimate role of men and women is to serve as vicegerents on earth, to worship God and follow His commands so that we may return to Him. Both men and women share this responsibility, which constitutes our basic role in life. The Qur'an outlines the attributes believing men and women should try to live by, but in no specific way are we told in what capacity each individual man and woman should practice these: "Say: Behold, my prayer, and all my acts of worship, and my living and my dying are for God alone" (6:163). This verse, which was addressed to the Prophet but serves as an inspiration to all, reveals that our vicegerency is not only spiritual, but must be consolidated with actual service.

Salvation and ultimate felicity is a divine gift shared by both men and women by virtue of their faith, divine grace and virtuous deeds (33:35). Women are independent individuals, as exemplified by the fact that all human beings will be accountable for their own intentions and deeds on the Day of Judgment when no human being shall be of the least avail to another human being (82:19). If men were ultimately responsible for women (fathers for their daughters, husbands for their wives, etc.), then this accountability would be solely on men's shoulders to bear all the way until the Day of Judgment. But this is not the case: "And whatever wrong any human being commits rests upon himself alone; and no bearer of burdens shall be made to bear another's burden... For, He it is who has made you inherit the earth, and has raised some of you by degrees above others, so that He might try you by means of what he bestowed upon you" (6:164-165).

Imam Abu Hanifa recognized the right of the woman to contract her own marriage The Qur'an requires that spouses treat each other with love and mercy (30:21). Moreover, the Qur'an repeatedly warns against the use of injurious statements by a husband against his wife (58:2-4). Even the issue of which sex was created first is not specified, implying that for our purposes here on earth it may not matter (4:1). Qur'an, in a number of passages, has expressly said that the reward of the Hereafter and the proximity to God are not linked with sex (see for example: 16:97, 3:195). They depend on faith and deeds, and there is no difference between man and woman in this respect. In the Qur'an, side by side with every great and saintly man, a great and saintly woman has been mentioned. It has glorified the wives of Adam and Abraham and the mothers of Moses and Jesus. If it has mentioned the wives of Noah and Lot as unworthy of their husbands, it has not ignored the wife of the Pharaoh, and has mentioned her as a great woman who was in the hands of a wicked man. The Qur'an in its stories has maintained a sort of balance; its heroes are both men and women.

In many Muslim countries today, women are still negotiating their right to participate in the political process even though it is reported in the Qur'an that the Prophet himself accepted the '*bay'ah*' (a form of election) from women. There is sufficient historical evidence of participation by early Muslim women in the choice of rulers, in public issues, in lawmaking, in administrative positions, in scholarship and teaching, and even in the battlefield. Such involvement in social and political affairs was done without losing sight of the complementary priorities of both genders and without violating Islamic guidelines of modesty and virtue.

The veiling of Muslim women is a more complex issue. Certainly, the Qur'an requires them to behave and dress modestly-but these strictures apply equally to men. Only one verse refers to the veiling of women, stating that the Prophet's wives should be behind a 'hijab' when his male guests converse with them. Some scholars, however, claim that this does not apply to women in general, and that the language used does not carry the textual stipulation that makes a verse obligatory. In practice, most modern Muslim women appreciate attractive and graceful clothes, but avoid dressing provocatively. And if 'purdah' is introduced it is simply to protect the privacy of the Prophet's bedroom from the prurient gaze of male guests who stayed too long after dinner (33.54). Women imams also led the prayers for their households. Women fought on the battlefield and were entitled to own property in their name.

Each sex has the ability to contribute to successive generations, as implied by the term 'Caliph' (vicegerent), in

Qur'an 2:30. But that doesn't limit a woman's vicegerency solely to bear or rear children. There is no judgment made in the Qur'an against a barren woman, a woman who chooses not to have children, or a young woman who dies before childbearing with one that has many children. Only two of the Prophet's wives even bore children with him : Khadija and Mariya. Other wives such as Hafsa, Ayesha and Zaynab did not bear any children, and there is no evidence that they were discounted for this. In many Muslim cultures today, however, a woman's role and status are often defined and affected by her decision to delay childbearing, the number and gender of the children, or the inability or desire to have children at all. If childbearing is indeed the only role for women, then such cultural preoccupations are understandable; but Islamic teachings always have a way of putting things in balance, reinforcing the significance of motherhood, but not defining roles completely by biology.

Thematic Summary of Various Chapters

The Book of Genesis alludes to the idea that woman, not man, was the primary agent of what is customarily described as the 'fall' or man's expulsion from the Garden of Eden, and hence all daughters of Eve are to be regarded with hatred, suspicion and contempt. It further indicates that woman was created not only from man but also for man, which makes her existence merely instrumental and not of fundamental importance. The second chapter critically evaluates the story from the perspective of an enlightened Qur'anic vision, which is based on justice and compassion. It also ventures to show how the practice of patriarchal power in Muslim societies has been mediated through understandings of the Qur'an. It analyzes Qur'anic exegesis related to the creation of human being in order to focus on how the practice of religious power is defined and reflected in the existing gender ideology and gender relations. The essay further argues that the ideological tenets embedded in a patriarchal understanding of the Qur'an and Islam fosters a mode of gender relations, which practically disempowered Muslim women.

Islam brought radical changes regarding women and society, despite the deeply entrenched patriarchy of seventh-century Arabia. It commands people to pay attention to the concept of balance, harmony, compatibility and inter-human unity as well as to their environment. The concept of gender relations in Islam is more than merely the managing of gender justice, but theologically and teleologically arranging the relation mode between microcosmic (human), macrocosmic (environment) and God. Only through this can humans perform their functions as caliph (vicegerent), and it is only the successful caliph who can achieve the level of a true worshipper (*abid*). Gender is an undeniable aspect of human creation, which has inherently divided the human race into women and men. There are some individual distinctions between the male and female sexes of all living beings in the universe. This intrinsic distinction between the sexes sets the basis for human reproduction and the continuation of human generations and on the other hand, it has created a continuous debate and conflict of identity and hierarchy. Even though human societies and their legal systems have evolved towards perfection, the issue of the subordination of one sex by the other and the oppression of women persists in different forms in many societies in the world. Islam principally regards men and women on an equal footing in creation and in human dignity and value. The reality of the gender difference does not in any way effect their ontological position. Gender difference does not always signify inequality as many feminists themselves now agree who initially postulated women's liberation in terms of the identical treatment of women and men. The third chapter seeks a balance between the claims of Radical Feminism and Misogynic Religionists. The Qur'an provides hermeneutic keys for reading the text, in line with the principles of holism, contextual legitimacy, and analytical reasoning.

The Qur'anic recognition of its own thematic unity is clear from its warning not to break it "into parts", or to "change the words from their right places and the contexts and forget a substantial part of the Message" (4:46). The Qur'an praises those who comprehend the text as a totality. Every reading of it may not be appropriate emerges from the Qur'anic approval of those "who listen to the Word and follow the best (meaning) in it" (39:18), and its criticism of those who focus only on its "allegorical verses for its hidden meaning" (3:7, 11:1). One has to make a clear distinction between the Qur'an, on the one hand, and the human interpretations of the Qur'an, on the other, which reflects the particular historical contexts from which they emerged. That distinction opens up the possibility of alternate, progressive and gender-sensitive readings of the Qur'an. God, who speaks through the Qur'an, is characterized by justice, and it is stated clearly in the Qur'an that God can never be guilty of "zulm" (unfairness, tyranny, oppression, or wrongdoing). Hence, the Qur'an, as God's Word, cannot be made the source of human injustice, and the injustice to which Muslim women have been subjected cannot be regarded as God-derived. The fourth chapter not only argues that such readings and representations of Islam and the Qur'an as patriarchal rest on a number of faults, but also that the Qur'an can be read as an anti-patriarchal text, that is, as undermining the fundamental claims of patriarchies with detailed examples.

In the discourse on the actualization of gender justice in society language and the perception of language influence the understandings, conclusions, implementations and indications that arise from the actual living relationship between the males and females in society. It is often said that human language is insufficient for discussion about the Divine. Therefore, understanding both the strengths and shortcomings of language is important in changing restrictive policies and laws. Muslims traditionally use 'Allah' as the Arabic name of God. Descriptions of 'Allah' abound in the

Qur'an and the *Sunnah*. Islamic theology confronts us with the spectacular absence of a gendered Godhead. However, like other Scriptures the Qur'an also uses 'He' to refer to Allah, while making it clear that Allah transcends all dualistic traits. The Arabic use of the male gender for the generic does not mean that God is male. A theology, which reveals the divine through incarnation in a body, also locates it in a gender, and inescapably passes judgment on the other sex. This is the pertinent question dealt in this paper: while male and female are aspects of duality, Allah is unique. Nothing else resembles Him. He has no counterpart. So why is the male pronoun used to refer to Allah? The fifth chapter argues that the use of the pronoun "He" is only due to linguistic inevitability, and not an epistemological claim about God's Being.

In Islam lawful sex (i.e., sex within marriage) is viewed highly positively for both the pleasures and the procreative function. It is regarded as an act of religious devotion (*'ibadah'*) for which rewards in the Hereafter are acknowledged. While the Qur'an emphasize on reciprocity of the spouses, Muslim world negates it by the acceptance of certain male-centered *ahadith*. This creates marital discordance and socio-psychical problems among the couples. The sixth chapter explores the idea in greater detail arguing that disadvantageous circumstances of women should always be countered in conjunction with an attempt to alleviate those factors, which adversely affect both genders. In the essay egalitarian interpretations are being used not only in relation to women's rights and position, but to call upon men to give more in the family, and to end abuse of power over and scapegoating of women. It is a tragedy for Muslims that we find no problems today with projecting our own ignorance, misogyny, obscurantism, and hatred onto the Qur'an, and thus onto God. The good of the group or totality is always more crucial than the good of any one sector of the society. In fact, the society is seen as an organic whole in which the welfare of each member or organ is necessary for the health and well being of every other part. Any radical change, which is to succeed in an Islamic environment, must be one, which does not work chauvinistically for male's interest alone. Islamic traditions should be re-read in order to achieve women's progress in tandem with the wider struggle to benefit all members of the society. An analysis of the classical '*fiqh*' texts on marital life shows that the model of gender relations in the early texts of Islamic jurisprudence is grounded in the patriarchal ideology of pre-Islamic Arabia, which continued into the Islamic era in a modified form through a set of male-dominated theological, legal and social theories and assumptions, such as "women are created of and for men." These theories stood in sharp contradiction to the Qur'an, which holds that the relationship of men and women is one of equality, mutuality and cordiality.

Muslim intellectuals must be acutely aware of the distinction between the text, which is given, and objective, and the personal understanding of a scholar, which is inherently subjective. There is a difference between what is the revealed word of God and what is human understanding of the word of God. The former is divine; the latter is fallible and changeable in accordance with changing times and circumstances. The sources are a body of data and the 'fiqh' is a process for understanding that data. Islamic scholarship began with a clear distinction between text and 'fiqh'. However, from the middle of the second century A.H, 'fiqh' began to be treated as a body of knowledge, standardized and considered objective, as opposed to being treated simply as scholarly opinion. This assumption of scientific status elevated 'fiqh' for all intents and purposes to the level of Divine inspiration. While this was and is never claimed by jurists, the incorporation of 'fiqh' within Shari'ah as constituting the body of Shari'ah principles renders 'fiqh' objective, conclusive, and, in similar fashion to the Qur'an, inimitable. The very nature of 'usul al-fiqh' facilitated the internalization of the cultural norms of the communities in which the foundations of Islamic jurisprudence were laid. These cultural norms are evidenced in the body of 'fiqh' that Muslims have inherited over the centuries. The opinions of medieval jurists, which comprise a major proportion of the 'fiqh', are often referred to as falling within the Shari'ah. Orthodox Muslim 'ulema' resist readings of Islamic law that treat it like any other system of law, and disguise their resistance by mystification and misrepresentation. In chapter seven the case of blood money ('Diya') is taken as an example where there is a clear variance between Qur'anic norms of gender justice and 'fiqh' consideration of gender bias. What attempted here is an internal critique of traditional Islamic jurisprudence and the historical denial of equality of rights for women in the formulation and application of Islamic law.

History reveals that sexual oppression of women, in one form or another, exists in every society in the world. Nevertheless, it has been achieved by different methods : economically, intellectually, physically and psychologically. The control of women's bodies, or in other words physical mutilation, was raised with the rise of patriarchy. Islam, like any religious tradition, can be used to support human rights, democracy, and respect among different communities, or oppression, authoritarianism, and violence, depending on the choices and actions of Muslims everywhere. Majority of Muslims believes that the Qur'an itself teaches that men are superior to women and that women are inferior and subordinate to men. But that is not my own understanding of the Qur'an and enlightened scholars always felt that such readings of it are terribly irreligious because they reduce and corrupt our idea of God. My attempt in chapter eight is to recover the Qur'anic basis of gender equality and thus, to provide a convincing case about why Islam is not inherently a patriarchal religion and why Muslim women and men can jointly struggle for fairness and equality from within an Islamic framework itself.

End Notes

1. Jan Goodwin, *Price of Honor: Muslim Women Lift the Veil of Silence on the Islamic World*, Little Brown & Co: London, 1994, p. 27.
2. Hina Jilani, "Whose Laws? Human Rights and Violence Against Women in Pakistan" In *Freedom From Violence: Women's Strategies from Around the World* (Ed. Margaret Schuler), Wild Books: New York, 1992, p. 71.
3. *The Pakistan Penal Code*, p. L.D. Publishers: Lahore, 1975, p. 183.
4. Amina Wadud, *Quran and Woman: Rereading the Sacred Text from a Woman's Perspective*, Oxford University Press: New York, 1999, Ch. 1.
5. A.D. Ajijola, *Introduction to Islamic Law*, International Islamic Publishers: Karachi, 1981, p. 134.
6. Qur'an 3:195, 4:124, 33:35, 57:12.

2

Was Eve Created from the Rib of Adam?

An attempt at exploring the role of women in Islam has the potential to offer a profound understanding of the truth, of the world and of our place in it. To get to the root of the position of women in Islam we need to go back to the story of Adam and Eve. Theologically, the history of women's inferior status in the Muslim (as well as the Jewish and Christian) tradition began with the story of Eve's creation from Adam's rib. Changing her status requires returning to the point of creation and setting the record straight. Given the way the 'rib' story has been used, it is impossible to overemphasize its importance. The starting point is simple enough in that it asserts that God's primary creation is man, not woman, since woman is believed to have been created from man's rib. Hence she is derivative and secondary ontologically. I suggest that the reader leave aside any preconceived notions regarding the origin of woman for a few minutes and start afresh. This practice has the advantage of opening certain new vistas without any loss of perspective: if the new doors do not open, one can always go back, to the older constructions.

Nietzsche, a great philosopher, believed that man and woman were two different creatures. By and by they evolved and came to resemble each other. So they are thought of as two different races. It must be emphasized, however, that those philosophers and scientists who believe that Adam and Eve are of the same race have always despised the female's nature. However, the position of the Qur'an is that man and woman are of the same nature. Contrary to all the past philosophies, the Qur'an contends that both male and female are of the same nature, and was created simultaneously by God. They are of the same race and are, therefore, brothers and sisters.

The Qur'an is the Magna Carta of human rights and a large part of its concern is to free human beings from the bondage of traditionalism, authoritarianism (religious, political, economic, or any other), tribalism, racism, casteism, sexism, slavery or anything else that prohibits or inhibits human beings from actualizing the Qur'anic vision of human destiny. The goal of Qur'anic Islam is to establish peace, which can only exist within a just environment.

Ample historical evidence portrays women in the Prophet's Medina raising their heads from slavery to claim their right to join, as equal participants, in the making of their Islamic nation. Women such as Khadija and Ayesha (wives of the Prophet Muhammad) and Rabi'a al Basri (the outstanding woman Sufi) figured significantly in early Islam. Khadija, herself a business entrepreneur, was the foremost patron of the Islamic movement, in its nascent phase, and the person of Prophet Muhammad. Ayesha was one of the main sources of oral information about the Prophet, which evolved into the ahadith. She played a leading political role. However, the Islamic tradition has, by and large, remained rigidly patriarchal until the present time, prohibiting the growth of scholarship among women particularly in the realm of religious thought. This means that the sources on which the Islamic tradition is mainly based, namely, the Qur'an, the Sunnah, the Hadith literature and 'Fiqh' have been interpreted only by Muslim men who have arrogated to themselves the task of defining the ontological, theological, sociological and eschatological status of Muslim women. In certain ahadith texts, we can find the discriminatory and oppressive rules governing women. Girls are much less likely than boys to receive an education in Muslim society today. They are often deprived of their share of family inheritance, they are held under a much higher level of scrutiny to behave modestly compared to their brothers. The Muslim world is fraught with political tyranny and corruption, great economic backwardness and a high degree of intellectual stagnation. There is an enormous gap between what Islamic scriptures say and the way these texts are practiced today.

The issue of woman's creation is more fundamental theologically than any other. This is so because if God who is the ultimate giver of value has created man and woman equal, then they cannot become unequal, essentially, at a subsequent time. On the other hand, if God has created man and woman unequal, then they cannot become equal, essentially, at a subsequent time. If one upholds the view that man and woman were created equal by God-which is the teaching of the Qur'an-then the existing inequality between men and women cannot be seen as having been mandated by God but must be seen as a subversion of God's original plan for humanity.

The Qur'anic Revolution

In order to fully comprehend the phenomena of Qur'anic revolution, with regard to the status woman, one has to realize the theological concept prevalent among the most 'advanced' faiths, viz., Judaism and Christianity. Both the Bible and the Qur'an tell the story of the creation of the first man, Adam. This story is significant for its universal appeal, as it tells how mankind began its earthly existence.

Just a quick study of the way the Bible treats Eve would explain the reason behind all the problems that the women are suffering today. When God asked Adam why he ate from the forbidden Tree, he answered, according to Genesis: "And the man (Adam) said, the woman (Eve) whom thou gavest to be with me, she gave me of the Tree, and I did eat. And the Lord God said unto the woman, what is this that thou hast done? And the woman said, the serpent beguiled me, and I did eat. And the Lord God said unto the serpent, Because thou hast done this, thou art cursed above all cattle, and above every beast of the field; upon thy belly shalt thou go, and dust shalt thou eat all the days of thy life: And I will put enmity between thee and the woman, and between thy seed and her seed; it shall bruise thy head, and thou shalt bruise his heel. Unto the woman he said, I will greatly multiply thy sorrow and thy conception; in sorrow thou shalt bring forth children; and thy desire shall be to thy husband, and he shall rule over thee" (3:12-16).

Women are from the origin (Eve), sinful and so they must pay. All this came from the belief of Original Sin. Bible states: "Of the woman came the beginning of sin, and through her we all die" (Ecclesiastes 25:22). "I find more bitter than death the woman who is a snare, whose heart is a trap and whose hands are chains. The man who pleases God will escape her, but the sinner she will ensnare.... while I was still searching but not finding, I found one upright man among a thousand but not one upright woman among them all" (Ecclesiasticus 7:26-28). One has to ask what is the wisdom in denying the existence of even one upright woman on earth? In another part of the Hebrew literature, which is found in the Catholic Bible, we read:" No wickedness comes anywhere near the wickedness of a woman...Sin began with a woman and thanks to her we all must die" (Ecclesiasticus 25:19, 25:24). The Genesis narration implies that the source of all moral degradation, and decadence is the woman's deceit. She carries the unwanted burden of her sin and is eternally cursed upon for this reason.

The Bible states that the period of the mother's ritual impurity is twice as long if the child born is a girl than when it is a boy (Leviticus 12:2-5). The Catholic Bible does state explicitly: "The birth of a daughter is a loss" (Sirach 22:3). In contrast to this shocking statement, boys receive special praise: "A man who educates his son will be the envy of his enemy" (Ecclesiasticus 30:3). A daughter is considered a painful burden, a potential source of shame to her father:

"Your daughter is headstrong? Keep a sharp look-out that she doesn't make you the laughing stock of your enemies, the talk of the town, the object of common gossip, and put you to public shame" (Ecclesiasticus 42:11).

It is clear in the Old Testament that uncovering a woman's head was a great disgrace and that's why the priest had to uncover the suspected adulteress in her trial by ordeal (Numbers 5:16-18). St.. Paul in the New Testament made some very interesting statements about the veil: "Now I want you to realize that the head of every man is Christ, and the head of the woman is man, and the head of Christ is God. Every man who prays or prophesies with his head covered dishonors his head. And every woman who prays or prophesies with her head uncovered dishonors her head-it is just as though her head were shaved. If a woman doesn't cover her head, she should have her hair cut off; and if it is a disgrace for a woman to have her hair cut off or shaved off, she should cover her head. A man ought not to cover his head, since he is the image and glory of God; but the woman is the glory of man. For man didn't come from woman, but woman from man; neither was man created for woman, but woman for man. For this reason, and because of the angels, the woman ought to have a sign of authority on her head" (I Corinthians11:3-10). St Paul's rationale for veiling women is that the veil represents a sign of authority of the man, who is the image and glory of God, over the woman who was created from and for the man.

All the three religions of Judaism, Christianity, and Islam agree on one basic fact: God creates both men and women. But the Judeo-Christian tradition teaches that Satan appeared in the form of a serpent before Eve and tempted her to eat from the forbidden Tree and that it was Eve who seduced Adam to eat with her. A careful look into the two accounts of the story of the creation reveals some essential differences.[1] In 20:120, the Qur'an tells us "... the Devil whispered to him: O Adam! Shall I show thee the Tree of immortality?" Then in the next verse (20:121), using the pronoun 'huma', it is clear that both Adam and Eve ate from the Tree. The same verse then ends with "and Adam disobeyed his Lord, and went astray." In 20: 123, God again speaks to both Adam and Eve: "Go down hence, both of you." The Qur'an in 7:19-25 clarifies that it was both Adam and Eve at fault, equally: "fa-waswasa lahumaa ash-shaytaan" meaning "So Satan whispered to them (dual)". It is clear that the Qur'an, contrary to the Bible, places equal blame on both Adam and Eve for their mistake. It does not say that Eve tempted Adam to eat from the Tree or even that she had eaten before him. Eve in the Qur'an is not a seducer or deceiver. God, according to the Qur'an, punishes no one for another's faults. Both Adam and Eve committed a sin and then asked God for forgiveness and He forgave them both. So there is no question of a hereditary sin called Original Sin in Islam. Eve, like Adam, was not restricted from the Tree in order to follow God's commands by default. She was tested, chose to disobey God and went to the Tree on her own free will. She also paid the price. There is nothing wrong with making a wrong decision, for it is better to learn, repent and be stronger for it than never to be challenged at all and remain meek all our lives. In short, the whole story clearly teaches us the divine directive for equality of the sexes, fairness, and justice in matters relating to men and women. The following Islamic principles are also brought to light: that humans have freedom of will, responsibility for their choice of action and the consequent accountability before God. Islam does not contribute to any theory of the 'fall of Adam' symbolizing the fall of Man. There was no 'fall' in that particular sense. Human being was created for the purpose of acting as vicegerent on the earth and he came to the world to fulfil this mission. It, actually, represents the 'rise of man' to a new assignment, his tryst with destiny, and not a 'fall' (2:30-39).

Once Adam is held responsible for the sin he committed, he cannot blame it on Eve, since he is as responsible a human being as she. Both Adam and Eve were punished for their sin by being ousted from Paradise. In the Qur'anic story, Eve did not receive any harsher admonition than Adam and was not threatened by misery for herself and all her female offspring as the Bible depicts. The Qur'an, while referring to the rewards of the pious in the Hereafter, has categorically stated that: all persons-men as well as women-shall be fully rewarded for their deeds and shall not be wronged in the least [2]; they shall get all that they may desire and all that they can ask for, as a first gift from God. His blessings would follow subsequently (41:31); and they-men as well as women-shall have perfect counterparts/spouses as a reward of their deeds.[3]

As should be obvious from the above points, and as mentioned in the Qur'an, there is absolutely no difference in the reward of men and women. The Qur'an has offered women dignity, justice, and protection, which, for long, have remained out of their reach. Every human being is born pure and untainted and thus there is no need for a saviour to come and be sacrificed in order to save humanity from our sinful nature.[4] Women in the Qur'an are not portrayed as the cause of humanity's downfall and corruption. In this way the Qur'an and Islam can be seen as part of a tradition that significantly increased the status of women from a religious and theological standpoint. God no longer depicted women as corrupters of the human race. They were no longer created out of men for men's benefit.

The Qur'an is not less clear in commanding equality for men and women in its directives regarding religious obligations and rewards.' We read: Lo! Men who surrender unto God, and women who surrender, and men who believe and women who believe, and men who obey and women who obey, and men who speak the truth and women who speak the truth, and men who persevere (in righteousness) and women who persevere and men who are humble and women who are humble, and men who give alms and women who give alms, and men who fast and women who fast, and men who guard their modesty and women who guard (their modesty), and men who remember (God) and women who remember-God hath prepared for them forgiveness and a vast reward' (33:35). It reveals to mankind the desired equality of the two sexes by establishing the same ethical obligations and rewards for women and men: 'And who so does good works, whether male or female, and he (or she) is a believer, such will enter Paradise and they will not be wronged the dint in a date-stone' (4:124). "Whosoever does right, whether male or female, and is a believer, him verily We shall quicken with good life, and We shall pay them a recompense according to the best of what they do" (16:97). The Qur'an grants woman a share in the inheritance of the family (4:7-11), warns against depriving her of that inheritance (4:19), specifies that the dower ('mahr') of her marriage should belong to her alone and never be taken by her husband[5] unless offered by the woman as a free gift (4:44). As with any privilege, these rights of women carry corresponding responsibilities. If she commits a civil offence, the Qur'an tells us, woman's penalty is no less or no more than that of a man in a similar case (5:41, 24:2).

The Qur'an says: "O you who believe! You are forbidden to inherit women against their will. Nor should you treat them with harshness that you may take away part of the dower you have given them-except where they have been guilty of open lewdness; on the contrary live with them on a footing of kindness and equity. If you take a dislike to them it may be that you dislike a thing and God brings about through it a great deal of good" (4:19). "And how could you take it when you have gone in unto each other and they (your wives) have taken from you a solemn covenant? "(4:21). A contract or covenant ("meesaq") requires the free consent of both parties in agreeing to that contract. An agreement in which a person is forced to do something against his or her will do not constitute a "meesaq". If the woman has been forced into getting married or the will of the man has been manipulated by coercion then such an agreement does not become a contract or "meesaq". Thus for a contract of marriage to come about, both parties, i.e., the man as well as the woman have to use their free will in coming to terms and agreeing to live the rest of their lives with each other. If out of these two any one is forced or does not have their free will involved then such would not constitute a "meesaq".

Qur'an, in addressing the believers, often uses the expression, 'believing men and women' to emphasize the equality of men and women in regard to their respective duties, rights, virtues and merits.[6] In Islam, women are neither viewed as being biologically warped nor are they seen, generally speaking to be of criminal mentality (crooked). They are human beings of a similar nature (4:1) similar to that of men and were also created "in the best of moulds" (95:4). The Islamic duty is to "forgive and overlook and cover up their (women's) faults" (64:14) and not to treat them with harshness, on the contrary, live with them on the footing of kindness and equity (4:19), are particularly relevant in this context.

It was this very same idea of considering daughters as being a source of shame that led the pagan Arabs, before the advent of Islam, to practice female infanticide. Qur'an severely condemned this heinous practice (16:59). It has to be mentioned that this sinister crime would have never stopped in Arabia were it not for the power of the scathing manner the Qur'an used to condemn this practice.[7] The Qur'an, moreover, makes no distinction between boys and girls. In contrast to the Bible, the Qur'an considers the birth of a female as a gift and a blessing from God, same as the case with the birth of a male. It even mentions the gift of the female birth first (42:49).

The Qur'an never considers any woman to be the possession of any man. It eloquently describes the relationship between the mates by saying, "And among His signs is that He created for you mates from among yourselves, that you may dwell in tranquility with them and He has put love and mercy between your hearts: verily in that are signs for those who reflect" (30:21). This is the Qur'anic conception of marriage: love, mercy, and tranquillity, not possession and double standards. It speaks of the intimate and close relationship of the two mates in these words: "They are like garments unto you as you are like garments unto them" (2:187). This verse; by using the simile of garments, has explained two basic facts. First, dress is considered to be one of the most fundamental needs of human beings in all stages of life. Second, dress covers the nakedness of human beings and hides those parts, which are to be kept hidden. Every person has his weakness and frailty and does not want them to be disclosed to others. The two sexes working together, not only cover each other's weakness and frailty, but also enhance each other's capabilities and help each other make up their deficiencies. Men are told to be generous and liberal in their treatment of women under all circumstances, especially when the relations between the two are not very amicable. The Qur'an refers to this in these words: "And do not forget liberality between yourselves" (2:237). It describes very gentle conversations between the Prophet Solomon and the Queen of Sheba (27:42-44), and between Moses and two young ladies (28:23-26), which symbolize the civilized social relationship between the two genders. Among the pagan Arabs before Islam, inheritance rights were confined exclusively to the male relatives. Qur'an abolished all these unjust customs and gave all the female relatives their just share.[8] Among the pagan Arabs, before Islam, the widow was considered to be a part of her husband's property to be inherited by his male heirs and she was, usually, given in marriage to the deceased man's eldest son from another wife. Qur'an scathingly attacked and abolished this degrading custom (4:22). There is no stigma attached with divorce or widowhood in the Qur'an.[9].The Islamic veil, unlike the veil of the Christian tradition, is neither a sign of man's authority over woman nor is it a sign of woman's subjection to man. It, unlike the veil in the Jewish tradition, is not a sign of luxury and distinction of some noble married women, but only as a symbol of modesty with the sole purpose of protecting women, in fact, all women.[10] In fact, Qur'an is so concerned with protecting women's bodies and women's reputation that a man who dares to falsely accuse a woman of sexual infidelity will be severely punished (24:4). In Islam there is absolutely no difference between men and women as far as their relationship to God is concerned, as both are promised the same reward for good conduct and the same punishment for evil conduct. Qur'an says: 'And for women are rights over men similar to those of men over women' (2:226). 'Believers, men and Women, are protectors, one of another: they enjoin what is just and forbid what is evil, they observe regular prayers, practice regular charity, and obey God and His Messenger. On them will God pour His mercy: for God is exalted in power and is wise' (9:71).' And the Lord answered them: Truly I will never cause to be lost the work of any of you, be you a male or female, you are members one of another '(3:195). It proclaims that women have souls exactly the same way as men and will enter Paradise if they are righteous. Who so does that which is right, and believes, whether male or female, him or her will We quicken to happy life (16:97).[11]It admonishes those men who oppress or ill-treat women (4:19). While the Bible forbids women from speaking in church (I Corinthians 14:34-35), the Qur'an illustrates how a woman can argue with the Prophet (58:1).

Subversion of the Qur'anic Spirit

Nowhere in the Qur'an can one find even the slightest hint that Eve tempted Adam to eat from the Tree or even that she had eaten before him. Eve in the Qur'an is no temptress, no seducer, and no deceiver. Moreover, Eve isn't to be blamed for the pains of childbearing. Indeed, childbearing is a sacrifice, which improves her status rather than resulted from a curse (31:14, 46:15). God, according to the Qur'an, punishes no one for another's faults (59:12, 95:18). Paradoxically, the myth of Eve as temptress is widely prevalent in the Muslim world. The ordinary Muslim believes, as seriously as the ordinary Jew or Christian, that Adam was God's primary creation and that Eve was made from Adam's rib.

Since all Muslim scholars agree on the principle that any hadith, which is in contradiction to the Qur'an, cannot be accepted as authentic, (these) ahadith ought to be rejected on material grounds. There are no "ifs" and "buts" regarding this principle. Unfortunately, when it comes to women, there are many ahadith that conflict either with other hadith literature or with verses of the Qur'an. We have a very sad situation: most Muslims say that they hold the Qur'an as the most important source for all Islamic issues, but when it comes to practice, it seems that "traditions" determine how we conduct our lives. Nowhere is this more noticeable than in the treatment of women. And apparently it all stems from the perception that Eve, or Hawwa, who was supposedly created from the rib of Adam, was the cause of the downfall of man.

In ahadith we find statements like: If a woman could prostrate to another person (besides God) it will be her husband (Abu Dawud 11.2135); Women, house and horses are evil omens (Bukhari 7.62.30); Majority of women are in hell (Bukhari 1.6.301); A prayer is annulled by a passing woman, dog and a monkey. (Bukhari 1.9.490); Women, house and horses are evil omens (Bukhari 7.62.30); and, the urine of a male baby is cleaner than that of a female (Ibn Majah). The reason cited for the last one is: "He (the Prophet) said, 'Verily, God, the exalted, created Adam and, Hawwa was created from his small rib. Thus a lad's urine became from water and clay and urine of a lass [girl] became from flesh and blood." But the continuing popularity of these "ahadith" among Muslims in general, also indicates that they articulate something deeply embedded in Muslim culture, namely, the belief that women are derivative and secondary in the context of human creation.

Myth of the 'Rib of Adam' in the Bible

The Bible describes the creation of Eve in these terms: "The Lord God said: 'It is not good that Man should be alone; I will make him an help meet'... the Lord God caused a deep sleep to fall upon Adam...and He took one of his ribs... and made He a woman ... and brought her unto the man...and...Adam said, She shall be called woman" (Genesis 2:18,21-3).

The term "helper" has historically been interpreted as implying an inferior role for Eve. The Hebrew word translated "helper" is used twenty-one times in the Old Testament: twenty of these cases refer to help from a superior. Adam later asserts his authority over Eve by naming her. According to Genesis 3:16, Adam's role is to become Eve's master. The King James Version (KJV), New International Version (NIV), and Revised Standard Version (RSV) use the term "rule" to describe Adam's rule over Eve. The Living Bible substitutes "master" for "helper". The Modern Language Bible uses "dominate". By implication, all of their descendents would have the same power imbalance between spouses. 1Timothy 2:11-14 reads: "Let a women learn in silence with all submissiveness. I permit no women to teach or have authority over men; she is to keep silent. For Adam was formed first, then Eve; and Adam was not deceived, but the women was deceived and became a transgressor." In 1 Corinthians 14: 34-35 we are told: "...women should remain silent in the churches. They are not allowed to speak, but are in submission as the law says. If they want to inquire about something, they should ask their own husband at home; for it is disgraceful for a women to speak in church." And 1 Corinthians 11: 3-9 says: "A man ought not to cover his head, since he is the image and glory of God; but the women is the glory of man. For man did not come from woman, but woman from man. Neither was man created for woman, but woman for man." How can a woman learn if she is not allowed to speak? How can a woman grow intellectually if she is obliged to be in a state of total submission? How can she broaden her horizons if her onc and only source of information is her husband at home?

Myth of the Rib in Ahadith

Only later, under Jewish and Christian influence, did the ordinary Muslim come to believe that Adam was first created and that Eve was made from him. The hadith related to 'rib' reads: 'Women were created crooked; if you try to straighten her you will break her and breaking her is divorcing her' (Muslim 8:3467). "He who believes in God and the Hereafter, if he witnesses any matter he should talk in good terms about it or keep quiet. Act kindly towards woman, for woman is created from a rib, and the most crooked part of the rib is its top. If you attempt to straighten it, you will break it, and if you leave it, its crookedness will remain there. So act kindly towards women." (Muslim 8:3468). 'A woman is like a rib—that is why she has the crookedness.' (Bukhari 7.62.113).

Without entering the polemics regarding the authenticity of the hadith referred to, one can be sure that the statement ascribed to the Prophet should be construed as a general statement, based upon general exposure and experience. In the hadith, there is no mention of Eve. It is the female sex that has been mentioned in general. Even if one takes it literally the hadith does not indicate that 'rib', from which 'woman' was created, was taken from Adam. If all the texts of the hadith referred to be analyzed, it becomes evident that it compares the nature of a woman with a rib. The comparison subtly alludes to the fact that a woman's nature is very delicate and tender as well as a bit stubborn. It advises men to handle women tactfully keeping in view this nature. Instead of forcing them to accept a particular point of view, which will only bring out their obduracy, men should try to convince and persuade them. At the maximum, the hadith is indicative of the behavioral traits of women, rather than their anthropological origin.

Qur'an does not discriminate against women despite the sad and bitter fact of history that the cumulative (Jewish, Christian, Hellenistic, Bedouin, and other) biases which existed in the Arab-Islamic culture of the early centuries of Islam infiltrated the Islamic tradition, largely through the hadith literature, and undermined the intent of the Qur'an to liberate women from the status of chattel or inferior creatures, making them free and equal to men. Not only does the Qur'an emphasize that righteousness is identical in the case of man or woman, but it affirms, clearly and consistently, women's equality with men and their fundamental right to actualize the human potential that they share equally with men (16:97, 23:35). In fact, when seen through a non-patriarchal lens, the Qur'an goes beyond egalitarianism. It exhibits particular solicitude toward women as also toward other classes of disadvantaged persons. Further, it provides particular safeguards for protecting women's special sexual/biological functions such as carrying, delivering, suckling, and rearing, offspring.[12] We must remember that truth is often camouflaged in the very source of information we use as reference. Often the information at our disposal is imbedded in the indiscriminate use of isolated traditions or of groups of traditions emanating from single biased sources or from well-defined socio-political and religious groups. Each seeks to establish that version of "history" that is best suited to its own aspirations and prejudices. Conservatism, though a mental attitude, has a social base and finds anchor in intellectually bankrupt and stagnant societies, even when these societies give a superficial impression of being progressive. We must bear in mind that in these societies conservatism provides an inner defence mechanism for an externally perceived threat.

Notwithstanding the Qur'anic and Prophetic warrants for treating women and men with equality to the point of what would now be called positive discrimination against women, in many Muslim societies the survival of pre-Islamic mores or the influence of other cultures has led to girls and women being devalued, with all the consequences thereby entailed. Some Muslims-those who are commonly tagged 'fundamentalist' among them-seek to justify the abuses that result from this bias in Islamic terms; but it is not hard to find Muslim theologians, sociologists, historians, human rights lawyers and others who challenge such distortions.

Creation of Eve in the Qur'an

Certain Arabic nouns (as in French or Spanish) take a gender. Thus, a Muslim man is a 'muslim' while a Muslim woman is a 'muslimah'. The plurals reflect these gendered endings also, but less clearly. A group of Muslim women is 'muslimat'; a group of Muslim men is 'muslimun'. However, a group that includes both men and women is also referred to as 'muslimun'. Thus, when the collective noun 'muslimun' appears in the Qur'an in its male form, it cannot generally be assumed that it refers to men only; rather, in most cases it refers to all Muslims, male and female.

The word "ummah" comes from the root "umm" or "mother." The symbols of a mother and motherly love and compassion are also linked with the two attributes most characteristic of God, namely, "Rahim" and "Rahman," both of which are derived from the root "rahm," meaning "womb." The ideal "ummah" cares about all its members just as an ideal mother cares about all her children, knowing that all are not equal and that each has different needs. While showing undue favor to any child would be unjust, a mother who gives to a "handicapped" child more than she does to her other child or children, is not acting unjustly but exemplifying the spirit of "ihsan" (righteousness, benevolence and empathy) by helping to make up the deficiency of a child who is unable to meet the requirements of life. Thus "ihsan" shows God's sympathy for the "disadvantaged" segments of human society (such as women, orphans, slaves, the poor, deprived, the infirm, the minorities, etc.).

The words that we use normally have a relationship with the concepts that we have. The concept of Divinity has traditionally been one of perfection and absolute power and authority. It is for this reason that man has generally not used the feminine gender for God. The "He" that is normally used for God does not signify that we have ascribed to the concept of a male God as compared to a female God, it only signifies the concept of the power and authority that has traditionally been associated with Divinity. Masculine gender for God does not signify a male God just like the feminine gender for a country does not signify a female country.

An analysis of the Qur'anic descriptions of human creation shows how the Qur'an even-handedly uses both feminine and masculine terms and imagery to describe the creation of humanity from a single source: "O people, be careful of (your duty to) your Lord, Who created you from a single being, and created its mate of the same essence" (4:1). Some people translate the verse 4:1 as: 'It is He Who has created you from a single person (Adam), and then He created from him his wife (Eve)'. They explain this verse by saying that Eve was created from the rib of Adam. This misleading translation has probably arisen because of the Arabic words 'khalaqa minha zawjaha', which if literally translated mean 'created from that initial soul his/her mate' (16:72). Actually the word 'minha' (from the soul) does not imply that 'Eve was made from Adam'; they rather imply that Eve was made from the same species as Adam, meaning that both were human. Qur'anic translators disagree on the meaning of "nafs" in the above verse, which Muhammad Asad translated as "living entity." The literal translation of 'minha' as 'out of it' clearly alludes, in conformity with the text to biological fact that both sexes have originated from the 'one living entity'. Many claim that "nafs" translates as "person," that is, Adam. But according to Asad and other scholars, God created humankind and its sexual counterpart out of its own kind. The Arabic word referring to mate ('zawj'), in the above Qur'anic verse, is grammatically neutral and can be applied both to male and female interchangeably. So it is fallacious to assume that Adam was created first, Eve was created out of Adam, or that Eve/woman is innately subservient to Adam / man. The fact that this Qur'anic verse does not specify one specific sex over the other is proof of gender non-bias and equality. It is commonly (and mistakenly) argued that Adam was created first, and that by this gesture God finds the male dominant and superior to the female. However, the wording of the Qur'an in the aforementioned verse (4:1) does not support this claim. That God's original creation was neither man nor woman, but undifferentiated humanity, (who appeared simultaneously at a subsequent time) is implicit in a number of Qur'anic passages. The term 'Adam' is a masculine noun, but linguistic gender is not sex. If 'Adam' is not necessarily a man, then Adam's 'zawj' is not necessarily a woman. In fact, the term 'zawj' is also a masculine noun and, unlike the term Adam, it has a feminine counterpart, 'zawjatun'. (Here, it may be noted that the most accurate English equivalent of 'zawj' is not "wife" or "husband" or even "spouse" but "mate"). The Qur'an uses 'zawj' with reference not only to human beings but also to every kind of creation, including animals, plants and fruits.[13] If the Qur'an makes no distinction between the creation of man and woman—as it clearly does not—why do Muslims believe that Hawwa was created from Adam's rib?

One of the major themes of the Qur'an is that God's creation as a whole is "for just ends" (15:85) and not "for idle sport" (21:16). Humanity, consisting of both men and women, is fashioned "in the best of moulds" (95:4). We should understand that Adam here stands for Man in the generic sense. The Qur'an declares what it means: "We created Man from sounding clay, from mud molded into shape" (15:26). 'God began the creation of Man from clay, and made his progeny from a quintessence of fluid' (32:7-8). 'It is He Who created you from a single person, and made his mate of like nature, in order that he might dwell with her in love' (7:189). It means that the first man and woman (Adam and Eve) were created directly by the Almighty. The point is made clearer still elsewhere by the Qur'an.[14] Let me quote one verse: 'And God has made mates for you from among yourselves' (16:72). This lays down that our wives are of the same kind and essence as ourselves. No clearer announcement of the equality of the sexes, from the theological point of view, has ever been made. Both men and women alike are recipients of the "divine breath," because they are created with the same human spiritual nature.

Indeed, as the Qur'an states, God originated them both from a single person or "one soul" ('nafsin waahidah'). From two individuals, Adam and Eve, generations of human beings have inhabited the earth: "Oh humankind! We created you from a single pair of a male and a female, and made you into nations and tribes, so that you may know each other (not that ye may despise each other). Verily the most honored among you in the sight of God is the one who is the most righteous of you)" (49:13). In another verse, men and women have been described as the progeny of a single soul (39:6). It is important to note that the word for wife and husband in the Qur'an is 'zawja' and 'zawj' i.e., one of the couple, which again is indicative of, compete equality. 'Man' is not made in the image of God, nor is a flawed female helpmate extracted from him as an afterthought or utility. Dualism is the primordial design for all creation: 'And of every thing We have created pairs' (51:49). Therefore, when the proto-human soul, self or person ('nafs') is brought into existence, its mate ('zawj') was a part of the plan. The Qur'anic position is that Adam and Eve were created from a single 'nafs' (entity), so both of them had the same human spiritual nature (4:1). Syed Qutb, an eminent Qur'anic exegete, correctly identifies that the pair ('az-zawjayn') are two parts of the one 'nafs'.

The Qur'an tells the story of Adam and Eve in several places.[15] In the thirty or so passages pertaining to the subject of human creation, the Qur'an uses generic terms for humanity ('an-nas', 'al-insan', 'bashar') and there is no mention of any name in it of Eve. However Eve has been implicated in three chapters of the Qur'an (2,7, & 20).[16] The word 'Adam' occurs twenty five times in the Qur'an but it is used in twenty-one cases as a symbol for self-conscious humanity.[17] Here, it is pertinent to point out that the word 'Adam' is a Hebrew word (from 'adamah' meaning the soil) and it functions generally as a collective noun referring to the human rather than to a male person.

Secondly, in Arabic the words "created from" do not necessarily refer to the substance of creation; they can also refer to the nature of something. A literal translation of the words 'ja'ala lakum min anfusikum azwaja' used in verse 16:72 (which are very similar to 'khalaqa minha zawjaha' employed in 4:1) would mean 'it is God Who has created your mates from you' implying that every wife is made from her husband as Eve was. This of course is incorrect; the word 'anfus' (plural of 'nafs') in this verse means 'genre', 'species' and not 'physical being'. It needs to be appreciated that in Arabic the words 'created from' do not necessarily refer to the substance of creation; they can also refer to the nature of something. For example the Qur'an says: 'Man is a creature of hastiness' (21:37). This does not, of course, mean that man's substance is hastiness; it only refers to his nature.

There is no hint that the first woman created by God is a creature of lesser worth than the first male, or that she is a kind of appendage formed from one of his ribs. Instead, male and female are created, we read, 'min nafsin wahidatin' ("from a single soul or self") to complement each other (Qur'an 4:1, 7:189). The Qur'an taught that man is neither created for woman, nor woman for man, but sexes complement one another.[18] 'A single soul' is neither male nor female, although it could be understood to mean Adam; it is not necessarily so. In fact 'soul' is feminine and 'mate' is masculine! Not that woman came first, because in other parts of the Qur'an the creation of Adam is described. But the gender relationship here is ambivalent. And the mate was created from the 'soul' not the humble 'rib'.

The Fight for Gender Justice

The Qur'an makes no specific mention of gender during the early stages of creation. Adam is even considered as a symbol of humanity as a whole, and not as a figure of masculinity but as a human being transcending all divisions of sex and race. In all references of the Qur'an to the account of creation, in later stages the plural form of verbs has been used. This clearly implies that both Adam and Eve were involved in all of the stages of the event and no indication is given that Satan initially deceived Eve. Both repent together and pray to God, their repentance is accepted (20:117-123,

2:35-38). This implies no sexist or gender-biased attitude for the account of creation, which actually sets the conceptual framework for human contemplation. Riffat Hassan writes: "The creation of woman is as clearly defined in the Qur'an as the creation of man, and the Qur'anic statements about human creation, diverse as they are, leave no doubt as to one point: both man and woman were made in the same manner, of the same substance, and at the same time."[19] Al Hibri underscores the same argument while she wrote: 'God was declared male, and man was declared to be created in His likeness. Eve became the symbol of temptation and sin. The woman was consequently judged as a less likely candidate for salvation and an everlasting life in heaven than man.'[20]

All human beings are equally respectable in the eyes of God. It is obvious that word 'human' includes both men and women. Hence all the injunctions of the Qur'an are equally applicable, whenever human or people etc. are mentioned, to both men and women. Many Qur'anic verses subsume women and men in the broad terms of "human being" or "people" ('insan', 'nas'). Though these words take masculine pronouns in Arabic, and are often translated into English as "man," "mankind," or "men," in Arabic they are gender-neutral and apply to/include women as well, as with the term "humankind" in English. In Qur'an 15:28 and 32:7, the Arabic terms used are 'basharan' and 'al-insaan'. Both mean a human being or a person. English translations do not usually convey this meaning and commonly use the terms "man" or the pronoun "him" to refer to "person," which is actually without particular gender identification. Equally erroneous is the common translation of "bani-Adam" as "sons of Adam" or "men" instead of the more accurate translation, "children of Adam." The Qur'an teaches that creation originated in a single 'nafs' (feminine plural for 'self'); it does not state that man (Adam is a generic name for human) was created before woman, or that she was a product of his body, or that she was responsible for the 'fall'.

The Qur'an does not espouse a view of sexual difference or sameness that coheres with either the one-sex or the two-sex model. It does not consider woman a type of man in the presentation of its major themes. Man and woman are two categories of the human species given the same or equal consideration and endowed with the same or equal potential. In effect, the Qur'anic teachings on human ontology, agency, and subjectivity, show that women and men constitute part of a single totality-that of gendered pair-in which it is not the biological sex of either partner, or the specific nature of their sexuality, that is important, but the nature of their moral praxis. In other words, the only criteria for distinguishing between humans in the Qur'an are ethical-moral, not sexual. According to Qur'an, superiority depends on the individual qualities (developed personality, character, and one's deeds) and not by virtue of birth (49:13). Under Islam's basic principles, men and women are equal partners. According to Qur'an, dignity of the children of Adam is a divine bestowal, which is to be secured by all means, including the law and the state authorities, and is to be defended by all forces: 'We have conferred dignity on the children of Adam, and borne them over land and sea, and provided for them sustenance out of the good things of life, and favored them far above most of our Creations' (17:70). From the perspective of the Qur'an, human rights came into existence when we were created, as we were, by God, in order that our human potential could be actualized. These rights not only provide us with an opportunity to develop all our inner resources, but they also hold before us a vision of what God would like us to be: what God wants us to strive for and live for and die for. Any temporal ruler or human agency cannot abolish rights created or given by God. Eternal and immutable, they ought to be exercised since everything that God does is for "a just purpose." It is important to note that there is more Qur'anic legislation pertaining to the establishment of justice in the context of family relationships than on any other subject. The Qur'an allows her social,[21] political (3:159, 27:32-40), legal (2:233) and economic (4:32, 4:7) rights. According to Qur'an, a woman's role on earth isn't limited merely to childbirth. She is required to do as many good deeds as any other man is required to do. Qur'an never said that no upright women had ever existed. To the contrary, Qur'an has instructed all the believers, women as well as men, to follow the example of those ideal women such as the Mary and the Pharaoh's wife (66:11-13). The role of woman in the history of the world is demonstrated in the story of Bilquees, the Queen of Sheba (27:22-44). The Qur'an set, there by, a precedent that a woman in a political leadership is not offensive to religion. She represented a democratic ruler who consulted with her people before making important decisions (27:29). She visited Solomon, talked to him and made decisions for herself and her people. Here we witness one of the first Muslim women in charge of a nation, ruling them as the Queen of Sheba. Her history provides us lessons that God has placed no restrictions on a woman in a leadership role. Contrary to what the traditional Muslim scholars advocate, a woman as a political leader or Head of State is not against God's system or against the Qur'an.

Islam does not consider woman "an instrument of the Devil", but rather the Qur'an calls her 'muhsana'-a fortress against Satan because a good woman, by marrying a man, helps him keep to the path of rectitude in his life.[22] The Qur'an has given the *raison d'être* of marriage in the following words: 'And among His signs is this, that He has created for you mates from among yourselves, that you may dwell in tranquility with them; and He has put love and mercy between you. Verily in that are signs for those who reflect' (30:21).

With the advent of Islam woman's dignity and humanity were restored. Islam considered the woman as a worthy human being, with a share in humanity equal to that of the man. Both are two branches of a single tree and two children from the same father, Adam, and mother, Eve. Their single origin, their general human traits, their responsibility for the observation of religious duties with the consequent reward or punishment, and the unity of their destiny all bear witness to their equality from the Islamic point of view (Qur'an 4:1). There is no reference in the Qur'an to the Biblical story of creation: that Adam was created first, and Eve was created from his rib. It is incredible that the language which is used to refer to the first beings created is clearly gender-neutral.

The Qur'an has instructed us to say the truth even if those who are very close to us don't like it: "Whenever you speak, speak justly, even if a near relative is concerned" (6:152). "O you who believe! Stand out firmly for justice, as witnesses to God, even as against yourselves, or your parents or your kin, and whether it be (against) rich or poor" (4:135). It blamed the Jews, in their dealing with the Scriptures, basically for two things: sometimes they altered the words, sometimes the contexts of these words and sometimes the meaning and interpretation of these words. As a result they lost a part of the guidance given to them. The Christians, on the other hand, are basically charged only with the second thing. These charges have been made specifically in the Qur'an.[23] Since the Qur'an is immune to such adulterations,[24] mullahs adopt the same technique using wild interpretation as well as fabricated and spurious ahadith. All the prevalent ideas of man's superiority are the creation of the "Islam" manufactured during the era of Muslim monarchy, when the women were auctioned off in the markets. The classical books of Muslim jurisprudence are full of rules and regulations about their trade. A literalist interpretation, taking verses in isolation, may find justification for beliefs or behavior that those who appeal to the ethos, and the spirit of the Qur'an would find entirely indefensible. Many verses of the Qur'an refer to the innate spiritual and moral equality of men and women; starting from the creation itself.[25] The orthodox 'ulema' (religious scholars) treat the question of women in Islam with hypersensitivity. They are opposed (to any kind of change in general and women's question, in particular. They imitate quite mechanically all the provisions, in this respect, formulated by the ulema more than thirteen hundred years ago. Any re-thinking on the issue is considered no less than a sin. The ulema, with all their sincere commitment to Islam, were after all product of their time and interpreted the Divine word from male perspective. They were also influenced by dominant male attitude of their times and took for granted in right earnest the prevalent male attitude towards women. One of the prevailing assumptions in medieval ages was that women had deficient intelligence ('naqis al-'aql') and hence should not be entrusted with responsible jobs. Time and again, the Qur'an reproaches those who used to believe woman to be inferior to man.[26]

What is shocking is that despite evidence to the contrary, the orthodox ulema's assumptions acquire divine status and are thought to be immutable. Though the Qur'an nowhere says that a woman's duty is to look after her husband and children and do household work, the whole Muslim literature is full of such assertions. Such assumptions come not from the Qur'an but from the prevailing social ethos. Both, male and female, have been created from one 'nafs' (soul, being, entity) and both are each other's mates. There is no concept of husbanding in the Qur'an. Husband is 'zawj' and wife is 'zawja', the feminine gender of 'zawj'. There is no question of lording or husbanding over ones own mate. However, unfortunately, the Muslims never adopted this culture of sexual equality. They relied more on ahadith of doubtful authenticity rather than on clear and normative pronouncements of the Qur'an.

Many Muslim apologists argue that Islam liberated women more than fourteen hundred years ago. However, this theoretical emancipation is not manifest in the Muslim world. When it comes to Muslim women, sometimes no amount of modesty is ever enough. Women are almost always segregated from their families at Islamic functions, and some mosques have solid partitions so that they can be visually and audibly isolated. Some men also discourage women from going to the mosque or leaving their homes. This mentality stems from traditional baggage that has no place in Islam anywhere. During the Prophet's time, women actively participated in Muslim society. However, since that period, the Biblical tradition of "the woman being inherently evil" has managed to infiltrate Islam. This ideology is perpetuated by some questionable ahadith, which proclaim that the majority of the occupants of hell will be women. This is contrary to the teachings enshrined in the Qur'an, which invites everyone to do good deeds, and promises both men and women their just rewards. When Muslim woman are denied their legitimate human rights, and that too, in the name of shari'ah, it is absurd to repeat the mantra, 'Islam has elevated woman status', without doing anything to change their present predicament. Muslim women continue to be subjected to discrimination and theology has been effectively used to perpetuate this unequal treatment. When 'triple talaq', and unlimited polygamy is widely practiced, in the name of 'shari'ah', the spirit of the Qur'an is under threat. When marriage, instead of being the contract between two free minds, made out of free volition, is reduced to being a one-sided choice, the Qur'anic spirit of gender justice is under fire. Within the contemporary Muslim culture, in most societies, the husband is regarded as the way to heaven for the wife, and not vice versa, the Qur'anic spirit of gender justice is ignored. Women are systematically prohibited from the actualization of their personalities, and are confined to their homes, using 'religious' restrictions.

The memory of Umm Salama, Ayesha, Fatima and Sukayna awakens the Muslim woman and prompts her to take action in claiming her legitimate rights. Any man who believes that a Muslim woman who fights for her dignity and right to equal citizenship necessarily excludes herself from the 'umma' and is a brainwashed victim of Western propaganda is a man who misunderstands his own religious heritage and cultural identity. Muslim woman can walk into the modern world with pride, knowing that her dignity and human rights and full participation in the political and social affairs of the Muslim community, stems from no imported Western values, as often asserted, but is a true part of her own tradition, that goes upto Prophet's time.

The Qur'an only sets down principles. Indeed, these principles can, and should, be interpreted by each successive generation to fit its particular circumstance and culture. But they often seem to have been progressively forgotten in favour of a traditional, andocentric Islam, based as much on self-interest as on myth, and on a partial and biased reading of what, nevertheless, remains a potentially radical document and tradition, precisely because of its egalitarian ethos. It is the duty of the Muslim intellectual to develop a viable theology based on the Qur'anic wisdom of gender justice. They should teach the community to regard the Qur'an as an open book, rather than a closed text, and continue to find its inner meanings by way of 'Ijtihad ' (reasoning from the Qur'an)-a method that is eminently applicable for the modern context.

End Notes

1. See Qur'an 3: 195, 4: 124, 16: 97, and 40: 40.
2. Qur'an 2:31-36, 7: 19-25, 20:115-123.
3. Qur'an 2: 25, 3: 15, 4: 57.
4. Qur'an 95:4, 6:164, 17:15,-59:12, 53:38, 39:7, 35:18, 20:117-122.
5. Qur'an 2:229, 4:19-21,25.
6. Qur'an 4:124, 9:72, 16:97, 40:40.
7. Qur'an 16:59, 43:17, 81:8-9.
8. Qur'an 4:11-14, 4:178, 4:127.
9. Qur'an 2:231, 232, 234, 240.
10. Compare Qur'an 33: 59 with Numbers 5:16-18, and 1 Corinthian 11:3-10, 1 Timothy 2:11, 12, 1 Peter 3:7.
11. See also Qur'an 43:70.
12. Qur'an 2:233, 31:14, 46:15.
13. Qur'an 43:12, 6:143, 22:5, 55:52.
14. See Qur'an 30:21, 39:6, 8:8 and 16:72.
15. Qur'an 2:30-39, 7:11-25, 15:26-44, 17:61-65, 20:115-124, 38:71-85.

16. Qur'an 2:36, 2:26, 7:19, 7:20-23, 20:117, 20:121-123.
17. Qur'an 3:33, 20:121-2, 7:23, 3:59, 5:27, 2:31, 2:34, 7:11, 17:61, 18:50, 15:28-33, 20:116-117, 38:71-75, 7:172.
18. Qur'an 3: 195, 9:71, 66:19-21, 33:35-36.
19. Riffat Hassan. "The Issue of Women-Men Equality in the Islamic Tradition." In *Women's and Men's Liberation-Testimonies of Spirit* (Edited by Riffat Hassan, Leonard Grob, and Haim Fordon), Greenwood Press: New York, 1991. p. 77.
20. Azizah Al-Hibri, Capitalism is an Advanced Stage of Patriarchy, In Lydia Sargent (Ed), *Women and Revolution: A Discussion of the Unhappy Marriage of Marxism and Feminism*, South End Press: Boston, 1981, p. 176.
21. Qur'an 30:21, 2:228, 17:23-24, 20:114.
22. Qur'an 24:4, 4:24-25, 5:5, 24:23.
23. Qur'an 2: 75, 4: 46, 5:13, 5: 41, 5:66, 3:71, 3:78, 2:78.
24. Qur'an 41:42, 5:48, 10:61, 75: 16-19, 22:52, 15:9.
25. Qur'anic verses 2:228 and 33:35 declare sexual equality in no uncertain terms.
26. Qur'an 16:57-59, 62; 42:47-59; 43:15-19, 53:21-3.

3

Gender Equity and Gender Difference

The very word 'woman' had been for many Church Fathers a metonym for concupiscence; and patristic Christianity's consistent preference for celibacy as a calling higher than marriage had entailed a particular attitude towards women. The model was, of course, Christ himself, not the historical one, but as later figured and interpreted by the Church's imagination.

Barbara Stowasser, documents the role of Muslim exegetes (many of them Christian and Jewish converts), in introducing into Islam ideas originating in Biblical traditions by way of their exegesis of the Qur'an (*tafsir*), and the narratives recording the life and sayings of the Prophet Muhammad (*ahadith*). As a result, the Qur'anic teachings are overlaid by an exegesis that often misrepresents them in fundamental ways.[1] For instance, the secondary religious texts (like 'tafsir' and 'seerah' literature) assert that Eve was created from Adam's rib (as a way to establish a "hierarchy of being" based on its temporalization), and that she brought about the 'fall', a sin for which all women are said to have been punished by painful childbirth and menstruation. In contrast, indeed, there is no concept in Islam of the 'fall', which is based on Biblical temporalizations of the rift between God and humans and incarnates the moment of their mutual rupture and alienation. In Islam, on the other hand, Expulsion of humans from Paradise also opens up the possibility for them to receive immeasurably of God's Mercy (2:37). Nor does the Qur'an treat childbirth or menstruation as punishments for women or for designating them inferior to men or as inherently unclean. Similarly, the Muslim tendency to deny "female rationality and female moral responsibility" also derives from "Bible-related traditions," and contradicts the Qur'anic definition of women and men as equally responsible moral agents.[2] In the same vain, Muslim representations of certain women figures in the Qur'an is also "achieved by way of adaptation of Bible-related wisdom" rather than by adherence to the Qur'anic teachings.

Duality: the Fundamental Reality

It was believed that only animal life was divided into two genders, masculine and feminine, then this phenomenon of complementarity was found in plants and vegetation. In fact, this reality exists in every creation, animate as well as inanimate. The Qur'an describes the dual nature of all created things, using the term 'complementary pairs.'[3] Opposites as a function of duality are the basis of the Universe. One cannot exist without the other, nor can we appreciate one without the other. Would we be capable of understanding pleasure if we did not experience pain? And the same goes for male and female, happiness and sadness, health and disease, remembering and forgetting, new and old, spirit and body, strength and weakness, success and failure, beauty and ugliness, youth and old age, etc. all expressions of this complementary duality that works toward forming a complex, inter-related and beautifully balanced whole. Understanding duality as an axiom makes it possible to view human problems in their fullness from several perspectives: co-operation, co-existence and collaboration become the focus and not a 'me against them' or 'better than thou' stance. The divine ordering of the universe makes binary existence one of its characteristics. This principle is manifested in the presence of male and female in the inanimate world, also, with its phenomena of magnetism, electricity and others. Even in the atom, there are positive and negative charges, that is, the proton and the electron. There is nothing wrong with an electron or right with a proton-they simply are. Similarly there is nothing right with a man or wrong with a woman. Most opposites are relative and observer dependant. An observer who remains mentally and emotionally blocked cannot see balance and symmetry of the whole, nor can he appreciate the necessity of both, hence his insistence on making one better than the other. Our study of duality gives a view of the world that is deeper and broader. The discovery of the positron may be regarded as a major turning point in contemporary physics. It was Paul Maurice Dirac (1902-1984) who first postulated parity or pair-wise creation, now recognized as a basic principle of modern physics. Every particle in the universe has a certain charge. When a particle is formed, its opposite twin or antiparticle is produced together with it, for beings are always created in pairs. The most famous of these parities are-electron and positron; proton and anti-proton; neutron and anti-neutron, neutrino and anti-neutrino. It is basic principle of nuclear physics that every particle exists together with its opposite twin.

The word 'zawjain' is translated into the English language as 'pairs.' In scientific literature its meaning is extended to incorporate such concepts as 'duality', 'complementarity', 'opposites', 'inverses' and several other concepts reflecting conjugate and/or reciprocal properties. In simple terms, parity suggests that for every situation that exists there is always a mirror image. The applications in science are statements such as these: (1) for every negative particle that exists there will be a corresponding positive particle (and vice versa). (2) For every mass that exists there will always be an anti-mass. (3) For every motion or spin there will always be an opposite motion or spin.God created two different and distinct genders as a pair.[4] Ultimately both genders are from the same source.[5] Each gender is encouraged to maintain its biological, psychological, emotional, and social identity. This is for the purpose of facilitating and regulating relations between the two genders for the good of the whole society. Parity, a basic phenomenon of creation, requires that men and women complement one another each bringing to the relationship unique features of the respective gender identity. This complementation would be meaningless if the two genders lost their separate identities. On the demographic level, there should exist equal numbers of men and women. This is maintained in a normal social setting. In abnormal situations the balance may be lost leading to social problems.

Gender separation has been used in a wrong way to discriminate against women on the basis of their sexuality. In contemporary Western society the woman's body is sometimes treated as a sexual object to be exploited in the commercial advertisement and entertainment industries. In pre-Islamic period, in Arabia, there was despising for females. There was preference for male births and hatred for females.[6] Parents were sad on birth of a daughter.[8] Infant daughters were considered a blemish[7] and were even buried alive.[9]

In the creation of human beings, as mentioned earlier, the male and the female make up the pair. This means that men and women are equally necessary, as an essential condition of their creation. Neither one precedes nor does either have priority or superiority over the other. Those biological differences that do exist between them do not mean that women and men are of unequal value. The natural features that men enjoy do not make them better than women, and the natural features of women do not make them any worse than men. This is the only way that the age-old dialectic argument of the supremacy of man or woman comes to a logical conclusion. Men and women cannot live independent from each other and are constantly affected by physical and metaphysical attractions of the other, and form each other's character through physiological interactions.

There is not a single verse in the Qur'an to the effect that men's social roles are a function of male biology or that biological differences between women and men make them unequal. It is true that in some things, the Qur'an treats women and men differently, but difference does not necessarily imply inequality, as many feminists themselves argue; moreover, the Qur'an does not ascribe its different treatment of women and men to the fact that they are male or female. Indeed, one cannot deduce a theory of gender from the Qur'an because even though it recognizes biological differences, it does not assign them any gender symbolism. This is a crucial point because most theories of sexual inequality do in fact confuse biology with its social constructions (gender). In the sight of God, Muslim women and men are equal participants in all aspects of Islamic life. The Qur'an (49:13) states that within the pairs in which humankind is created, the one to be most honored is the most righteous, be it man or woman. The Qur'an further describes Muslim women and men as each other's garments (2:187) and each other's protecting friends and guardians (9:71). It explains this phenomenon in the most lucid manner: "Hallowed is He, Who created pairs in all things, those that grow from the earth and of themselves, and what they know not" (36:36). "And all things have We created in pairs in order that you may reflect on it" (51:49).

In the broadest sense, the idea of complementarity is at the center of the conception of gender and genderization in Islam. The male and female genders complement each other and to act in accordance with the nature, function, and role of one's own gender in the absolute sense and toward each other in the relative (or relational) sense is the secret of harmony between and the happiness of either sex. In his 'Sexuality in Islam', Abdulwahab Bouhdiba writes: "The bipolarity of the world rests on the strict separation of the tow 'orders', the feminine and the masculine. The unity of the world can be achieved only in the harmony of the sexes realized with full knowledge. The best way of realizing the harmony intended by God is for the man to assume his masculinity and for a woman to assume her full femininity. The Islamic view of the world removes any guilt form the sexes, but it does so in order to make them available to one another and to realize a 'dialogue of the sexes' in a context of mutual respect and joie de vivre.'[10]

Members of One Another

Her human nature is neither inferior to nor deviant from that of man. Both are members of one another. The Qur'an informs us that never will God cause to be lost the work of any human beings, all are members, one of another.[11] How have woman, as mythic "complements" of man's desire (Adam) suddenly been admitted as equal before God and given equal rights and duties as heaven's occupants (2:35)? How have woman (Eve, for example) who had been imagined as the tempter of men (Adam) suddenly becomes disinfected through the vindication that it was both of them who were involved in the cosmic sin (7:20)?

Some fourteen centuries ago Umm Salama is said to have asked her husband, Prophet Muhammad, why God was not addressing women directly in the Qur'an. Perhaps she was concerned at the number of verses addressed to men, or perhaps she did not take the references of the Qur'an to men to be inclusive of women, even though in Arabic that is often the case. Umm Salama's critique became the way for God to correct an entire community. Among the remarkable features of the Qur'an, particularly in comparison with the scriptural texts of other monotheistic traditions, is that women are explicitly addressed; one passage in which this occurs declares by the very structure of the utterances, as well as in overt statement, the absolute moral and spiritual equality of men and women: 'For Muslim men and women, for believing men and women, for devout men and women, for true [truthful] men and women, for men and women who are patient and constant, for men and women who humble themselves, for men and women who give in charity, for men and women who fast (and deny themselves), for men and women who guard their chastity, and for men and women who engage much in God's praise,-for them has God prepared forgiveness and a great reward' (33:35).The verse shows clearly that all spiritual and moral obligations of men and women are the same and that the ones capacity is not inferior to the others. It stresses the moral rights and moral obligations of men and women. And if God has given men and women the same obligations it is only because they have the same potential. God is Merciful. He won't apply greater responsibility than one can bear. If she's not spiritually whole or morally whole then one can't expect her to be equally moral and equally spiritual. And this verse says that both, man and woman, are equally so.

Most anti-women ideas among Muslims, as well as practices like female circumcision, predate Islam and do not originate in, nor does the Qur'an and authentic ahadith endorse them. But this does not mean that Muslims have not derived theories of inequality and male privilege from the Qur'an. Specifically, its different treatment of women and men with respect to marriage (especially polygyny), divorce, evidence, inheritance, etc., and a couple of lines in the text ("men have a degree above women," and "men are in charge of the affairs of women [in that] God has preferred them"), are all read, as establishing the Qur'anic advocacy of sexual inequality and patriarchy. However, there are a number of problems with such readings which will be analyzed in the next chapter.

The Qur'an says absolutely nothing about Eve's temptation and her being prime responsibility of 'fall'. There are no rib, no apple, no serpent, and no Original Sin. The Book is not simply silent about such matters rather it negates such concepts. Yet, within a hundred years of Prophet Mohammad's death, Islamic literature had made its own the Christian theory that Eve was created from Adam's rib. We are certainly a long way from the Prophet's mosque, open to all, welcoming all those interested in Islam, including women. The mosque now suffers a betrayal of Prophet Muhammad's ideal community: women are declared strangers to the place of worship. Early Muslim women had the privilege of access to the mosque as companions of the Prophet. In the period immediately following the death of the Prophet, women were active participants at all levels of community affairs–religious, political, social, educational, intellectual. They played key roles in preserving traditions, disseminating knowledge and challenging authority when it went against their understanding of the Qur'an or the prophetic legacy.

Here Islam extends its feminizing of sacred spaces to its own epiphany of the Word which resonates within them. For the *shari'ah*, the word made Book is open to female touch and scintillation. Symbolically, the custodianship of the first Qur'anic text was entrusted to the Prophet's wife Hafsa, not to a man. Ayesha, from whom Prophet Muhammad said we should learn 'half our religion', was sought after as an advisor to the early jurists. In the famous 'Battle of the Camel' she was an army general. The prophet even received revelation while resting his head on her lap. Unfortunately, this period passed before it could establish a pattern sustainable as historical precedent. And the name of Ayesha cannot erase what was to happen to the status of women in the following thousand years. Islam acknowledges the multiple roles of women in all spheres of society. An example is the first wife of the Prophet Muhammad, Khadija. She owned an international trading business and the Prophet, her husband, worked for her. She was the owner and he was the manager of her affairs. Contrary to popular perception, women were key participants in the public sphere as well as the private sphere. Another example is that in Islam, women do not take their husband's name. This recognizes that women do not lose their identity.

Islam, since the beginning, has affirmed that gender discrimination is a human rights violation for the misery it brings to women (4:75). The source of all human creation is one living entity, unlike the Biblical interpretation or understanding that men were created first and thereafter women, and women were created from men. There was this one "entity" and God created men and women from it. What we know is that from one 'entity' multitudes of men and women were created. All individuals are born from one entity, according to verse 4:1, and have the same status and equal potential to do good and evil. The Qur'an says: 'O Humankind! Be conscious of your Sustainer, who has created humanity out of one living entity, and out of it created its mate, and out of the two spread abroad a multitude of men and women. And remain conscious of God, in whose name you demand [your rights] from one another, and [reverence] the wombs [that bore you]. Verily, God is ever watchful over you' (4:1). In Islam sexual equality is ontological in that the Qur'an teaches that humans originated in a single self ('*nafs*'). It does not privilege the man by prioritizing his creation or by endowing him with attributes or faculties not given to women. Indeed, the Qur'an does not define men and women in terms of masculine or feminine traits since it takes humans to "manifest the whole." In a world where women were no more than objects of sexual gratification for men, and at a time when the religious circles argued over whether women were human or not, possessing souls, Islam proclaimed: "O mankind! We created you from a single (pair) of a male and a female" (49:13). Men and women are of the same family, and as such have similar rights and duties, and their Lord promises them in the Qur'an: "Never will I waste the work of a worker among you, whether male or female, the one of you being from the other" (3:195). It teaches us that believing women can be leaders of nations (27:23).

When a couple enters into a marriage, they commit to and agree to fulfill certain functions in each other's lives. If one party break those agreements, dishonor, disrespect or show no care for the family unit, measures must be taken. This is completely natural and just. It is reported in the Qur'an that woman not only expressed her opinion freely but also argued and participated in serious discussions with the Prophet himself as well as with other Muslim leaders

(58:1-4, 60:10-12). Islam grants woman equal rights to contract, to enterprise, to earn and possess independently. Her life, her property, her honor are as sacred as those of man. If she commits any offense, her penalty is no less or more than of man's in a similar case. If she is wronged or harmed, she gets due compensations equal to what a man in her position would get.[12] As a mother, she enjoys more recognition and higher honor in the sight of God.[13] The Qur'an provides women with explicit rights to inheritance, independent property, divorce and the right to testify in a court of law. It prohibits reckless violence towards women and girls and is against compulsion in marriage and community affairs. Women and men equally are required to fulfill all religious duties, and are equally eligible for punishment for misdemeanors. Finally, women are offered the ultimate boon: Paradise and proximity to God: 'Whoever does an atom's weight of good, whether male or female, and is a believer, all such shall enter into Paradise' (40:40).

As Islam spread and came into contact with well-established, patriarchal cultures to its North-Judaism, Christianity, and Zoroastrianism-it assumed many of their values and assumptions. Though the branding of women as "the devil's gateway" is not at all the intent of the Qur'anic narration of the "fall" story, Muslims, no less than Jews and Christians, have used the story to vent their misogynistic feelings.

Another example is the veil. The Qur'an clearly and unequivocally recommends veiling only for the wives of the Prophet, as a precaution against lewd attacks in the streets of Mecca and Medina (33.54). The Scripture also enjoins both men and women not to display their bodies shamelessly (24: 31-32). But the practice of veiling and 'purdah' were already common means of segregating the sexes throughout the Mediterranean, Persian and South Asian worlds, although amongst upper-class women the veil is still adopted as a mark of status.

During the Abbasid period, when Muslim civilization was developed, leading scholars and thinkers were exclusively male. They had no experience with revelation first hand, had not known the Prophet directly and were sometimes influenced by intellectual and moral cultures antithetical to Islam. In particular, they moved away from the Qur'anic ethical codes for female autonomy to advocate instead women's subservience, silence and seclusion. If women's agency was taken into consideration it was with regard to service to men, family and community. Women came to be discussed in law in the same terms as material objects and possessions. (This is today reflected in Pakistan's rape laws, which treat the offense as one of theft of male private property with no consideration for the woman's rights.)

Not until the post-colonial 20th century would Muslim women re-emerge as active participants in all areas of Islamic public, political, economic, intellectual, social, cultural and spiritual affairs. What enlightened Muslims are less happy about is the new feminism of the past three decades, the militantly ideologised worldview of Betty Friedan, Greer and Daly. These radical feminist thinkers initiated a new phase by attacking not only structural unfairness in society, but also the most fundamental assumptions about male and female identity. "Until the myth of the maternal instinct is abolished, women will continue to be subjugated", wrote Simone de Beauvoir; French feminist, in her acclaimed book, *The Second Sex,* and similar noises could be heard from the radical feminists everywhere. In this view, the traditional association of femaleness with feminity and maleness with manhood was biologically and morally meaningless, and was to be attacked as the underpinning of the whole traditional edifice of "patriarchy".

Feminism, as represented in Western society, has generally denied any type of gender differentiation and has demanded a move toward a unisex society in order to achieve equal rights for women. 'Unisex society,' mean one in which a single set of roles and concerns are given preference and esteem by both sexes and are pursued by all members of the society regardless of sex and age differentials. By gender equality, feminists who want to create a unisex society, presume, that the equality of sexes on every aspect to the point that the gender differences should become totally immaterial in determining the laws and values. It implies that the concept of moms and dads, brothers and sisters, husbands and wives etc. should cease to have any meaning with time. Similarly, the distinction between homosexual and heterosexual relationship would also vanish. In the name of gender equality they would reach a point where the only distinction remaining would be the bodily organs. In the case of Western feminism, the preferred goals have been those traditionally fulfilled by the male members of society. The roles of providing financial support, of success in career, and of decision making have been given overwhelming respect and concern while those dealing with domestic matters, with child care, with aesthetic and psychological refreshment, with social interrelationships, were devalued and even despised. Both men and women have been forced into a single mold which is perhaps more restrictive, rigid and coercive than that which formerly assigned men to one type of role and women to another. Islam instead maintains that both types of roles are equally deserving of pursuit and respect and that when accompanied by the equity demanded by the religion, a division of labor along sex lines is generally beneficial to all members of the society.

Liberal feminism is partially (and subliminally) influenced and directed by male chauvinism. Liberal feminists claim that man sees motherhood as inferior and tries to fit women into that role. As a reaction, they try to deny the importance of this vital feminine quality. Instead of denial, they should fight for its dignity and value. An argument can be very compelling on behalf of economic appreciation and support of motherhood. If a husband and his business benefit from the emotional and physical effort of a housewife, then why not she split the salary? Besides, the job of bearing and nurturing the next generation is one of the biggest assets for human society. In a society where capitalist economy is valued, women, as the vital half of human race ought to be empowered economically. This is not just a utilitarian concern or a pragmatic solution, but the result of a universalized maxim. There are already signs that women are rebelling against the feminist orthodoxy that demands an absolute parity of function with men, and that "dropping out" to look after a child is less outrageous in the minds of many educated women than the media might suggest. But much real damage has been done. The campaign to turn fathers into nurturers and househusbands shows little sign of success; and many houses have become more like 'dormitories' than 'homes'.

'Scientific Evidence' 'to Prove' 'Female Inferiority'

Although the inferiority of women doctrine was long believed, it was increasingly scientifically investigated from the 1970s on as never before. Modern critics of the conclusion that females were less intelligent because the female brain was smaller were often motivated by the women's movement. These critiques demonstrated major flaws in the evidence that "proved" women's inferiority, and indirectly, of major aspects of evolution theory itself.[14] Even though Darwin's theory gave birth to biologically based racism and sexism, some argue that he would not approve of, and could not be faulted for, the results of his theory. It is true that many researchers went far beyond Darwin-especially his cousin, Galton, who concluded from his life long study of the topic "women tend in all their capacities to be inferior to men."[15] These conclusions of Darwinian biology about females "squared with other mainstream scholarly conclusions of the day. From anthropology to neurology, science has demonstrated that the female Victorian virtues of passivity, domesticity, and greater morality (less sexual activity) were rooted in female biology."[16] The Darwinian conclusion that women are inferior has had major unfortunate social consequences. Darwin hypothesized that sexual selection, an important evolutionary method, along with the data he and his followers gathered supporting their view of the inferiority of women, were major evidences of natural selection.[17]

Hubbard goes further and calls Darwin guilty of "blatant sexism" and places a major responsibility for scientific sexism and its mate, social Darwinism, squarely at Darwin's door. Advancing knowledge has shown many of his ideas were not only wrong, but also tragically harmful, and many still adversely affect society. In Richards' words, Hubbard concluded that Darwin "provided the theoretical framework within which anthropologists and biologists have ever since been able to endorse the social inequality of the sexes." Consequently, "it is important to expose Darwin's androcentrism, and not only for historical reasons, but because it remains an integral and unquestioned part of contemporary biological theories."[18]

Acceptance of Gender Difference

The Islamic theory is that in the beginning, there was only one entity, which were, later, split into two human beings out of which the whole humanity emerged (4:1). The Qur'an presents the position that when Adam and Eve were created and sent to enjoy God's gifts in Paradise, they were neither man nor woman, but only human beings as such. They were friends or partners, but not husband and wife. Prompted by satanic machinations, they were seduced into committing the first sin, after which their shame (their sexual organs) appeared before them (7:20-22, 20:121). If we examine the literal meaning of the Qur'an, it can be perceived that God has created man in two different forms: As an independent creation, and as a creation that exists to perpetuate itself. It is from this standpoint that gender differences begin to play a definite role. Muslim philosophers have claimed that women and men are not just superficially similar to each other. They argue that the soul does not recognize any sexual differences. If we remove their material bodies from consideration, the argument goes, then we will find that women and men are actually identical. Hermeneutics of suspicion directed against either sex are irreligious from the Qur'anic perspective. God, as a sign, 'has created spouses for you, from your own kind, that you may find peace in them; and He has set between you love and mercy' (30:21). Theologically, as we have seen, Islam tends to assert the equality of the male and female principles, while in its practical social structures it establishes a distinction. To understand this paradox is to understand the essence of the Islamic philosophy of gender, which constructs roles from below, not from above. Women's functions vary widely in the Muslim world and in Muslim history. In peasant communities, women work out of doors; in the desert, and among urban elites, womanhood is more frequently celebrated in the home. Modernity, refusing to recognize gender as sacred sign, and delighting in random erotic signaling, renders the public space 'domestic' by coloring it, and makes war on all remnants of gender separation, crudely construed as disparaging. It is a fact of biology that woman's physical design is not the same as man's. In fact, the Friday prayers or even prayers in a mosque are not compulsory for any woman-importantly; they have been exempted, not prevented, from coming to mosque for regular prayers. Islam recognizes and provides for the biological, psychological and functional differences between the two sexes.

There is no inherent value placed on man and woman, there is no arbitrary preordained and eternal system of hierarchy. The Qur'an does not strictly delineate the role of women and the role of men to such an extent as to propose only a single possible outcome for each gender. Islam has always appreciated the femaleness of the woman and regarded her as playing a role integral to that of the man, and similarly regarded the man as playing a role integral to that of the woman. Neither is a foe, adversary or a competitor to the other. Rather, each is a help to the other in attaining the relative perfection of his or her person. Woman is usually smaller than man. She is usually lighter, has higher water content, a higher center of gravity, a slower metabolic rate. God created male and female to be of equal value and equal importance. He created us all with certain talents and certain abilities. In His wisdom He has identified definite responsibilities commensurate with the abilities He has placed within us. Some of these are physical abilities dependent upon our biology. The role of being a mother is physically impossible for a man. God's wisdom has also ordained that the physical and psychological construction of the woman should carry elements that enable her to attract and be attracted by the man. Fundamental to this purpose was God's equipment of the female with an instinctive desire and a strong natural passion that leads to their mutual attraction and communion so that life would continue and generations would spring forth. One has to remember that the message of the Qur'an is universal to all humanity at all times. The "custom" of a race or a nation in a specific time and place regarding "functions" of the two genders has evolved and changed and would continue to do so depending on many factors. The 7th century Arabian society culture and tradition has influenced the male dominated interpretation and understanding (or misunderstanding) of many Qur'anic verses in a way that has never been intended by the Qur'anic message. Women occupied the back rows of the Prophet's mosque where they could be seen and heard by the rest of the congregation. During the Prophet's own lifetime, men and women worship together in the mosque. Women take part as equals in all debates. In a *hadith* recorded by Imam Bukhari, the Prophet stresses that the mosques of Allah are not forbidden to women. The institutionalization of the exclusion of women from such crucial places as a mosque should end. A very interesting point to note is that in Islam, unlike any other religion, a woman can be an Imam, a leader of communal prayer, for a group of women. All the laws and regulations pertaining to prayer, fasting, charity, pilgrimage, doing good deeds, etc., apply to women, albeit with minor differences having mainly to do with female physiology. There are countless Qur'anic verses stressing the essential fact that human society is built upon the idea of the male and female pair and that both are equal partners on their own merits in their own fields. Where any distinction is made, it is a natural and not an imposed one, as, for example, the rule relieving a woman of certain religious duties during menstruation, thus lessening her distress (2:222).

From a Qur'anic perspective the difference between the sexes is not reducible to anatomy or biology, but in terms of a microcosmic reflection of a higher reality. The view of male and female differences, in terms of a dualism, is not Islamic. Islam provides the framework for a polarity, which is not hierarchical, but based on mutual fulfillment. Female nature within this perspective is held at a high value and as necessary and integral to the nature of man. The relationship between the sexes is not hierarchical but rather mutually interdependent. It is through the unity of these two aspects that one attains inner contentment. Women are the gender capable of bearing children in human race. This capability is not the "primary function" of women on earth. All Messengers sent by God were men; this does not make the "primary function" of men to deliver messages. Both the choice of messengers and the fact that women are capable of bearing children are God given. However, with the latter throughout pregnancy, delivery, suckling and motherhood instinct for child's care and protection requires more presence, support and care from men towards women. If we hadn't noticed it before, the Qur'an confirms that men and women are endowed with unique and distinct qualities, and we need each other to achieve a balanced and harmonious life (4:32). We should not covet the qualities bestowed upon each other by God; the men enjoy certain qualities, and the women enjoy certain qualities. We may beseech God to shower us with His grace. Such differences become very obvious when the woman becomes pregnant and gives birth. They are also very obvious immediately after the birth, when the infant is in special need of closeness to the mother for nourishment and bonding for some time. In these situations, a woman becomes very dependant on others to provide food and protection for her and her baby. It is the man's responsibility to provide the protection and provision required. This requirement of "qiwama" (being fair/standing out for) of men towards women who need this care, attention and support would be fair, equitable and logical. Because men were spared the physical and emotional difficulties associated with pregnancy, this statement of fact gives true believing men the opportunity to be "even" with women when it comes to "Caliph" (vicegerent) on earth and taking their responsibilities in society. In the Qur'an, reference to men and women is through attributes and deeds, by which we will be judged. The most pious of us, or those who follow God's commands, are referred to as "believers" or "mu'mineen" (plural) in the Qur'an. In many references, in fact, the Qur'an resonates this equality by eloquently repeating "men and women" with ethical and practical qualities throughout the verses, and even emphasizes this ten times in the verse 33:35. One must mention here that although there were no women Messengers, however, at least, two women received divine inspiration ('*wahy*') from their Lord: Mary and Moses' mother.[19]

Unfortunately, many women of today have been misled to think that the way to become equal with men is to become more like men, and vice versa. True equality is when we can be fully equal while still allowing and enjoying all the different characteristics God gave us. Biologists point out that males and females have different reproductive strategies. The 'parental investment' is massively higher in the case of females than of males. This has nothing to do with social conditioning: it is a genetic and biologically determined. The human female, for instance, makes a vast investment in a child: beginning with nine months of metabolic commitment, followed by a further period for weaning. The male's 'parental investment' is enormously less. Biology also helps us understand why the female hormonal pattern, dominated by estrogen and oxytocin, generates strong nurturing instincts which are far less evident in the male androgens and in adrenaline, which is useful for huntsmen and warriors, but of considerably less value in the rearing of children. Simply put, mothers have a far greater investment to lose if they neglect their children. Men have less of the 'nurturing' neurotransmitter oxytocin than do women. Androgens ensure that men choose mates for their youth and their apparent childbearing abilities, estrogens impel women to choose mates who are confident and powerful, as more likely to provide the food and protection that their offspring will need. These androgens, however, do more than shape the reproductive organs of the unborn child. Between the sixteenth and the twenty-eighth week of pregnancy, they also trigger fundamental divergences in the male and female brains.

The male and female fetuses begin life in the womb almost identical. The key difference is the XY chromosome couple, which signifies the male, where the female has an XX pair. The function of the Y chromosome is to trigger the release of androgens which approximately two months into pregnancy initiate the development of the male gonads. (Hence the view of many biologists that the female is in fact the basic human shape, and the male a divergence from it—the opposite of the Aristotelian view.) The Qur'an treats sperm and ovum as equal partners in conception,[20] advises the spouses to render mutual satisfaction (30:22), implicitly endorses birth control and uncouples sex from procreation (2:223). The Qur'anic position on human sexual natures and praxis also is revolutionary inasmuch as it teaches that women and men have the same sexual natures. It does not, for instance, claim that a particular type of sexual identity, drive, or penchant for certain types of behaviors is specific to either sex. Further, the Qur'an recognizes the importance of sexual desire and the need for its fulfillment, but it also establishes a framework for the expression of desire. And while the Qur'anic emphasis on chastity reveals some anxieties about sex, the Qur'an does not treat sex itself as dangerous or dirty. Rather, it views sex as fulfilling, and natural.

The male is not like the female, says the Qur'an (3:36). It further holds, much to the astonishment of the modern biologists, that it is the male sperm that is responsible for the sex of the child.[21] Absolute egalitarianism (in the sense of intending to create a unisex society) is reductionism, and diminishes the bivalence of our kind, whose fertility is apparent in many more ways than the merely reproductive. Our own bodies mirror this. Human reproductive glands, for example, manufacture both male and female hormones. Women's ovaries produce small, but significant amounts of androgen (a male hormone). Likewise, men's testicular canals produce not only testosterone, but also a small but significant amount of estrogen (female hormones). God has also designed the human anatomy so that both sexes have vestigial equipment of the opposite sex. No one is 100 per cent male or 100 per cent female-not even the most muscular man or the curviest woman can claim this distinction. The biologists describe this as 'gender dimorphism'. That is to say, just as procreation bears fruit through the shaping received from androgens and estrogens, so too creation itself is bathed in androgens and estrogens. The entire cosmos is gendered; in fact, it comes into being, and attains the complexity of manifestation after the experience of undifferentiated unity, through the interaction of the Divine names, where the supreme and governing category is the polarity of 'Jalal' and 'Jamal' (the principles of magnificence and beauty).

Science is currently affirming an innate distinction between the sexes, a distinction that God clearly calls us to celebrate rather than to suppress. The social architecture of Islam is very different to that of the modern secular West: that it should be a source of pride to us. We are permitted to speculate, however, that the disastrous social problems now overcoming the West, and westernizing classes elsewhere, will combine with the new science to provide a revised definition of gender and social roles which will, in the longer term, convince our critics of the superior wisdom and compassion of the Prophetic social model. Theologically, Islam tends to assert the equality of the male and female principles, while in its practical social structures it establishes a distinction.

Although many feminists condemn Islam's "uncompromising monotheism," it is this very inflexibility about the primacy of God's Rule that opens up possibilities for radical equality for women inasmuch as God's Rule is not based in the idea of sexual differentiation, hence in a theory of sexual inequality. That is, while the Qur'an recognizes sexual (biological) differences, it does not assign sex or biological difference symbolic or normative value. It does not link sex with gender. Consequently, the Qur'an does not teach biology of sexual incommensurability, i.e., the notion "that there are two stable, incommensurable, opposite sexes and that the political, economic, and cultural lives of men and women, their gender roles, are somehow based on these 'facts'. This "two-sex model," which is at the core of modern Westernized misogyny, assumes that biological differences between males and females, hence between men and women, render them "different in every conceivable aspect of body and soul, in every physical and moral aspect." The tendency to ascribe "psycho-social distinctions" between women and men to biological differences is common not just to "patriarchal religions" (monotheism), as feminists charge, but also to Western secularism, which also claims that women's biology renders them deficient in morality and reasoning.

The Qur'an does not define women and men in terms of gender attributes, much less in terms of binary oppositions; e.g., man as logical, woman as illogical; man as intelligent, woman as emotional; man as the Self, woman as the Other. In fact, inasmuch as humans commence from a single 'self' in the Qur'an, there is no real or 'symbolic Other' (4:1). Moreover, in the Qur'anic definition of the human pair, neither half is privileged, as is clear from its teachings on variety of issues ranging from marital relations to moral personality to sexual modesty. In no context does the Qur'an say that men have attributes or faculties that women do not; indeed it does not even describe men and women in terms of masculine or feminine traits because it does not associate sex with gender. Thus, while the Qur'an recognizes biological differences, it does not assign them any gender symbolism. Not a single verse suggests that female and male gender roles are a function of their biology or that biological differences make the two unequal or one subordinate to the other.

The Qur'an, however, does not take up a view of sexual difference or sameness that coheres with either the one-sex or the two-sex model. It does not consider woman a type of man in the presentation of its major themes. Man and woman are two categories of the human species given the same or equal consideration and endowed with the same or equal potential. In effect, teachings of the Qur'an on human ontology, agency, and subjectivity, show that women and men constitute part of a single totality-that of sexual pair-in which it is not the biological sex of either partner, or the specific nature of their sexuality, that is important, but the nature of their moral praxis. In other words, the only criteria for distinguishing between humans in the Qur'an are ethical-moral, not sexual (49:13). To clarify: morally purposeful action in accordance with Qur'anic teachings and not sexual identity, defines human agency and subjectivity in Islam. Not only does the Qur'an make no claims about sexual sameness or difference that portray women as lesser or defective men or the two sexes as incompatible, unequal, or incommensurable, in the tradition of Westernized patriarchal thought, but-unlike the latter-it also does not equate sex with given social meanings (gender), or assign specific attributes to either sex.

Why Homosexuality is Disapproved?

Basically human beings have a biological need to be coupled in heterosexual relationships. Our culture meets that need through marriage. In a similar way, human beings have a biological need to be communal, and we meet that need culturally by forming communities, cities, states and nations. The Qur'an evidently considers homosexuality as unnatural, unethical and immoral (66:10, 54:33-34, 21:77). It also considers such tendency as a sexual deviation leading to a perverted act, which goes against the natural order God intended for mankind. It is a corruption of the man's sexuality and a crime against the opposite sex (Qur'an 29:29, 26:165-166, 29:29, 26:173). Because heterosexual unions are built into nature, cultures have a mandate to protect and strengthen the male-female concept of marriage. To do otherwise would violate man's purpose and would be wrong. Where the Association of Psychiatrists considered homosexuality an illness, it is now removed from the list and replaced by homophobia (the dislike of homosexuals and homosexuality). The consequence of AIDS is enough to prove that homosexuality is evil and dangerous to society. The early spread of AIDS was concentrated among the homosexual community. It later spread to the heterosexual community through blood transfusions and intravenous drug usage and so-called bisexuals. And continues on a rampage among promiscuous heterosexuals. Were homosexuality a product of genetic destiny, it would be unfair for God to criminalize it and punish those who practice it. Currently, some scientists are even claiming that murder is of genetic origin. To accept that would mean to excuse murderers and tolerate murder. The argument against same-sex marriage is based on the nature of human persons as gendered beings who have a purpose that is derived from that nature. That is to say, male-gendered human persons are meant for coupling with female-gendered human persons, even if their coupling does not result in procreation. This argument is not based on a human person's current function, ability, or desire, each of which could be inconsistent with how human persons ought to be by nature. For example, a person who is blind is lacking something physically, though he or she is still a human person who by nature ought to be seeing. In the same way, a sterile, aged, or willingly childless person is still a gendered human person whose purpose for marital union with someone of the opposite gender. This remains true even if he or she has desires that are contrary to what he or she ought to desire by nature. Within the past several years, in the western world, there has been a tendency by some psychologists to classify homosexuality and lesbianism as normal behavior. The argument is frequently stated that nature has built into some people a sexual desire, which is as naturally satisfied with members of the opposite sex. Now scientific evidences are becoming available which demonstrate that is strongly supported by the knowledge that we are gaining in science. Obviously God has equipped us with stimuli that are built into our body mechanisms. These stimuli are very definitely sexually oriented. To maintain that males sexually attracting males are normal for nature is a violation of the evidence. Obviously there are very definite opposites built into our biological systems. Men and women are not the same; they are different. This is not to say that there is superiority in on case or the other, but it is to say that to maintain that homosexually and lesbianism are normal modes of human behavior is unsupported by the evidence and strongly opposed by it. God has created man and woman with biological drives which can be chemically stimulated. The close identification of a man and a woman in marriage puts all of this in a healthy, creative, pleasurable, and rewarding contest. No such balance and no such satisfaction can possibly occur when two individuals are sexually united in contradiction to their biological make-up and also in contradiction to God's word.

We can infer from our physical makeup (the fact that we are male and female) the need to reproduce which can only occur with a union of a man and a woman, as well as our specific nature to be heterosexual that humans were created to be heterosexual and not homosexual. If morality is just a arbitrary social convention with no objective basis, then two people can hold diametrically opposed viewpoints and claim they are both moral. It makes no sense to say since some believe homosexual marriage is right and some believe it is wrong that it is therefore both right and wrong at the same time. That is logically contradictory. Together, men and women make up a composite image of the living God. Individually, we are incomplete, partial, and lacking something in our personality. One of the reasons God gave us marriage state is to learn how the other half of the God-image behaves. We learn from our mate's traits and characteristics of the opposite sex in order to become complete spiritual-beings. The theological case against homosexuality is related to our understanding of the "dyadic" nature of creation. Human sexuality is an incarnation of the divine-willed polarity of the cosmos. Male and female are complementary principles, and sexuality is their sacramental and fecund reconciliation. Homosexuality is therefore the most extreme of all possible violations of the natural order. Its biological sterility is the sign of its metaphysical failure to honor the basic duality. Marriage is a partnership based on love and mutual respect, in which both parties enjoy equal rights, at the same time enjoying different qualities and obligations in that partnership. Recognizing our differences, and achieving equal respect for the different obligations and responsibilities men and women have towards each other, is not a defeat, but a victory for women.

The Qur'an strongly guarantees all fundamental human rights, without reserving them to men alone. These rights are so deeply rooted in our humanness that their denial or violation is tantamount to a negation or degradation of that which makes us human (17:70). These rights came into existence with us, so that we might actualize our human potential. These rights not only provide us with the opportunity to develop all of our inner resources, but they also hold before us a vision of what God would like us to be, what God deems to be worth striving for. The abandonment of a God-given right would be no more virtuous than the refusal to utilize a God-given talent.

End Notes

1. Barbara F. Stowasser, *Women in the Qur'an: Traditions and Interpretations*, Oxford University Press New York, 1994, p. 28.
2. Qur'an 11: 124, 16:97.
3. Qur'an 11:40, 13:3, 23:27, 31:10, 36:36, 51:49 and 53:45.
4. Qur'an 75:39, 53:45, 92:3.
5. Qur'an 4:1, 7:189, 16:72, 30:12, 39:6.

6. Qur'an 6:137, 6:140, 6:151, 17:31, 60:12, 81:8-9, 16:58-59.
7. Qur'an 16:58-59, 43:17.
8. Qur'an 16:58-59, 43:17.
9. Qur'an 6:137, 6:140, 6:151, 16:58-59, 17:31, 60:12, 81:8-9.
10. Abdelwahab Bouhdiba. Sexuality in Islam, Routledge & Kegan Paul, London, 1985. p. 30.
11. Qur'an 3: 195, 9:71, 33:35-36, 66:19-21.
12. Qur'an 2: 178, 4:45, 92-93.
13. Qur'an 31: 14-15, 46:15.
14. FIavia Alaya, *Victorian Science and the 'Genius' of Women*, Journal of the History of Ideas 38 (1977): 261-280.
15. Stephanie A. Shields, *Functionalism, Darwinism, and the Psychology of Women: A Study in Social Myth*, American Psychologist 30, no. 1 (1975): 739-754, p. 743.
16. Gloria Steinem, *Revolution from Within: A Book of Self-Esteem*, Little, Brown and Company: Boston, 1992, p. 133.
17. S. Sleeth Mosedale, *Corrupted-Victorian Biologists Consider 'The Women Question'*, Journal of the History of Biology 9 (1978): 1-55.
18. Ruth Hubbard, "Have Only Men Evolved?" In *Women Look at Biology Looking at Women* (Ed: R. Hubbard, et al), Schenkman Publishing Co: Cambridge, 1979, p. 16.
19. Qur'an 20: 38, 28:7.
20. Qur'an 35:11, 32:8, 76:2.
21. Qur'an 53:45-46, 75:37-39.

4

Abused Verses of the Qur'an

The Qur'anic law upholds the dignity and the worth of women more reliably than secularity ever can. Male chauvinism thrived prior to the advent of the Prophet Muhammad, and continues to do so in our own era. A materialistic worldview, which measures human worth in terms of earning power and status and access to sexual fullness, will inexorably glorify the male. For the male, conditioned by the androgens from the time he was almost invisibly small in the womb, is assertive: his metaphors are projection, conquest, and single-mindedness. As the facts of science trickle down into popular culture, and as old-style equality feminism breaks down, the male is going to be magnified as never before in history. Materialistic civilizations will, in the longer term, favor and revere male traits. In the shorter term women may appear to be overtaking the men, because of the energy generated by the congratulations of modernity, and because of the reciprocal atrophy of male identity and self-regard. But in the longer term, unless the logic of Adam Smith's capitalism is mysteriously terminated, the future belongs to the androgen. Because of a belief in a liberated, equitable and dignified position of women outlined in the Qur'an, many Muslims, men and women alike, are calling for reevaluation of attitudes and practices that, although done in the name of Islam, are actually contrary to the basic messages found in the primary sources. Muslims today are facing great challenges from within and without. Most often calls for change are seen as tools of an outside power that is seeking to undermine the efforts of Islam and Muslims. Certain geopolitical realities lend credibility to this view. However, the current desire for change on the part of Muslim women is perhaps more borne out of the fervent belief in the image of the Muslim woman as communicated by God in the Qur'an of a liberated, vital human being who can work in cooperation with men on many levels to contribute to the betterment of society. They seek to expose this concept which has been buried by the persistence of attitudes that focus on competition and subsequent subjugation of one sex over the other in direct conflict with the spirit of the Qur'anic verse: "And thus does their Lord answer their prayer: I shall not lose sight of the work of any of you who works (in My way) be it man or woman: You are members, one of another" (3:195).

How to Read the Qur'an Properly?

One may argue that in the absence of a complete application of Islamic law, where the rights of women will have no teeth, Muslims should turn to the spirit of that law, which is justice, and find ways to accomplish this goal. With all these unequivocally positive and elevating references to women (or to be humble male equating), why then do we see all eyes focused on three of four verses in the Qur'an that carry controversy and that are always (in my experience) explained out of context? In fact such verses are sometimes taken literally and others figuratively but always to disadvantage women. The explanations offered by scholars suffer from the lack of methodology. They are contrasting with the over all message of the Qur'an, they are even incongruent with some obvious linguistic rules. Often, such explanations defy logic and insult the intelligence of the reader: as if the rest of the Scripture is not important and as if no intelligent man or woman will ever ask how can the Scripture 'contradict' itself? And how is it that God 'allows'

His male human creatures abuse His female creatures? And if females are so 'inferior and incompetent' then why does the Almighty who is Just and Merciful give them the same religious and social obligations as He measure to His more 'superior' males?

The Qur'an should be used as the basic interpreter of the Qur'anic text.[1] While we may hesitate on the issue of the best meaning of every verse, we cannot regard a reading, which imputes injustice (*'zulm'*) to the Qur'an as the best. The Qur'an also distinguishes between itself and its misreading by condemning those "who write the 'Book' with their own hands and then say: 'This is from God'" (2:78). It urges believers to use their own intelligence and reasoning to decipher the signs of God while condemning priests for leading people away from truth.[2] Historically, Islam has addressed serious issues openly and sought to correct actions that constitute harm or 'zulm' (i.e., cruelty and abuse) to the dignity of humankind. Human life and respect for it has been stressed unstintingly, regardless of age or gender. As a general rule, Islam forbids all 'zulm', be it physical, mental, emotional or spiritual (6.120). What Muslims do stress is that Islam valorizes women by making the basic duties of the faith equally incumbent upon both sexes. The suspension for a few days each month, during menstruation, is seen as a pragmatic and generous dispensation, which does not vitiate this basic principle. Even radical feminists now agree that simple equality principles have proven inadequate for feminist practice, especially in the "area of sexuality". Moreover, a growing literature suggests that treating women and men differently does not by itself amount to treating them unequally, particularly if differences in treatment are not premised in claims about biological differentiation.

Just like any text, the Qur'an is not immune from possible misinterpretation: Arabic allows for gender endings that can be both masculine and feminine, depending on the context. But context reintroduces the human element, subjectivity, and the possibility of different interpretation. Some Arabic words, like in English, may have more than one related meaning. Thus ascribing the 'wrong' meaning may sometimes create contradictions between verses in the Scripture or give a strange understanding to the topic the verse is addressing. In such cases, the advice from the Qur'an itself is to follow the best meaning derived: "The ones who listen to what is being said, and then follow the best of it. These are the ones whom God has guided, and these are the ones who possess intelligence" (39:18). As such, the best meaning which can be used and which will then give a logical and consistent meaning to the issue of working towards the resolve of matrimonial strife is that the husband yields by 'leaving' / 'separating' rather than letting the wife carry out her wish to leave. It is violence against female gender to interpret the Qur'an in ways that support disempowerment of woman. Interpreting of the holy texts is one of the most important ways for Muslim women to assert their rights. What can one say about those people who, in their utter ignorance and maniacal arrogance, subjugate even the word of God to their ugliness and deformities? Muslims need to be proactive in self-critical reexamination of its classical works including Qur'anic exegesis. Such reexamination is not for wholesale repudiation and discrediting of the past contributions of many noble Islamic personalities. Rather, they must accept the fact that they were human beings and not without personal biases or various influences and experiences that had shaped their positions. Conscientious Muslim scholars would engage in critical reexamination like divers seeking pearls. In the deep ocean of knowledge and understanding, those who seek pearls must sift through more than just piles, separating pearls from empty shells and also watch out for shells that can be harmful.

We should realize that Islam does not establish sacred spaces inaccessible to women. Women can and do enter the Ka'ba. The Inner Court of the Temple in Jerusalem before its demolition by the Romans was out of bounds to women, who faced the death penalty if they penetrated it. Under Muslim patronage, it was thrown open to both sexes. Hence the Dome of the Rock, is allocated on Fridays exclusively to women, so that men pray in the nearby al-Aqsa mosque hall. Here, as elsewhere, the sexes are segregated during congregational prayers, and the reason given for this is mere pragmatism. Examples illustrate that Muslims read inequality and even oppression into the Qur'an by generalizing what is specific in it and by de-contextualizing it. A patriarchal exegesis originates generally from a faulty hermeneutics and the resultant inconsistent theology. Patriarchy is really a politics of male privilege and sexual differentiation, which equates sex with gender and prioritizes the male while making the woman different (unequal), less than, or the 'Other.' The attribute of God's Justice maintains that though "severe, strict and unrelenting" in justice (4:89), God "never does any *'zulm'* to anybody" (4:40). In other words, God does not act in such a way as to transgress the proper limit and encroach upon the right of some other person, which is the meaning of 'zulm' employed in the Qur'an. Whatever way we define *'zulm'*, we cannot regard inequality, discrimination, and hatred as not being *'zulm'*. As patriarchy is based on all these evils, it can be considered a manifest case of 'zulm' and one must assume, again as a hermeneutic principle, that the Qur'an cannot overlook it.

The interpretive discourses of gender employed by classical exegetes provide a window into the gender relations of their socio-historical contexts. Their hermeneutical lenses are evidently created by a patriarchal worldview and thus their interpretations are the ideological products of a male-centered society. These texts constitute the religio-cultural legacy of Islam, which provide the vehicle for the reception of the Qur'an in the minds of Muslims. They are instrumental in the transmission of a consciousness and worldview that implicitly and at times explicitly legitimates violence against women. These exegetical studies are indicative of the presence of structural complicity of religion in discourses of violence against women.

Does Biology Favors Male?

The themes of femininity and the natural earth being noted, in the verse: "Your wives are a tilth unto you" (2:223). The verse describes the process of tilling which the sower performs before sowing the seed, which is to germinate and produce a new plant. Through this image therefore, stress is indirectly laid on the importance of bearing in mind the final purpose of sexual contact, i.e., reproduction. What emerges very clearly from this analysis is the complete lack of warrant for coercion, dictatorship, and domination. We should explore another side of this root, reflected in the word 'qayyim', meaning 'righteous, true, reliable', i.e., this verse establishes a husband's responsibility to treat his wife well, to be kind, caring, and just. This takes it further away from dictatorship and makes it a partnership. The verse, also, indicates that women in the society are the guardians of your future generations, just as a garden keeps the seeds and turns them into flowering plants. So, whenever you meet with women socially, treat them with respect, keeping the aforementioned principle in mind. This conduct will go a along way to insure the betterment of the future generations: send forth good today for the sake of tomorrow.

In addition to some of the physical realities that make menstruation unpleasant for some women, a general negative interpretation of Islamic literature may contribute to an overall sense of distaste regarding a normal bodily function, which further promotes a negative self-image of women. Indeed, in Yusuf Ali's translation of 2:222, reads as follows: "They ask you concerning women's courses. Say: they are a hurt and a pollution ('azan')" The same word "azan" translated by Yusuf Ali as "hurt and pollution" is translated by Muhammad Asad as "a vulnerable condition." To the person reading in English, each translation has an entirely different effect. The large volume of *ahadith* regarding menstruation reflects the need for practical guidance on the part of the Muslim community at the time of the Prophet Muslim women today can view menstruation as a simple fact of life that has no negative bearing on her value as a human being. Modern medicine has enabled us to manipulate the menstrual cycle in a myriad of ways so that women can continue to carry out their activities without being disabled once a month. Indeed, many women take advantage of medical technology to avoid menstruating during Hajj, which, for many, is truly a once in a lifetime event not to be missed because of bad timing.

Another common misconception is about the so-called 'houries' of Paradise, believed to be available for companionship of male believers. However, it should be understood that the Arabic word "Hoor" which occurs four times in the Qur'an is plural of "Ahwar" which is for the masculine gender and "Hawrau" which is for the feminine gender. Thus the word "Hoor" is not restricted to the female gender only, but represents both men as well as women (44:54, 37:46-49). Its basic meaning is the whiteness of the eye, and also signifies a clean and pure intellect of a person, free from vile intentions. From this word also comes the word "Al-hawariyun" which has been used in the Qur'an (3:52-53) for the disciples of Jesus Christ, as they were persons having purified souls. In the Qur'an, where it is mentioned for the believers in a state of heaven: " And We shall pair them with companions of pure eyes" (52:20). Then it does not imply a relationship as a husband and wife, but simply means that in "Jannah" the believers will have companions of pure intellect, which will include, men as well as women.

Does the Law of Inheritance Proves Male Supremacy?

To question and possibly oppose ingrained positions that are based on archaic laws, weak ahadith, or cultural trends, requires courage and conviction on the part of religious leaders. But this is necessary and worth any risks in order to enable women to achieve liberation through Islam as originally intended. A brother inherits twice the share of his sister from their parents' property (and a mother twice that of a father from the property of their children), but this unequal division has to be seen in the context of the fact that husbands, not wives (even if independently wealthy), have been charged with the responsibility of maintaining their families. Bearing in mind that these verses were revealed in Arabia over 1400 years ago, when women had no financial security other than what was provided by men, these verses demonstrate the care and respect given to the family unit, and ensured that women's rights would continue to be protected. Hence, brothers with sisters were given larger shares than their sisters, together with the legal obligation to spend a portion of this wealth on those sisters. According to Muslim Family Law, the responsibility for the wife's maintenance always remains with the husband. According to the Qur'an, the provision for maintenance of a married woman is exclusively the responsibility of her husband (4:5), and a husband is required to pay the dowry for his wife upon marriage (4:4). This dowry is exclusively owned by the wife, and the husband has no right to take it back even upon divorce (4:20-21). Upon divorce, a husband is required to pay for her maintenance (2:241) and during *'iddah'* (65:6). The responsibility for the maintenance of the children upon divorce is on the shoulder of the husband (2:233). If in the matter of inheritance, men have been given the larger share, this is not because of a male superiority but rather due to his greater economic responsibility. The wife has no corresponding obligation to support her husband. There are scholars who argue that these rules apply only if the deceased left no will and that the division can be changed by a will. Presumably, the will would be analogous to a debt and would be paid prior to any other disbursement of property (4:11). Furthermore, a tradition of the Prophet Muhammad states that a person can will up to one-third of his or her property in any manner, thus allowing equalization of gender-based default presumptions. (It should be noted that a majority of the *Sunni* schools of thought state that more than the one-third share cannot be bequeathed to natural heirs; however, others, including the *Shiite* school, disagree with this limitation.) Moreover, transfers of property can be made during the life of the testator. In the secular world, men are not likely to fulfill their Qur'anic obligations, and women may not be provided for. Therefore the Qur'an has empowered the deceased the full right to distribute his/her belongings as he/she chooses through a Will. The proportions of inheritance fixed by the Qur'an are only applicable when one dies without making a Will or if the Will does not cover the whole of the estate of the deceased.

Should Woman Cover Her Face?

One of the practices aimed at strengthening the home and minimizing promiscuity is that of the seclusion of women. The verses of the Qur'an on which those who practice it base their custom reads: "Say: O wives of the Prophet, you are not like any other women. If you would keep your duty, be not soft in speech, lest he whose heart contains malice may thereby be encouraged. Employ suitable speech. Stay in your houses and do not dress to display your finery in the way they dressed during the time of primitive ignorance; and keep up prayer, and give welfare due and obey God and His Messenger; for God desires only to remove from you abomination (of vanity since you are) the household (of the Prophet) and to purify you by a perfect purification" (33:32-33). Literally these verses are addressed only to the wives of the Prophet and some authorities maintain that it applies only to them. Other theologians and legists however interpret it by implication to apply to all Muslim women, and this opinion is widely accepted in a number of Muslim countries where women generally stay at home, coming out only for some over-riding reason. The predominant Muslim notion that women who wear a veil are more pious and moral is rejected in the Qur'anic message (7:26).

Contemporary Islamic code regulating women's dress is far less precise than many assume. A conservative translation of the verse 33:59 would read: "O Prophet! Tell your wives, daughters and women of the believers to lower or possibly draw upon themselves their garments. That is better so that they will not be known and molested. And God is forgiving and merciful." This translation seems to be worked under a very different set of assumptions. It seemed to be under the assumption that the Qur'an aims to eliminate all sources of temptation in society, and that women should bear the brunt of the burden in this process. Hence, women should be covered from head to toe except perhaps for one roaming eye, and men may happily prance around undisturbed by delectable female parts. Worst of all, this fundamentally male-indulgent view is presented as God's unquestionable truth. The authors of the translation, however, seem to be working under a very different set of assumptions. The operative words in Arabic are 'yudnina alayhinna min jalabibihinna'. This could mean 'lower their garments' or 'draw their garments closer to their bodies'. 'Jalabibihinna' literally means, 'their garments'. A 'jilbab' is a garment, like a dress or Arab robe, which has stitches and thread. A single piece of cloth like a chador or 'abayah' which some women wrap around their bodies in the modern age, would normally be called a 'jilbab'. 'Yudina' literally means to bring closer or to lower something, in this case a garb. Therefore, one can interpret this verse to require the covering of the legs, or a more vigilant covering of the torso, or, simply, modesty, but the original text docs not support this rendition into English.

According to the authoritative lexicon of 'Lisan al-Arab' by Ibn Manzur (d. C.E 1311), a 'khimar' is a piece of cloth that is worn on the head. A man's turban may be called a 'khimar' as well, and a man wearing a turban may be called a 'mukhtamir'. A 'jayb' is a bosom of a human being. It could also be where the neck and chest meet or the beginning of the cleavage area on a woman's chest. Furthermore, a shirt, garment, or pocket may be called a 'jayb' as well. The jurists add that the 'khimar' did women wear a cloth in pre-Islamic times on the neck and that it was normally thrown toward the back leaving the head and chest exposed. The verse apparently instructs that the piece of cloth normally worn on the head (the 'khimar') or neck be made to cover the bosom or to descend down to the point of touching the cloth. In the era of ignorance, 'Jahiliya' period, women used to go out in public with naked breasts and would reveal their necks in order to show off their adornments in this period the women wore dresses that revealed their necks and chests as well as other parts of their bodies. They also drew their veils backwards while leaving the front parts wide open. Consequently, they were commanded to draw their veils forward in order to cover their chest. The institutionalization of the veil and the separation of woman from public space crystallized when the Muslim world came into contact with Hellens and Persians in cities. In these contexts, the veil, which was formerly used as an occasional costume, became institutionalized and women became obligated to wear it. Qur'anic commentators repeatedly emphasize that women in Mecca and Medina were in the habit of exposing all or most of their chests, even if their hair was covered. Consequently, it is quite possible that the point of the revelation was to call upon women to cover their chests. But whatever may be the case; nothing in the verse indicates that the 'khimar' is to cover the face or hands. If the verse intended that the face be covered, it would have stated 'wal yadribna bi khumurihinna ala wujuhihinna' (instruct them to place the 'khimar' on their faces). But the verse does not allude or refer to the face in any way. In fact, what partially covers the face is usually referred to as 'niqab', and what covers the head is normally referred to as 'khimar'. But the Qur'anic verse doe not use the word 'niqab' anywhere. The only truth here is that the authors simply forced their idiosyncrasies of their own culture upon Divine text. Consequently, none of the richness and equanimity of the text is reflected in their translation. Rather, the text is made to represent and embody their authoritarian and despotic constructions.

Although the verse does not explicitly require the covering of the hair, it is possible that the verse assumes it. But to extract more than that from this verse requires an incredulous degree of creative reconstruction at best, or conceited and malevolent misogyny at worst. One should also note that the verse states that women should not display their ornaments except what would normally appear. The Arabic is 'illa ma dhahara minha' which is an ambiguous phrase. The closest rendering in English of this phrase is 'that which would normally appear'. This phrasing leaves open the question of whether customs or social standards may influence notions of propriety and modesty. The vast majority of Muslim jurists asserted that the phrase 'what would normally appear' refers to two distinct elements. The first is 'urf' or 'adat' custom and established practice and the second is 'haraj' (adversity). Meaning, this phrase refers to what are admittedly adornments and perhaps objects of temptation, but they are adornments that do not have to be covered because they normally appear either as a matter of custom or because they need to appear to avoid and alleviate potential hardship. Modesty does not mean removing all forms of adornments or enticements. One, that is not possible without excluding women entirely from society, and two, the Qur'an acknowledges that certain adornments ('zinah') are permitted to appear. Modesty, at a minimum, does mean lowering one's garment and covering the bosom area. Most Muslim jurists concluded, from this discussion, that the face and hands are adornments that do not have to be covered because it would create hardship to ask that they be covered, and because established social practices do not necessitate that they be covered.

Literally, the word 'hijab' means, 'curtain'. In the Qur'an the term 'hijab' is not used as a reference to women's clothing; rather, it was the screen behind which the Muslims were told to address the Prophet's wives. (The term is also used to describe the "screen" separating God from Moses, as he received divine revelation.) When the Prophet's wives went out, the screen consisted of a veil over their face. It does not appear that covering the face was adopted by the other Muslim women at the time since it was a special injunction for the Prophet's wives as is clear from verses 33:53, and 33:32.

Therefore an honest and accurate translation of the verse 33:59 would read: "And say to the believing women to lower their gaze, and guard their private parts, and that they should not display their adornments except what would ordinarily appear. And, that they should draw their veils over their bosoms and that they should not display their beauty except to their husbands." The Qur'anic Arabic instructs that women should take their 'khimars' and covers their 'Jayb' (pl. 'juyub'). The Arabic is 'wal yadribna bi khumurihinna ala juyubihinna' which means that women should take their 'khimars' and strike with it or place it upon their bosoms. The Qur'an does not demand or expect that all sources of 'fitna' (temptation) be eradicated in society. It balances the various rights, and unlike our trivializing friends, the Scripture does not expect women to bear the full burden of modesty. The weakness of men cannot be the source of hardship and suffering for women, and any approach that does not acknowledge this fact, in my view, is not true to the spirit or letter of the Qur'an. All historians agree that at the advent of Islam men and women attended social affairs and ceremonies together and communicated with each other, while observing ethical codes. The issue of Islamic dress is in fact a negation of the idea of seclusion. Women and men are invited to abide to chastity in codes of conduct and dress, since this would enable them to engage in ethically "clean" interactions at the level of their social and occupational necessities. Nevertheless being with men does not necessarily cultivate the identity of women (24:30-31).

Does the Testimony of Female Half of a Male?

Likewise, the Qur'anic stipulation (2:282) that two women, in place of one man, can serve as witnesses to the transaction of a debt, does not mean that it regards the woman's testimony as being half a man's, as patriarchal 'mullahs' hold. The only verse in the entire Qur'an to equate the testimony of two women to that of one man is the so-called verse of debt, which occurs in Qur'an 2:282. This verse contains a significant amount of material that later jurists categorized variously as recommended or merely instructional ('irshad') and without legal import. However, a very few jurists opined that the recording of debts, witnessing, and all other matters dealt with in the verse may be categorized as obligatory ('wajib'). The Qur'an, in its own delicate manner and with characteristic sagacity, places the reclassification of women as fully participating members of society on its agenda for reform. The overall objective was to end the traditional perception of women by including them, "among such as are acceptable to you as witnesses," and to bring about their acceptance as full partners in society by means of this practical recognition. In this way, the Qur'an seeks to overcome the psychological impediments of men that prevent them from accepting women as their equals in society. There is another interpretation: the two women are not both witnesses, only one is a witness. The other really plays the role of an attorney or advisor. Instead of not allowing women as witnesses, the law enables a woman to act as a witness; it does not disable her. It is a historical fact that at the time of revelation, the question of numbers was irrelevant, as it was the equality of women that the Qur'an sought to emphasize. In the far more consequential matter of adultery, when a husband accuses his wife but is unable to produce four witnesses to the fact, the Qur'an gives greater weight to the wife's testimony on her own behalf than the husband's against her. If a man accuses his wife of unchastity, he is required by the Qur'an to bear witness with oath five times as evidence of his wife's guilt. If the wife denies and bears witness with oath similarly five times, she isn't considered guilty and in either case the marriage is dissolved (24:6-9). If the wife swears her innocence, in the case of the accusation of adultery, the husband can have no further legal recourse against her. Actually in this case the final judgment is based on the wife's oath not the husband's. So her witness has more weight than his in this case. From this description it is clear that the verse 2:282 cannot be used as an argument that there is a general rule in the Qur'an that the worth of a female's witness is only half the male's. This presumed "rule" is voided by the above reference (24:6-9), which explicitly equates the testimony of both genders on the issue at hand. The context of 2:282 relates to testimony on financial transactions, which are often complex and laden with business jargon. The passage does not a make blanket generalization in that this would otherwise contradict the verses of 24:6-9. The only reason given is to corroborate the female's witness and prevent unintended errors in the perception of the business deal. The Arabic term used in this passage, 'tadhilla', literally means "loses the way," "gets confused," or "errs." But are females the only gender that may err and need corroboration of their testimony? No, and that is why the general rule of testimony in Islamic law is to have two witnesses, even when they are both male. Another possible interpretation of the requirements related to this particular type of testimony is that in numerous societies, past and present, women generally may not be heavily involved with and experienced in business transactions. As such, they may not be completely cognizant of what is involved. Therefore, corroboration of a woman's testimony by another woman who may be present ascertains accuracy and, hence, justice. It would be unreasonable to interpret this requirement as a reflection on the worth of women's testimony, as it is the only exception discerned from the text of the Qur'an. This may be one reason why a great scholar like Al-Tabari could not find any evidence from any primary text (Qur'an or hadith) to exclude women from something more important than testimony: being herself a judge who hears and evaluates the testimony of others.

In other mentioning of witness, the Qur'an does not differentiate between man and woman.[3] The jurist Ibn Al-Qayyim points out that the rule enunciated in 2:282 is the exception to the general rule that the testimony of a woman is equal to that of a man.[4] It must be added that unlike pure acts of worship, which must be observed exactly as taught by the Prophet, testimony is a means to an end, ascertaining justice as a major objective of Islamic law. Therefore, it is the duty of a fair judge to be guided by this objective when assessing the worth and credibility of a given testimony, regardless of the gender of the witness. A witness of a female graduate of a business school is certainly far more worthy than the witness of an illiterate person with no business education or experience. Furthermore, this verse states a reason behind the rule, in case one forgets, the other may remind her. Within Islamic jurisprudence, as some eminent Islamic jurists argued, once the reasoning behind a rule is no longer applicable, then the rule itself may not be applicable.

Polygyny: Promoted or Restricted?

Similarly, although the Qur'an permits polygyny in certain cases, it is not because it privileges males but, strange as it may sound to us today, because it wishes to ensure justice for the most vulnerable women in society: the orphans (4:3). An erroneous conception that males have stronger sexual urge, compared to women, was put forth, in early times, to justify the practice of polygamy even though the Qur'an makes no mention of sexual desires in the verses on polygyny (4:3-5). Another Qur'anic verse shows how almost impossible it is to maintain such an equal fairness among co-wives, and how difficult it is to be even close to such equal fairness (4:129). It is often argued that polygyny saves men from restoring to illegitimate relationship with other women. The Qur'an does not refer to any such argument. Injustice would be suffered not only by the co-wives but also by their children who have to live as half brothers and sisters. Yet the ulema throughout history made it almost a privilege for men to marry up to four wives and justice never remained an issue. The required spousal "love and tenderness" (30:21) would certainly be undermined in such complicated "partnership. " Monogamy-one man with one woman-is, therefore the normal rule according to the Qur'an. There might, however, arise an occasion in which a relaxation of this rule becomes a necessity in the over-all interest of the society. For instance, prolonged war may reduce considerably the number of young men in the society thereby leaving a large number of widowed women, generally with children, and unmarried girls un-provided for. These women and girls must be protected and looked after in the fulfillment of their human needs without hurting or undermining their dignity and honor. Establishing orphanages, or "old age homes," or even making these destitute otherwise economically independent, are only parts of remedy. Obviously, the problem is not economic only: it is much wider and deeper. It would be for the society to handle this delicate situation protecting the individual dignity of those affected, as well as the moral fabric of the society. The concern is with the protection and economic support of orphans so the women then have to be the mothers of orphans. The reference to context is very clear. Multiple marriages are allowed when the welfare of orphans is an issue. As is obvious by this verse, the permission for polygamy was to do justice to orphans (whose Muslim fathers had been killed in the wars defending Islam). In the old Arabian society of Prophet Muhammad, there was no other way of doing except by men taking in their mothers as their new wives. Although polygyny was intended by the Qur'an to be for the protection of orphans and widows, it is often used in Muslim societies as the Sword of Damocles, which keeps women under constant threat. Misrepresentations of the Qur'anic position on polygyny reveal another problem with patriarchal readings: the tendency to quote selectively from the Qur'an, thereby distorting and, in some cases, subverting its real intent and teachings. The Qur'an clearly does not condone polygamy. Nor does it encourage it in any way. At best, the Qur'an resignedly tolerates polygamy under very special and limited circumstances. Even so, it cautions against it and prohibits it if it is at all feared that the man in question may not deal in an equitable manner among the wives. Finally, the Qur'an counsels that even if the man feels he can be fair, it is better and advisable for him to maintain only one wife. It is therefore abundantly clear that the Qur'an frowned upon polygamy even at a time when having more than one wife was considered normal and ordinary behavior. Extrapolating to today's norms one can logically conclude that polygamy, in normal course, is against the egalitarian and liberating spirit of Islam. Scholars have correctly pointed out that a woman can protect herself from polygyny at the time the marriage contract is performed even in the Muslim countries where it is legal.

Does Male the Preferred Gender?

The claim that the Qur'an establishes males as superior to women often derives from misreading a reference to a husband's rights in a divorce: The 'darajah' (degree) for men over women occurs in this Qur'anic verse: "And women shall have right similar to the rights against them according to what is equitable. But men have a degree (of advantage) over them. God is Exalted in Power, Wise" (2:228). It would be contradictory to conclude from the statement "li rijaali alayhinna daraja" "men are a degree above them" that men are superior to women, as at one hand the verse says that women and men have rights similar to each other, and the implication that men are superior, will contradict this impression. Women who are divorced shall wait, keeping themselves apart, three (monthly) courses. And it is not lawful for them that they conceal that which God has created in their wombs if they believe in God and the Last Day. And their husbands would do better to take them back in that case if they desire reconciliation. And (the rights) due to the women are similar to (the rights) against them, (or responsibilities they owe) with regard to the kindness ('ma'ruf') and men have a degree ('darajah') above them (feminine plural). Read in context, the 'degree' refers not to men's rights in general, or to their biological or ontological status as males, but to the husband's right either (a) to divorce his wife without outside arbitration (the wife requires such arbitration even though the Qur'an does not stipulate it), or (b) to cancel a divorce. Obviously, an advantage in a peculiar situation does not mean one is superior to the other. Only in the matter of "iddah", that man has a degree higher than woman, but apart from this both have equal rights. Since the Qur'an mentions kindness and reconciliation in the same verse, the latter seems to be a more plausible reading. But the verse speaks of excellence; it does not allocate it to any particular sex. Much less it does associate excellence with men exclusively. So in this case, excellence is attributed to some generalized men and women. This would be on the basis of Arabic grammatical rule of 'Taghleeb'. Then it would indicate that some of them, men and women, are endowed with what others, men and women, lack. When a level is granted to male or female on the basis of their good deeds or piety, there can be no discrimination as the Qur'an argues: "Unto men a fortune from what they have earned and unto women a fortune from that which they have earned" (4:32). "Whoever works righteously; man or woman, and has faith: verily to him/her will We give a new life, a life that is good and pure. And We will bestow on such their rewards, according to the best of their actions" (4:124). So when it comes to who has greater advantage with God in terms of deeds, there is no level or degree given to the male or female over the other. Thus, in a superb manner, the Qur'an has untied the knot of this problem by saying that while men have a degree of 'darajah' (advantage) in holding the key to divorce; in the enjoyment of human rights, both men and women stand equal. This verse occurs among a series of verses referring to the required period of separation before claiming a divorce. The degree of advantage refers to man's being able to individually initiate divorce, whereas a woman can seek divorce only after intervention of an authority. So the advantage is limited to the circumstances of divorce only. Why this advantage? Most likely, because it is he who is duty bound to support to the wife and unborn baby, and the previous verses are referring to the possibility that during separation the woman may be expecting, and if so, the man needs to give due consideration to taking her back because of his responsibility towards the unborn child. Hence, he has the responsibility about validating the divorce or taking his wife back. This example illustrates that Muslims read inequality and even oppression into the Qur'an by generalizing what is specific in it and by de-contextualizing it. Yet, in the end, a patriarchal exegesis results not only from a faulty hermeneutics, but also from an incompatible theology. How incredible it is that, in Muslim cultures, an unrestricted value attached to this concept of "advantage" and men generalize it to all aspects of life, claiming superiority over women. If a woman becomes economically sufficient, say by inheritance or by earning wealth, and contributes to the household expenditure, the male superiority would be that extent reduced, since as a human he has no superiority over his wife. Religiously speaking, men and women have absolute parity: Whoever does good deeds, whether male or female, while being believers, they shall enter Paradise.[5]

Significance of a Coherent Worldview

Tawhid is usually understood to refer to God's absolute unity. However, a number of scholars are increasingly reflecting on the implications of that unity for humankind in particular and for creation in general. For those committed to progressive values it has also come to mean a principle of holism that permeates all of creation and a struggle to repair the wholeness of creation destroyed by racism, environmental mismanagement, economic exploitation and sexism. A belief in the unity of God can only become meaningful if we display a concern for the way in which manifestations of it are being damaged. Sexism and the discrimination against women fly in the face of the holism of *Tawhid*, which is in direct contrast to the misogynist worldview where man replaces God for a woman and where a male-female relationship is expected to mirror that between males and God. There is thus no place for alleged sayings of the Prophet such as "if prostration were permitted for any of God's creation then women would have been ordered to prostrate to their husbands." Often times we hear the "hadith" that when the Prophet went to Hell he saw more women in Hell than men. If women were more prone to evil, why would God give them equal obligations to do moral good? This form of unrestricted value for all circumstances contradicts the equity established in the Qur'an, "that each 'nafs' (man or woman) is responsible for what it earns" (4:32).

Ayesha was asked, after the Prophet's death, what he used to do at home when he was not at prayer; and she replied: 'He served his family: he used to sweep the floor, and sew clothes' (*Bukhari*). On this basis, 'Shafi'i' jurists defend the woman's right not to perform housework. In the 'Hanafi madhhab', by contrast, these acts are regarded as the wife's obligations. Hanbali School allows women to stipulate terms restricting the husbands right to polygamy. Maliki School of law will allow a woman to obtain a judicial divorce based on different reasons such as desertion, failure to maintain cruelty. Hanafi Sunni School, unlike the other Sunni schools, gives women the legal capacity to be her own 'wali', in other words, to marry without the consent of her 'wali' or male guardian. This is another sufficient reminder of the difficulty of generalizing about Islamic law, which remains a diverse body of rules and approaches. Islam's theology of gender thus contends with a maze, a web of connections, which demand familiarity with a diverse legal code, regional heterogeneity and with the metaphysical no less than with the physical. This complexity should warn us against offering facile generalizations about Islam's attitude to women.

Family laws pertaining to marriage and divorce that reinforce the image of relationships based on a hierarchy with the rights of the husband superceding those of the wife and that prevent women from being in control of their lives. Violence against women, which occurs in the home, community, and as a consequence of warfare which is claimed by some to be allowed by Islam when it is not. Abuse of certain Islamic practices affect women negatively, such as polygamy, when applied out of context and without abiding by Islamic restrictions. Excluding women from religious activities such as attendance in the mosque, which has clearly been established as the Muslim woman's right. The concept is prevailing that failure to promote the importance of a woman's contribution to society beyond childbearing. There is a drastic failure to enable women to take advantage of rights of property ownership and inheritance outlined by Islam. The focus is always on the behavior of women as a marker for morality in society and subjecting them to harassment, intimidation or discrimination.

The Qur'an teaches that a woman has every right to disobey a man if his orders are not righteous (58:12). A man can only be righteous if his orders are in accordance with and in consideration of all of God's laws, not only the ones he likes. One of the laws in the Qur'an decrees that the believers shall decide their affairs on the basis of due consultation among themselves (42:38). Without the woman in this equation, there is no due consultation. Thus, it is a duty upon the righteous man to consult his wife before making important decisions. Ultimately it is not the voice of the man that weighs heavier in the relationship of a couple that has decided to abide by God's laws, it is the word of God. Thus, regardless of how highly a man regards himself or his opinions, God gives him no right to make decisions that opposes His commands. Thus, a righteous man will heed a reminder from the wife based on righteous expectations. Thus, a woman should learn the Scripture to be able to give her husband those reminders. She should also carefully examine the belief of a man before choosing him as a husband to make sure he respects the rights God has granted her. Another law in the Qur'an commands us to treat each other in the best possible way (17:53). We are also told that love and care are two essential ingredients of a healthy married life (30:21).

It is a fact of life that for people to be able to function well together they need to agree on whom should be in charge.

We accept this arrangement in all other aspects of our lives, such as when we choose government, when we are employed, and so on, and so forth. We do not feel oppressed for example, because we have to submit ourselves to a legal system that demands of us that we behave a certain way or else holds us responsible. We understand the logic and need for such a system and generally don't mind following it because we want others to follow it as well, that we may feel safe where we are. Why should it be any different in a marriage situation, which in itself is an institution that must have certain rules and laws?

The order that God decreed for decision making in the family is this: children are obligated to obey their parents, unless they advice them to worship other than God.[6] The parents are together responsible for making balanced decisions for the whole family. When no agreement can be reached between the husband and the wife on what course of action to take, one must have the heavier vote. This is simple logic; the only other option is if someone else decides for your family. Verse 4:34 teach us that God gave the man the final word in the family. Again, this must be after due consultation, without abusing his right, considering what is in the best interest and most fair for all. This is a huge responsibility to carry, especially considering the seriousness by which the Qur'an regards oppression. It says oppression is worse than murder (2:190).

Ruler or Maintainer?

The Qur'anic verse 4:34 has attracted great attention from both within the believing community and without: "Men are the protectors of women, because God has given the one more strength than the other, and because they support them from their means. Therefore the rightcous women are devoutly obedient, and guardian absence that God would have them guard. As regards those women on whose part you fear defiance and ill-conduct, admonish them (first), (next) separate in bed, (and last) 'idribuhunna' (if they still persist in their defiance); but if they cooperate and pay you heed, do not look for excuses to harm them. Note well that there is God above you all" (4:34).

It is often assumed that the above verse (4:34), gives unquestioned authority to the husband over the wife, prescribes obedience by the wife, and gives the husband the right to beat her in case of her disobedience to him in order to make her to submit to his authority and control.In different ways the classical exegetes have deduced from the verse: a) that men are superior b) that this superiority is both functional and essential to their maleness and c) that while it is not intrinsic to their beings, it is nonetheless a gift from God. The claim that God has preferred men to women and made them rulers over women arises from reading only parts of a verse and from misinterpreting three words in it: Men are (*'qawwamuna 'ala'*) women [on the basis] of what God has [preferred] ('faddala') some of them over others, and [on the basis] of what they spend of their property (for the support of women). As for those from whom you fear [*'nushuz'*] admonish them, banish them to beds apart, and scourge them. Most of the Urdu translations have translated that word 'qawwam' as "hakim"-which means sovereign, which immediately has connotations of a master-slave relationship.

The key word in the above portion of the verse is: 'quwwaamuuna'. This word is variously interpreted and understood to mean different things by different interpreters of the Qur'an. It is, therefore, important to form some idea of its meaning, connotation, and implications for the cultural and social construction of gender and genderization in Islam. Liberal Muslim scholars such as Abul Kalam Azad and Muhammad Asad have emphasized the caring and social responsibility dimensions to 'qiwamah' and suggest that this verse is, in the first instance, a statement of the social fact as it existed in 7th century Arabia. The primary meaning of 'qawwamun' is financial maintainer, not ruler. The verse is thus charging husbands with the responsibility of maintaining women in those cases where they have a larger share in inheritance than the women (in which some of them have been preferred), and they are supporting women from it. Since men can only be 'qawwamun' over women in matters where God gave some of the men more than some of the women, and in what the men spend of their money, then clearly men as a class are not 'qawwamun' over women. Both men and women are from God's creatures, and God never intends to oppress anyone from His creation. Since childbearing is among the functions of the woman, it is only fair that the husband's responsibility is to provide for the woman and take care of her. So this 'qiwamah' is a responsibility on men, not a preference given to them by God over women. The equality of women and men is explicit in a large number of verses of the Qur'an. When speaking normatively, the Qur'an appears to take side on man-woman equality. Thus, 'qawwam' cannot be understood as to imply men's superiority or even being managers for women, as widely interpreted by conservative exegetes. As to gender relations, the Qur'an (9:71) has clearly appointed women and men each other's '*awliya'*, or mutual protectors, which it could not do if men were in fact more superior to women and become their 'managers'.

'Qawwamun' conveys the notion of providing for and that the term is used prescriptively to indicate that men ought to provide for women in the context of child-bearing and rearing. It also does not necessarily mean that women cannot provide for themselves in that circumstance. The term 'qawwamun' is not an unconditional statement of male authority and superiority over all women for all time, as traditional male interpreters have claimed. More competent exegetes thus show how classical male interpretations have turned the specific and contingent into universals. Concerning the misogynic argument that men have authority over women, while deconstructing particular verse such as the above, those exegetes also draw attention to other verse affirming mutuality of responsibilities as in 9:71 which says that "the believers, male and female, are protectors of one another."

'Qawwamun' does not convey the sense of governorship or rule over women, but rather signifies men's role as maintainers of women, because they support and meet their material needs from their wealth. The *shari'ah* has entrusted the responsibility of women's material needs to men, who are held liable for meeting all the economic needs of the family, while women are held responsible for looking after the children, their nourishment, education, training, etc. This division of the work of the household between husband and wife is based on their respective natural abilities. Fulfilling these responsibilities are the primary duties, though not exclusive, yet allowing free and full participation in all social, political and ethical activities with due propriety. The distinctiveness between man and women is related to the woman's pregnancy, delivery, and nursing, which make it necessary that the man should have the responsibility to provide for her needs and the needs of the children, at least when she is hindered with such a distinctive function, that of reproduction.

Qur'an 2:233 describes the notion of co-responsibility for childrearing, which is ostensibly talking about the period of lactation, but which demonstrates the wider principle of mutual consultation by parents. One can see nothing 'un-Islamic' in the father being the primary caregiver and the mother being the primary breadwinner. If "qiwama" is taken as "authority" or "being in charge of", one must ask if this "authority" would shift from one gender to another if, say, the husband looses his eyesight and job and the wife becomes the sole capable adult in a family to earn a living and be in charge of husband and children and what does "qiwama" or "authority" mean in this case? It is only normal in any couple of situation that partners support each other and in exceptional cases, more support is needed from the community and society. The majority view among the founding jurists of Imam Shafii, Malik and Ibn Hanbal regarded women as being disqualified as judges based on an interpretation of 4:34, that men are 'qawwamuna' (protectors) over women. The minority view of Imam Abu Hanifah, however, opined that the authority of a judge is not valid unless he possesses the qualifications necessary for a witness. Thus this opinion allows women to be judges in all cases except 'hudud' and 'qisas' cases. This flows from Imam Abu Hanifah's interpretation of verse 2:282, on women's eligibility to be witnesses in commercial transactions. There were also the individual views of other jurists such as al-Tabari and Ibn Hazm, which stated that a woman could be a judge in all cases without exception as long as she fulfils the requirements for the position. This would also appear to flow from a reading of 9:71, that believing men and women are each other's 'awliyya' (protecting friends and guardians). Qur'anic verses 4:58 and 5:42 talk about the need for judges to conduct themselves with justice and equity in deciding between two disputing parties; no distinction is made between man and woman judges. Verse 3:104 enjoin both men and women to do well and prevent evil. Nowhere down the Qur'an state that one gender is superior to the other. The Qur'an makes it clear that the sole basis for superiority of any person over another is piety and righteousness not gender, color, or nationality (49:13). It is also to be noted that the Scripture, also, does not distinguish between a man and a woman's vicegerency (2:30).

"Nushuz" could be defined as animosity, hostility, rebellion, ill-treatment, discord, and violation of marital duties on the part of either husband or wife. In this context, a wife's "ill-will" implies a deliberate, persistent breach of her marital obligations. In the context of the above verse the most appropriate meaning for "nushuz" is marital discord (ill-will, animosity etc.). The process suggested is necessary, otherwise it is inviting the likelihood of divorce without any reconciliation procedure, and this will contravene the Qur'anic guidance. The separation could be temporary or permanent depending on the reconciliation procedure, and this fits in very well with the divorce procedure outlined in the Qur'an. The verse following the above verse gives further weight to the above translation (4:35): "And if you fear a breach between them (the man and the wife), appoint an arbiter from his folk and an arbiter from her folk. If they desire amendment, God will make them one of mind. Lo! God is Ever Knower, Aware." An added weight to the meaning outlined above is given by verse 4:128, where in the case of man the same word, "nushuz", is also used. Note too that as ill-treatment emanating here is from the husband, a process of reconciliation is encouraged: If a wife fears ill-treatment (*'nushuz'*) or desertion (*'i'raad'*) on her husband's part, there is no blame on them if they arrange an amicable settlement between themselves; and such settlement is best" (4:128). In the same chapter we read, "Whoever among you; men or women, are guilty of this crime (impropriety/ obscenity), punish them both; and then if they both repent and reform themselves, leave them alone, for God is Most Generous in accepting repentance, and Merciful in forgiving sins" (4:16).

Women could only be taken to task when they were guilty of open obscenity. The verse (4:16) clearly states that whoever commits open licentiousness, man or woman, must be punished. It may here be mentioned that this open obscenity or licentiousness (*'nushuz'*) means obscenity short of adultery and fornication. If a wife fears that her husband is going to be excessive, there is the same process for the wife too. She can advise him first: psychological pressure of withdrawing closeness and intimacy. She has use of an injunction, which is better than that to sit down with respected members of the community, (if need be with a judge), and draw up a contract with the man.

Obedience to Husband or to God?

Another crucial word in the verse 4:34 is 'qanitat', which is often interpreted by conservative exegetes as 'wifely obedience.' The verse mentions that good women are 'qanitat', guarding the secret that God has granted. "Qanitat" ("the obedient"), here, refers to obedience to God. However, most of the traditional interpreters have viewed this as obedience to the wishes of the husband and suggest that the obedience to one's husband is, in fact, an extension-even a condition, of righteousness. In the Qur'an, 'qanut' is used for both women and men[7] and non-humans.[8] 'Qunut' does not refer to the obedience of a wife to a husband or of any human to another. It refers to the spirit of humility before God. When the verse goes on to say "if they obey you," the Qur'an uses the term 'ta'a', which means for one human to follow the orders of another, referring not just to women obeying men, but men following orders as well (4:59). It is clear that the Qur'an does not order women to slavishly obey their husbands.

Let us analyze the word 'faddala' with Qur'anic wisdom. The first condition is usually misinterpreted as: God preferred men to women. However, the Qur'an states in this verse: "some over others" meaning, some women over other men, some men over other women, some men over other men, and some men over other men. This verse does not read 'they' (masculine plural) are preferred over 'them' (feminine plural). "Excelled some on other", occurs several times in the Qur'an, e.g., for crops and fruits (13:4) where no superiority is indicated. Just as women have uniquely feminine qualities, men also do have uniquely masculine qualities.

The Qur'an says that good women are 'qanitat'. The Qur'an uses this word with good men (3:17, 33:35) and with non-humans (39:9). 'Qanitat' does not refer to the obedience of one human to another-no matter what gender. In addition to the verse 4:34; there are three more places in the Qur'an in which exactly the word "faddala" has been used. Variation of this word, such as "faddaltukum," "faddalkum," "faddalna," has been used in many other places in the Qur'an. Verse 4:32 reads: "And in no wise covet those things in which God has bestowed His gifts more freely on some of you than on others: to men is allotted what they earn, and to women what they earn: But ask God of His bounty, for God has full knowledge of all things." In this verse, bestowing His gifts "more freely" does not imply any superiority. Unless, we accept such implication that those who are rich are superior to those who are poor. Indeed, Allah very clearly points out that what men and women will get is based on what they earn. They should not be judging themselves in comparison to others as to who has "superior" provisions. Such would be a perversion of the very fundamental precepts of Islam, indeed. Verse 4: 95 reads "Not equal are those believers who sit (at home) and receive no hurt, and those who strive and fight in the cause of God with their goods and their persons. God has granted a grade higher to those who strive and fight with goods and persons than to those who sit (at home): to all (in faith) has God promised good: but those who strive and fight has He distinguished above those who sit (at home) by a special reward." In this verse, a sense of superiority is implied by the word "faddala," but not on the basis of any "inherent distinction". Rather it is an "earned" distinction. Also noticeable is that "ba'dukum ala ba'd" (one over the other) clause is absent in this verse. Lastly, the verse reads: "God has bestowed His gifts of sustenance more freely on some of you than on others: those more favored are not going to throw back their gifts to those whom their right hands possess, so as to be equal in that respect. Will they then deny the favors of God?" Once again, unless we accept the implication that the rich are better than or "superior" to the poor, one needs to treat the word "faddala" in a neutral sense. Allah has not created men as "superior" to women! Translating the verse (4:34) with "superiority" simply indicates a person's interpretive bias. It should not be attributed to the Qur'an either, as it is a gross injustice to the Qur'an.

Linguistically, 'faddala' means "having a distinction" or "a preferred difference over another." The preference is between men, and is material in the sense that God has preferred some men to others in terms of wealth: the verse reads as 'faddala alah ba'duhum' (masculine). If men were preferred over women the verse would have read: 'faddalahum lahu alay hunna' (feminine). The phrase 'bima faddala alah ba'duhum' can be interpreted as meaning some whom God 'faddala' over some others. A broad linguistic interpretation of the phrase is to the effect that God 'faddala' some men over some other men and women and 'faddala' some women over some other women and men. The pronoun 'hum' in Arabic refers to both male and female. Therefore it is wrong to conclude from this that as men (or women) have some "advantage" in one respect, they are therefore superior to the other.

The right attitude should be for each gender to think that it is deficient in certain aspects, which can only be complimented by the collaboration and co-operation of the other as essential for its perfection and healthy growth. In other words, it should never fancy such ideas as its own excellence, but should consider itself dependent upon the other for its own perfection. The Qur'an has beautifully described this relationship of the two sexes in these words: "And among His signs is that He created for you mates from among yourselves, that you may dwell in tranquility with them, and He has put love and mercy between your (hearts). Surely in that are signs for those who reflect" (31:21).

Sanction for Wife-beating?

The problem of abuse comes from the word "idribuhunna" which is usually translated as "beat them". The verse 3:34 is often quoted for justifying the ruthless dominance of patriarchal males demanding obedience from their wives-to the point of disciplining them through physical punishment! A verse in the Qur'an can be broadened or narrowed in scope by another verse in the Qur'an. That is why in translating the verse (4:34), one observes the phrase "beat them lightly." The word "lightly" is not implied by this verse itself. This limitation of meaning on "fadriboohoonna" is based on other verses in the Qur'an and authentic narrations from the Prophet. Otherwise, literal translation would be not "beat them lightly," but "beat them." But any knowledgeable Muslim would agree that Qur'anic interpretation should be based on the totality of the Qur'an and in light of the authenticated Prophetic narrations. The verse instructs a husband whose wife causes problems in their marriage to first talk to her about it, then leave the marital bed, then ("adriboo") his wife, and all of this in view of pursuing a reconciliation as is evident from the subsequent verse 4:35 The Arabic word used here, (*'adriboo'*), from the root (d-r-b), has several dozens of meanings, such as: 'to beat', but also: 'to forsake', ' to avoid', 'to leave'. What verse 4:34, actually, does, is give a righteous man specific commands when dealing with a wife who is behaving in an unrighteous way, posing a threat to the safety of herself or the family. The verse is there to help him restrain his violent tendencies in tense situations by giving him strict guidelines to go by.

The root of this word is "daraba". If one consults an Arabic dictionary one would find a long list of meanings ascribed to this word. In the Qur'anic text, itself, depending on the context, one can ascribe different meanings to it: to travel to get out[9], to strike,[10] to beat,[11] to set up,[12] to give examples,[13] to take away, to ignore (43:5), to condemn (2:61), to seal, to draw over (18:11), to cover (24:31), to explain (13:17). A clear example of a multi-meaning word and how its incorrect application can cause serious problems is the word 'Daraba' which occurs in 4:34 and is primarily used to mean 'beat / strike'. The choice of 'beat' / 'strike' in this example creates a bizarre meaning as the verse is dealing with the issue of resolving a husband / wife dispute, and that if the final step were to 'beat' ones wife then that is a sure guarantee for ending the marriage rather than fixing it! As explained, the word 'Daraba' has multiple meanings in Arabic and are all used within the Qur'an: "O you who believe, if you attack ('Darabtum') in the cause of God then make a clear declaration, and do not say to those who greet you with peace: 'You are not a believer!' You are seeking the vanity of this world; but with God are many riches. That is how you were before, but God favored you, so make a clear declaration. God is expert over what you do" (4:94). "So how will it be when the Angels put them to death, striking

('Yadriboona') their faces and their backs?" (47:27). "So We sealed ('Darabna') upon their ears in the cave for a number of years" (18:11). "Shall We take-away ('Na'drib') the reminder from you, because you are a transgressing people?" (43:5). "Have you not seen how God cites ('Daraba') the example of a good word is like a good tree, whose root is firm and its branches in the sky" (14:24). "As for the poor who face hardship in the cause of God, and they cannot leave ('Darban') the land; the ignorant ones think they are rich from their modesty; you know them by their features, they do not ask the people repeatedly. And what you spend out of goodness, God is fully aware of it" (2:273). Thus, in the Qur'an alone we witness the verb "daraba" having multiple meanings. "Daraba" has also other meaning, which are not mentioned in the Qur'an. For example in the Arabic language, you do not print money-you "daraba" money, you do not multiply numbers-you "daraba" numbers, and you do not cease the work-you "daraba" the work.

How do we know which interpretation to choose? One way to find out is to relate this verse to other verses in the Qur'an and to check if the meanings make sense. In this case, let us look at verse 24:2, which describes what should be done in case of adultery: "The woman and the man guilty of adultery or fornication, flog each of them with a hundred stripes" (24:2). This verse establishes the principle that for men and women, equal actions lead to equal punishment. When for adultery men and women must receive equal punishment, surely there is no reason why they should be treated differently for any lesser marital problem. Now let us take a look at the consequences of interpreting (*'adriboo'*) one way or another. Suppose "*adriboo*" means: 'to beat'. In this case, verse 4:34 says that when a wife causes a problem in the marriage, her husband should first talk to her about it, then leave their bed, then beat her and all of this in view of increasing his chances of reconciliation. On the emotional level, this certainly does not sound like a very promising course of action. So let us check this meaning against the bigger framework and in particular against the principle of 'equal behavior leads to equal punishment'. This would imply that when a husband causes a problem in the marriage, his wife could beat him. At which he could invoke verse 4:34 to beat her again, so that the result would be a perpetual physical fight between spouses! Surely, this makes no sense at all. And indeed, it is not what God prescribes for the situation where a husband causes a rift. Ahmed Ali translates the verse as 'go to bed with them' and cites Raghb's 'Mufridat fi Gharib al-Qu'an', 'Lisan al-Arab', and Zamakhshari. 'Daraba 'ala', according to Raghib is said for a he camel mounting over she camel and thus Ahmed Ali translates it as 'going to bed' rather than beating the wife.

Suppose (*'adriboo'*) means 'to forsake', 'to avoid', or, 'to part'. Now what do we get? Verse 4:34 says that when a wife causes a problem in the marriage, her husband should first talk to her about it, then leave their bed (forsaking his sexual satisfaction), then avoid her even more (not talking to her anymore, leaving the room when she enters it, and possibly even leaving the house for a while), in order to prevent things from getting worse, and on the contrary to let things cool down and create enough space in view of increasing chances for reconciliation. This sounds like a very logical chain of events. Qur'an does not support any type of wife beating: "Do not retain them (i.e., your wives) to harm them" (2:231). Also, application of the general rule of verse 24:2 ('equal actions, equal punishment') now means that when a husband causes a marital problem, his wife should forsake a few of her rights, avoid her husband in increasing ways, and try to work towards a reconciliation. And yes that is precisely what verse 4:128 says: "If a wife fears cruelty or desertion on her husband's part, there is no blame on them if they arrange an amicable settlement between themselves."

Understanding ("adriboo") as 'to forsake, to (gradually) avoid (more and more), possibly eventually leave altogether', clearly makes sense when relating several verses to one another. Beating a wife, would contradict a *hadith* of the

Prophet, which repeatedly said: "do not beat believing women!" It would also contradict the Prophet's instructions about anger–which he explained, to originate from Satan and which he described as "a living coal on one's heart". One should not act upon ones anger, lest one would do things one would regret later. When you are angry when you are standing, sit down, the Prophet said. And when you are still angry when you are sitting, then lie down. Interpreting this verse as allowing a husband to beat his wife, surely contradicts these rulings on anger. Furthermore, Qur'an says that one must meet bad behavior with something that is better, not with something that is worse, in order to turn a hostile situation into a friendly one: "Nor can goodness and evil be equal. Repel (evil) with what is better: Then will he between whom and thee was hatred become as it were thy friend and intimate!" (41:13).

Therefore the word ('adriboo') cannot really have meant, "to beat". It must mean something that is better than causing problems, and avoiding the problems. Based on the evidence presented above, it would seem that interpreting ('adriboo') as 'to beat', causes several internal conflicts with the meaning of other Qur'anic verses and ahadith, while interpreting it as 'gradually forsaking, more and more and possibly leaving altogether', is a much more logical interpretation that is entirely consistent with the interpretation of other rules in the Qur'an and the *Sunnah* of the Prophet Muhammad. What makes much more sense is that this verse does not allow a 'superior' husband to 'beat' his 'inferior, disobedient' wife. On the contrary, this verse appears to tell us that a husband must look after his wife (an equal partner who, like he, is obedient to God), and that when his wife is causing problems in their marriage, he should first talk to her about it, if that doesn't help, he should begin avoiding her by leaving the marital bed. If that still doesn't resolve the situation, he should forsake her presence even more, avoid conversations, leave a room when she enters it, avoid her company altogether, and possibly leave the house for a while, so that no problems are added to the conflict, and so that things can cool down a bit to maximize chances for a later reconciliation. When the problem is solved, when the wife is committed to the marriage again, then the husband is advised not to keep using the incident against her and to consider the incident closed.

Now if we read the aforementioned verse 4:34-35 together with 2: 231 it becomes clear that the meaning of the word 'daraba' cannot be beating. The Qur'an states: 'When you divorce women and they (are about to) fulfill the term of their (*iddat*), either take them back on equitable terms or set them free on equitable terms, but do not take them back to injure them' (2:231). Again in verse 49:33, the Qur'an has ordained husbands to release wives in a graceful manner. In another verse Qur'an states: 'The parties should either hold together on equitable terms or separate with kindness' (2:229). If separation between the spouses has to be made with grace and kindness, how the basis of reconciliation of disputes between the husband and wife can be beating? It is therefore evident from the above comparative study of the verses of the Qur'an that the meaning of the idiom 'daraba', which is an instrument of reconciliation of marital disputes, cannot be beating of wife by the husband. Further, women are the embodiment of beauty, by nature emotional and fragile and therefore question of resorting to beating wife by husband to resolve crack and crevice in conjugal life does not arise. There is no record that Prophet Muhammad ever slapped, beat, stroke or punched any of his wives. He gave models to his followers not to treat their wives roughly and not to beat them. He said that no one is allowed to beat his wife like he does his slave because at night he will be with her again. Some Islamic jurists believe that, given the way in which a number of ahadith have condemned beating *any* women, including wives, the act should be regarded as judicable offense in the first place. A righteous man will be extremely careful in being fair and equitable in his marriage, making sure that he fulfills his part of the agreement before claiming the full rights of verse 4:34. Thus, it is very unlikely that he will ever use the option to physically correct his wife, since he will be much too careful in examining his own motives first. As we learn from the verse immediately following 4:34, when it reaches this stage of considering this cause of action, the marriage is already falling apart, and divorce is the next option. For both men and women, Qur'an encourages arbitration with representatives from both families, if it comes to a point where the couple fears separation (4:35).

In the light of these evidences, the translation of verse 4:34 may be read as: "Men traditionally take care of women, since God has endowed each of them with certain qualities and men spend from their financial resources. The righteous women are obedient (to God) and during the absence (of their husband) they honor them according to God's commandment. As for those women whom you are experiencing a fear of disloyalty from, you shall first advice them, then (if they continue) you may desert them in bed, then you may strike them out. If they obey you then don't transgress against them. God is Most High, Supreme" (4:34). Another possible translation is: "The men are to support the women by what God has endowed them over one another and for what they spend of their money. The upright women who are attentive, and keep private the personal matters for what God keeps watch over. As for those women from whom you fear a desertion, then you shall advise them, and abandon them in the bedchamber, and separate from them; if they obey you, then do not seek a way over them; God is High, Great" (4:34).

Egalitarian Approach

The original Arabic text of the Qur'an does not refer to husbands as the recipient of women's obedience. It talks about women who are pious, humble before God, and observant of God's commands. The corrupted text not only inserts a reference to husbands, but also equates obedience to husbands with obedience to God. Furthermore, the translation leaves the reader with the distinct impression that husbands may punish their wives for what, in the husband's judgment, constitutes 'ill-conduct'. This leads to a separate discussion all together. The Qur'anic precepts must be seen as a function of social dynamics rather than used as a fixed text legitimizing rigid patriarchal claims. This is the case of Khadija, known for her economic independence, Ayesha, for her political skill and religious knowledge and Fatima, the daughter of the Prophet, who symbolizes morality and strength. Women were political leaders as well as leaders of scholarly thought. The best example is the wife of the Prophet, Ayesha. She was the main leader of the opposition when there was a problem of succession in the third Caliph. She is now a symbol of political participation. Ayesha is also the main scholar in the history of Islam. The main source of sayings of the Prophet in the Hadith; many of these sayings are attributed to Ayesha. Hundreds of scholars came from other countries to hear her lectures. She held discussions, lectured about issues and engaged in academic debate.

Certain social norms were assimilated into Islamic jurisprudence through a set of theological, legal and social theories and assumptions. Salient among them were propositions such as: "women are created of men and for men", "women are inferior to men", and "male and female sexuality differ and the latter is dangerous to the social order." These assumptions and theories are nowhere more evident than in the rules that define the formation and termination of marriage, through which gender inequalities are sustained in present-day Muslim societies. In classical 'fiqh' texts, gender inequality is taken for granted, *a priori*, as a principle. It reflects the world in which the authors of these texts lived, a world in which inequality between men and women was the natural order of things, the only known way to regulate the relations between them. It was a world in which biology is destiny, and there is no overlap between gender roles. Sadly, many Muslims have been manipulated by inauthentic narrations, or have misunderstood canonical texts, in such a way as to create the same sort of primitive mentality found in Medieval Europe. The same misguided souls are now presenting this distorted image as a picture of the true Islam. Muslims everywhere tend to view men as being ontologically superior to women and to believe that a woman is duty-bound to submit to the man in his capacity as her husband, father or brother. This ideology of male supremacy infuses Muslim cultures and consciousness to such an extent that it has given rise to representations of Islam as a religious patriarchy that professes models of hierarchical relationships and sexual inequality and puts a sacred stamp onto female subservience. However, even within a patriarchal discourse there persists a subversive element. It has been demonstrated how al-Razi consistently attempts to abrogate and minimize the violence inherent in 'daraba'. Both al-Razi and al-Zamakshari state explicitly that the verse 4:34 functions to place a limitation on the power and authority of men and to restrict their retributive action against their wives. A verse, which in contemporary understanding can be seen to create a space for the violation of women, in a medieval context, may be arguing to limit the physical violation of women. There is thus a dynamic interplay between context and hermeneutics. The hermeneutical lenses of the classical exegetes have and continue to inform authoritative Islamic discourses. However it is necessary to challenge and critically engage their gender ideology and interpretations of the Qur'an in the contemporary Muslim world. It is vital to provide alternative constructions of women and men if we believe in the dynamism of Islam and the continuing relevance of the Qur'an to people in their full humanity.

Azizah Al-Hibri goes on to argue: "Awliya" means 'protectors', 'in charge', 'guides'. It is quite similar to 'qawwamun'. How could women be "Awliya" of men if men are superior to women in both physical and intellectual strength? How could women be in charge of men who have absolute authority over their lives? The last passage (verse) clearly places male and female on equal footing. The traditional interpretation (mistakenly) raises the man above woman."[14] The usage of the word "fa'izuhunna" (which is from the root word "wa'az"), in verse 4:34 suggests that the rebellion of the women ("nushuz") is not against the husband's desires, but against the commandments of God. The Qur'an's discussion of 'Nushuz' is not restricted to this verse. It is used for women (4:34) and men (4:128). So "nushuz" cannot mean 'a woman's disobedience to her husband.' Obeying God is what makes a women righteous, not obeying her husband. Men are human and fallible: they are not better Muslims simply because they are male. They do not have to "keep us in check" because women are more prone to deviation than they are. Women are not the followers of the men who call themselves Muslims, but of God. No woman of any religion, including Islam, should believe that her husband, father, or brother is a degree above her.

Likewise, the allusion to what God has preferred is not to men, but to God's favor upon some of them, male and female, in terms of the worldly goods they possess. The charge to men to maintain their families does not carry with it the charge to rule over the wife, such a feudal concept being external to the Qur'an. Nor is its sanction for "wife-beating" as clear-cut as it is made out to be since 'daraba' also means 'to separate' and 'restrain' and we can read the disobedience to which the Qur'an refers as being to God and not to the husband. The Qur'an also does not treat polygyny as a universal model, or as a way for men to obtain children, or sexual release. In female witnessing the "two-for-one" formula is nullified by other cases of evidence-giving, one of which privileges the wife's testimony over the husband's and the other which promises that on Judgment Day baby girls who were killed by their fathers will be called upon to testify against them (81:8-9). Finally, the fact that the Qur'an treats women and men differently in some cases does not mean that it treats them unequally or that it views them as being unequal. Difference is not the same as inequality and the

Qur'an never suggests that women and men are opposites of one another or incompatible, incommensurable, or unequal, in the manner of Muslim misogynists. This new scholarship on the Qur'an opens it up to egalitarian and anti-patriarchal readings.

The Qur'an describes the spousal relationship as one of love, mercy, and harmony between two human beings who have entered into a mutual contract (7:189) According to the Qur'an, the relationship between husband and wife should be one of love, mercy and mutual understanding (4:19). Men are told to be generous and liberal in their treatment of women under all circumstances, especially when the relations between the two are not very amicable (2:229). So, it is through the institution of marriage that true expression is given to what the Qur'an refers to as "love and mercy" (30:21) between men and women; that men and women are like each other's garments (2:187), that "be you male or female, you are members of one another" (3:195), and that "men and women are protectors, one of another" (9:71).

The important role of men in contributing significantly in sharing household responsibilities and child rearing, as exemplified by Prophet Muhammad, is generally ignored in the Muslim world. The Prophet personally rejected any corporeal punishment of his wives.[15] The condition has so reached that, because of a pervasive sexist and oppressive presentation of women in Islam, Muslim women often felt the only way to be liberated intellectually, socially, politically and economically was by abandoning Islam. Fortunately, there appears to be a growing movement of Islamist women who are demanding that the rights guaranteed by Islam must be applied in their communities. In addition, women are joining the ranks of Islamic scholars, thus providing alternative points of view to what has heretofore been addressed by men. Reviewing Islamic history from an egalitarian perspective, recalling contributions of Muslim women over the centuries, exploring current practices and laws and criticizing them from an Islamic point of view, examining texts as they pertain to women specifically are a few examples of some areas addressed by these scholars today.

End Notes

1. Qur'an 13: 31,25:33,36:70,29; 47-51.
2. Qur'an 29:35, 9:34.
3. See for other Qur'an reference of witnessing to: property of orphan (4:6, 4:15); bequest (5:106-108): and divorce (65:2).
4. Fathi Osman, *Muslim Women in the Family and the Society*, Minaret Publications: New York, 1998, p. 39.
5. Qur'an 4:128, 40:40, 16:97.
6. Qur'an 17: 23, 24, and 28.
7. Qur'an 3:17, 33:35.
8. Qur'an 39:9, 2:117.
9. Qur'an 3:156, 4:101; 38:44, 73:20.
10. Qur'an 2:60, 7:160; 8:12, 20:77, 24:31, 26:63; 37:93, 47:04.
11. Qur'an 8:50; 47:27.
12. Qur'an 43:58, 57:13.
13. Qur'an 14: 24-45, 16:75, 76,112; 18:32, 45; 24:35; 36:78; 39:27, 29; 43:17, 21; 66:10-11.
14. Aziza al-Hibri. "A Study of Islamic Her Story: Or How Did We Ever Get into this Mess," in Aziza al-Hibri, (Editor), *Women in Islam*, Pergamon Press: New York, 1982. p. 217.
15. Murad Hofmann, *Islam: The Alternative*, Amana Publications: Maryland, 1997, p. 123.

5

Is God a Male?

Human beings have the right to develop their aesthetic sensibilities, the right to thrive, and to enjoy a good life. This requires self-actualization or development, which is not possible without social justice. Not only an end in themselves, women's rights are a basic component of social justice and a fundamental aspect of creating a just society, in which all people can actualize their God-given potential. Today more women are active in the discussion and reformation of identity than at any other time in human history. By going back to primary sources and interpreting them afresh, women scholars are endeavoring to remove the shackles imposed by centuries of patriarchal interpretation and practice. By questioning underlying presumptions and conclusions they are creating a space in which to think about gender. Drawing upon enduring principles of human rights, enshrined in the text, they extract meanings that can interact with the changing moral and intellectual circumstances of the reader. And women scholars and activists are also busy constructing a system of legal reforms that can be implemented today for the full status of women as moral agents at all levels of human society.

Language is not simply a communicative tool; it is power. It divides and constructs reality. This is true for all cultural domains, and not less so that of religious and theological discourse. Far from being genderless, "God" has acquired through the centuries different degrees of gender connotation. The science of scriptural exegesis has attempted to interpret this language recognizing its special symbolic features.

Gendered God?

The term 'sons of God' appears eleven times in the Bible as translated in the King James Version, although the idea appears a few more times in slightly different expressions. The term in the Hebrew Scriptures is limited to 'Genesis' and 'Job'. The expression in Genesis seems to be ambiguous, and it is susceptible to various interpretations. However, since both texts refer to human reproduction, one ought not to entertain the idea that the 'sons of God' in Genesis are other than human (Genesis 6:2-6). The text shows that there were giants in the earth in those days; and also after that, when the 'sons of God' came in unto the daughters of men, and they bare children to them, the same became mighty men, which were of old, men of renown. Whoever the 'sons of God' are, they are capable of mating with human beings and are therefore human beings themselves. The belief in mating between humans and divinities was widespread in the Mediterranean area, but there is no contextual evidence for this belief in Genesis 6. Any interpretation of the term 'sons of God' in this text as being other than human depends on either mere supposition or on the introduction into the text of material foreign to it. Isaiah 54:5 tell us that our Maker is the 'Husband of mankind'. The concept of God was reduced to human image and was referred to as a male, father god, in many cultures. Anthropomorphic views of the divine were necessary to Judaism, which was communally constituted in opposition to neighboring goddess-worship, whence the imagery of Israel as 'God's bride'. In the Eighteen Benedictions said by pious Jews every morning and evening, we find the words: 'Cause us to return, O our Father, to thy

Law,' while in Deuteronomy 8.6, we read: 'As a man disciplines his son, the Lord your God disciplines you.'

It is true that the Bible often uses masculine terms to describe God or His activities. Male names are applied to God, Christ, and the Holy Spirit throughout Scripture. The names for God like, 'Yahweh', 'Elohim', 'Shaddai', 'Seb-baoth', 'Adonai', 'Kurios', and 'Theos' are all masculine gender. Furthermore, male metaphors frequently are applied to God. The Psalmist cried, 'The Lord is king forever and ever' (10:16) and that 'like as a father pitied his children, so Jehovah pitied them that fear him' (Psalm 103:13). Nehemiah represented God as a warrior when he wrote: 'Our God will fight for us' (4: 20). Jeremiah portrayed God as a spurned husband (3:1-2). The feminist alternative to patriarchal religion is to resurrect the ancient cult of The Goddess. This was an ancient Mediterranean and European religion dedicated to a goddess of fertility known as The Great Mother. This nature-based religion was supposedly the original religion that was displaced and persecuted out of existence by the Catholic Church, which labeled its female priests as witches.

This continued in the Christian Church, the 'New Israel', the 'bride of Christ', as the Church Fathers waged war on the goddess cults of late antiquity, and also, increasingly, on 'woman' herself as the paradigm of responsibility for the 'fall.' St. Paul, the real founder of Christianity, pontificates this mindset very clearly: "A woman should learn in quietness and full submission. I do not permit a woman to teach or to have authority over a man; she must be silent. For Adam was not the one deceived; it was the woman who was deceived and became a sinner. But women will be saved through childbearing-if they continue faith, love and holiness with propriety" (1 Timothy 2:11-15).

As a result of hegemonic theologies, women lost their self-esteem, and voluntarily bowed down to a long lasting slavery. Being a homemaker was not a choice, but a consequence of being a member of Eve's party, the sinful party. Therefore, this thousands year of exploitation degraded the role of women in society. Child raising and housekeeping, two of the most important and difficult jobs in the world, were considered inferior by men. What is worse, women adopted this bogus perspective too. Such references to God as 'Father' are less common in the Old Testament than the New, but they are still abundant, and are thorns in the path of gender-sensitive liberal theologians. A theology that locates in a book makes no judgment about gender; since books are unsexed. In Christianity this has led in the Middle Ages to depreciation or mistrust of women, seen often as the seducers, the inheritors of Eve. Misogyny or an ambiguous attitude to women appears in important figures such as St. Paul, St. Jerome, St. Anthony, Tertullian and St. Augustine. Along with the depreciation of women, there has also been in Christianity mistrust of sexuality and of the values of the body and nature, which is absent from Islam. Only in the sixth century it was ruled that women had a soul, and they won by a single vote! This Christian devaluation of women in the Middle Ages is even more paradoxical when one thinks how Jesus Christ was indeed a great liberator of women. Christians went so far as to portray God as an old man with gray hair and a beard on the ceiling of the Sistine Chapel.

In contrast to Christianity, Islam has never depicted God as Father. Such a comparison is completely outside the boundaries of Islamic discourse. The Islamic understanding of salvation history did not require that God should be constructed as male and the believers never saw itself as a feminine entity, despite the interesting maternal resonance of the term 'umma' (community). Muslim theology, at a later period, like other major religions of the world, developed patriarchal cultures, has been used traditionally to deprive women of their God-created, God-given fundamental human rights. Somewhere in the dust of history, Muslim scholars ('ulema') adopted the Christian theory that women are the primary human source of Original Sin. They adapted the

Hebrew myth of the creation of Eve, from the 'rib' of Adam, as the basis of their gender perception. Most Muslims disregard textual injunctions on gender equity and the prophetic model these days, individually and collectively and a patriarchal theology was developed at its stead.

Women were relegated out of public life and back into the seclusion of the home. Men arranged marriages according to their whims. Women lost most of their rights to divorce or to remarry. Their worth was literally devalued. The efforts of believing women of the monotheistic faiths to subject their religious texts to a feminist re-reading, or to locate and emphasize the women-friendly and egalitarian precepts within their religious texts, are to be supported. This is a legitimate–and a historically necessary–strategy to improve the status of women and to modernize religious thought. Feminism, in that particular sense, is a theoretical perspective and a practice that criticizes social and gender inequalities, seeks to transform knowledge, and aims at women's empowerment.

Islam and Patriarchy

It is not a coincidence that in the era when the balance of power shifted from muscle to brain, women cried for their dignity and freedom. The feminist movement stretched out and created a rainbow with all colors, from purple to red, from pastel to neon. The feminist movement as an amalgamation of rational and irrational reaction has been forcing us to reevaluate and modify our concept of genders and sex roles. What need to be reexamined are fallible human interpretations and practices. This is not a violation of the integrity of Islam but rather a broadening of the Islamic possibilities. Diverse practices in Muslim countries often reflect cultural influences (local or foreign), more so than the letter or spirit of the *shari'ah*. Fortunately, there is an emerging trend for the betterment of our understanding of gender equity, based on the Qur'an and Hadith, not on alien and imported un-Islamic or non-Islamic values and not on the basis of the existing oppressive and unjust status quo in many parts of the Muslim world.

The Islamic worldview intends to defeat every form of injustice that is perpetuated on others so that no person is in a status that is greater than, or lesser than, another for the mere reason of their membership in any one category. The entire religion of Islam is based on the idea of getting closer to God. Not only does the Qur'an repudiate the patriarchal construct of God as Father, but it also condemns sacralizations of prophets as fathers. It also characterizes the rule of fathers ("following the ways of our fathers") as being antithetical to God's Rule. This emerges not only from the Qur'anic relentless denunciations, in dozens of verses and contexts, of the rule of unbelieving fathers, but also from its treatment of believing fathers as illustrated by the lives of the Prophets, Abraham and Muhammad. Thus, as Asma Barlas has correctly points out, Abraham's break with his own father and his vision, first to sacrifice his son and then not to, all illustrate this displacement of the father's will by God's Will.[2] Indeed, it is a believing father's "willingness to submit his will to God's Will; i.e., to yield up his rights as father" that establishes him as a believer, as Abraham's narrative illustrates.

The Qur'anic vision of the relationship between men and women within society is therefore neither hierarchical nor adversarial but one of equality and mutuality. Relations between men and women in the community ('umma') are to be characterized by mutuality, and so are the relations between husband and wife. In 2:137, the Qur'an describes the relationship of the husband and wife in more intimate, and yet still equivalent terms: 'your spouses are your garments, and you are their garments.' Affirming every person's right to work and insisting that the fruits of the labor belong to the one who has worked for them also undermines the patriarchal family structure (4:32). Under a patriarchal economy, the fruits of the labor of all family members rightfully belonged to the male head of household.

Insisting that women who work are due their earnings not only undercuts the husband's control of his wife's possessions, but also provides women with economic independence.

Language as Metaphor

In the Arabic language, we find the general term 'Allah', which is used to denote God and it, is used as such also by Arabic speaking Christians. The pre-Arabic 'Allah' had no gender connotation. Though the name 'Allah' is masculine, the entity it represents is thought as having neither gender, nor form whatsoever. Consequently, though 'Allah' manifests its presence in creation through "signs" in nature it is strictly forbidden in Islam to visually represent God in any form, and visual representations of an anthropomorphic God as commonly found in Christian art are shunned as a form of idolatry and blasphemy. It should also be noted that while 'Allah', the name of the God revealed and worshipped, is grammatically masculine, the name of the unknowable and inscrutable divine essence, *Dhat*, is grammatically feminine. This provides to theological discourse in Arabic a sort of gender counterpoint and dialectic.

The Islamic conception of God is neither male nor female. Male and female are aspects of duality, whereas God is unique. Nothing else resembles Him (Qur'an 112:4). He has no counterpart. So why is the male pronoun used to refer to Him? First of all, Arabic has no gender-neutral pronoun. Everything is either 'he' or 'she,' including inanimate objects. Even though English has the pronoun 'it,' to use 'it' to refer to God has a drawback, because 'it' is basically used for things and creatures that can't think. Likewise, to refer to God as 'she' has certain connotations of weakness in a human context. Like it or not, men have dominated public life and human societies throughout history. Therefore, the Qur'an uses 'He' to refer to Allah, while making it clear that God transcends all dualistic traits. Descriptions of Allah abound in the Qur'an or the Sunnah, but none of them gives the slightest inkling that He is masculine or feminine.

The Islamic concept of mankind's place in the universe hinges on the notion that God, is the ultimate reality. There is nothing permanent other than Him (55:27). God is considered eternal and "uncreated", whereas everything else in the universe is "created." God is not neuter or androgynous, but is simply above gender. The Qur'an describes Allah in Chapter 112: "Say: He is God, Singular. God, the Absolute; He begetteth not nor was begotten. And to Him have never been one equal." The Qur'anic emphasis on reading it holistically, hence intra-textually, also emerges from its praise for those who say, "We believe In the Book; the whole of it is from our Lord" (3:7). Allah is 'ghaniyy' or "absolutely free from need" of anything as the Qur'an says, "Verily Allah is absolutely free of need of anything in the worlds" (31:26). "Nothing is like Him and He is the Hearer, the Seer" (42:11). "No vision can grasp Him, but His grasp is over all vision" (6:103). Allah is greater than any gender construction or the inescapably human device of language. Patriarchal portrayals of God are thus also a negation of Allah's Transcendence ('subhaniyyat').

In this context one can note the significance of the name, 'Al-Rahman' which means, the Gracious-Compassionate One, the All Merciful. At a simple statistical level it is the most often repeated attribute in the Qur'an. Apart from its overwhelming presence in the text, every chapter, except one, begins with this name accompanied by its variant 'Al-Rahim'. Etymologically they are inextricably tied to the roots of the word for 'womb' in Arabic, making it a Yin / Feminine attribute par excellence. Drawing on this explicit identification of 'rahma' with the 'maternal' aspect of the phenomenal Divine, the developed tradition of Sufism habitually identifies God's entire creative aspect as 'feminine', and as merciful. Creation itself is the 'nafas al-Rahman', the Breath of the All Compassionate.

In Islamic mysticism, the Divine beloved is 'female'. The Sufi metaphysicians were drawing on a longstanding distinction between the Divine names that were called names of Majesty ('jalal'), and the names of Beauty ('jamal'). The names of Majesty included Allah as Powerful ('al-Qawi'), Overwhelming ('al-Jabbar'), Judge ('al-Hakam'); and these were seen as pre-eminently masculine. Names of Beauty included the All Compassionate ('al-Rahman'), the Mild ('al-Halim'), the Loving-Kind ('al-Wadud'), and so on: seen as archetypally feminine. The core is that neither set could be seen as pre-eminent, for all were equally names of Allah. In fact, by far the most conspicuous of the Divine names in the Qur'an is al-'Rahman', the All Compassionate The cosmic matrix from which differentiated being is fashioned is thus, as in all primordial systems, explicitly feminine; although God 'an such' remains outside qualification by gender or by any other property. Further confirmation for this is supplied in a famous hadith, collected for us by al-Bukhari, which describes how during the Muslim conquest of Mecca a woman was running about in the hot sun, searching for her child. She found him, and clutched him to her breast, saying, 'My son, my son!' The Prophet's companions saw this, and wept. The Prophet was delighted to see their 'rahma', and said, 'Do you wonder at this woman's 'rahma' for her child? By Him in Whose hand is my soul, on the Day of Judgment, Allah shall show more 'rahma' towards His believing servant than this woman has shown to her son'. And again: 'On the day that He created the heavens and the earth, God created a hundred 'rahmas', each of which is as great as the space which lies between heaven and earth. And He sent one 'rahma' down to earth, by which a mother has 'rahma' for her child' (*Muslim*). The veneration of aged mothers is a recurrent feature of the Prophetic vision, in which kindness and loyalty to the mother, a 'rahma' to reciprocate the 'rahma' they themselves dispensed, is seen as an almost sacramental act. Ibn Umar narrates that 'a man came to the Messenger of God and said: "I have committed a great sin. Is there anything I can do to repent?" He asked, "Do you have a mother?" The man said that he did not, and he asked again, "Then do you have a maternal aunt?" The man replied that he did, and the Prophet told him: "Then be kind and devoted to her" (*Tirmidi*).

Some other Ahadith are given below: 'Whoever kisses his mother between the eyes receives a protection from the fire' (*Baihaqi*); 'Verily God has forbidden disobedience to your mother' (*Bukhari*). Scholars also noted that when the meanings of the 99 names were analyzed, the root meanings in many instances refer to creation and fertility, which negates the specification of a gender for Allah. In her book "The Tao of Islam" the Japanese scholar Sachiko Murata has drawn parallels with the attributes of Allah (proverbial 99 names of God) in the concept of 'yin' and 'yang' whereby the names of Majesty can be considered yang / masculine / jalal as for example, the Avenger, the Destroyer, the Reckoner. Examples of yin/feminine/jamal names are the Great Bestower, the Most Indulgent, the Beautiful, and the Source of Peace.[1] The vast majority of what are called "The Most Beautiful Names of God" (Al-Asma al-Husna)–the proverbial 99 names of God–mostly falls into these categories.

God's Essence transcends all duality, all relationality, so it is beyond male or female. But even on the level of the Divine Nature, there are the roots of the masculine and the feminine. On the highest level, God is at once Absolute and Infinite. These two attributes are the supreme archetypes of the masculine and the feminine. "Masculine" and "feminine" are not simply equivalents of the human male and female, since all men and women have elements of both masculinity and femininity within them. That God is Absolute is the principle of masculinity, and that God is Infinite is the principle of femininity. God has revealed Himself in the Qur'an in the names of rigor and mercy, known as the names of Majesty ('Jalâl') and Beauty ('Jamâl'). The Generous, the Merciful, the Forgiving are names of mercy or Beauty, while the Enumerator and the Just are names of rigor or Majesty. On the level of the names are the principles of the masculine and the feminine: the names of Majesty are the prototype of masculinity, while the names of Beauty are the prototype of femininity. Some of the key terms associated with the Divine are in the feminine gender in Arabic. Three of them are essential to understand the feminine dimension in Islam. One of God's names is 'al-Hakîm', the Wise; Wisdom is 'hikmah'. In Arabic to say, for example, "Wisdom is precious," you could repeat the feminine pronoun: 'al-hikmah hiya thamînah', literally "Wisdom, she is precious." On metaphysical plane, femininity corresponds to interiority and masculinity to manifestation. In the traditional Islamic city, beauty is interiorized. All human beings contain both elements within themselves, in their souls and bodies and psyches. The perfection of the human state, 'al-insân al-kâmil', means the perfection of both masculine and feminine qualities together, the prototype of both male and female.

Removal of the Mist

While ontologically "God" in the Judaic tradition as well as in the other two monotheistic religions, Christianity and Islam, has no gender, is beyond gender, its nature being utterly unknowable, formless and nameless, epistemologically the absolute transcendence of God has been approached in analogical terms which lend a personality affected by anthropomorphic representations.

Nobody is able to escape altogether the strictures of one's own conceptualization, though an effort to be at least aware of the limitations of how our linguistic system affects mental representation can considerably extend and refine the range of our mental associations, and therefore both broaden and deepen our spirituality. The Highest Power is the one who is completely without sex or race, and thus completely non-patriarchal. Deity is completely above sexual identity, and thus completely outside the value system created by patriarchy. God is not neuter or androgynous, but is simply above gender. God is not gendered, really or metaphorically. The Qur'an continues Biblical assumptions on many levels, but there is a striking discontinuity: the imaging of God has been shifted into a new and bipolar register, that of the Ninety-Nine names.

Islamic theology is the one in which the Divine is truly gender-neutral, but gifts humanity with a legal code and family norms which are rooted in the understanding that the sexes 'are equal but different', and will naturally gravitate towards divergent roles which affirm rather than suppress their respective genius. Arabic has no neuter, and the use of the masculine is normal in Arabic for genderless nouns. No male preponderance is implied, any more than feminity is implied by the grammatically female gender of neuter plurals. "Shams", the sun, is considered feminine in Arabic and "qamar", the moon, is considered masculine while the opposite holds true in the English language, i.e., the moon is considered feminine and the sun masculine.

Muslims refuse any type of favoritism. Islam is a religion of absolute justice. But because it rejects any identification of human worth with conspicuous functionality, or power, or status, or consumption, Muslims are able to insist on the worth of women in a way that is not possible outside a religious context. Without denying the inherent genetic differences, enlightened Muslims claim that "aggression and power" should not be the dominant characteristics anymore. This historical crime should stop. We, as the generation of information and intellect, should appreciate and enjoy the natural diversity of sexes, without refracting or exploiting them.

By giving such clear and merciful guidance to human beings, God is establishing a universal and eternal Truth for the benefit of mankind. This eternal Truth is the bedrock of religious guidance, since once people begin to believe that Almighty God mixes with or can be represented by His creation; they can be duped into believing almost anything. Once someone accepts that God has become "incarnate" in His creation, or that someone or something is a "manifestation"-and thus representation-of Him, the floodgates are open and "Truth" becomes a matter of subjective guesswork. Once the first and most basic concept is violated-regardless of how complicated and sophisticated the justification for it might be-it is very easy to fall further and further away from the Eternal Truth of pure Monotheism. In the final analysis, it is not a question of whether God is capable of becoming a man, but rather a question of whether one bases their beliefs about God on clear, unequivocal and authentic Guidance. Once it is left up to the human mind to decide what Almighty God can and cannot do, the stage is set for misguidance to take root. Human speculation about God only ends up leading to misguidance and despair, since no clear conclusions can ever be reached. For example, is God capable of creating an object so heavy that He is incapable of moving it? If not, does that mean that He is incapable? It is because of such misguided questions that Islam clearly teaches that mankind should only say about God what He has said about Himself. This means all of our ideas about God must be based on Revelation-not human speculation. In short, the final prophet of Islam-Muhammad-was sent by Almighty God to preach the same unadulterated Monotheism that was preached by Noah, Abraham, Moses, David and Jesus. This unspoiled and pure Monotheism means not only believing that there is only One God in existence, but also realizing that He is transcendent above His creation and that all worship is due to Him alone.

Islam rejects characterizing God in any human form or depicting Him as favoring certain individual or nations on the basis of wealth, power or race. He created the human beings as equals. They may distinguish themselves and get His favor through virtue and piety only. The concept that God rested in the seventh day of creation,[3] and that God is an envious plotter against mankind,[4] or that God is incarnate in any human being are considered blasphemy from the

Islamic point of view. The unique usage of 'Allah' as name of God is a reflection of Islam's emphasis on the purity of the belief in God, which is the essence of the message of all God's messengers. Because of this, Islam considers associating any deity or personality with God as a deadly sin, which God will never forgive, despite the fact He may forgive all other sins. The Creator must be of a different nature from the things created because if he is of the same nature as they are, he will be temporal and will therefore need a maker. It follows that nothing is like Him. If the maker is not temporal, then He must be Eternal. But if He is Eternal, He cannot be caused, and if nothing caused to come into existence, nothing outside Him causes Him to continue to exist, which means that He must be self-sufficient. And if He does not depend on anything for the continuous of His own existence, then this existence can have no end. The Creator is therefore eternal and everlasting: "He is the First and the Last" (57:3). He is Self-sufficient or Self-subsistent or, to use a Qur'anic term, 'Al-Qayyum'. The Creator does not create only in the sense of bringing things into being, He also preserves them and takes them out of existence and is the ultimate cause of whatever happens to them: "God is the Creator of everything. He is the guardian over everything. Unto Him belong the keys of the heavens and the earth" (39:62-63). "No creature is there crawling on the earth, but its provision rests on God. He knows its lodging place and its repository" (11:6).

Islamic theology confronts us with the spectacular absence of a gendered Godhead. A theology, which reveals the divine through incarnation in a body, as in Christianity, also locates it in a gender, and inevitably passes judgment on the other sex. God is not neuter or androgynous, but is simply above and beyond any gender. When we turn to the Qur'an, we find an image of Godhead epiphytically stripped of metaphor. God is simply God, the God; and never a Father. Although commonly referred to as "He", God is genderless, as there is no neuter gender to express this in the Arabic language. When Greek or other polytheistic deities are discussed in Arabic, it is customary to use the expression *ilaah*, a "Deity" or "God." God transcends all dualistic traits. Descriptions of God abound in the Qur'an or the Sunnah, but none of them gives the slightest feeling that He is masculine or feminine. The doctrine of God's Incomparability, which states that God is Un-representable, encourages us to reject God's engenderment, even at a linguistic level ("He"). This is crucial since misrepresentations of God as Father/ male also underwrite sexual hierarchies and oppression in religious contexts. God is beyond any conceivable picture that may be in mortals' minds; He is completely beyond mortal descriptions. The Qur'an says: 'To Him belongs the loftiest similitude [we can think of] in the heavens and the earth: for He is Exalted in Might, Full of wisdom' (30: 27). So we see that the Qur'an sometimes refers to God in singular form or in plural form, like in 108:1: 'To thee have We granted the fount [of abundance]'. All this is just to indicate divine respect and honor He most deserves. This neither denotes masculinity or plurality to His divine entity.

The first and most basic right emphasized by the Qur'an is the right to be regarded in a way that reflects the sanctity and absolute value of each human life. Each person has the right not only to life but also to respect, not by virtue of being a man or a woman, but by virtue of being a human being. "Verily," states the Qur'an, "We have honored every human being" (17:70). Human beings are deemed worthy of esteem because, of all creation, they alone chose to accept the "trust" of freedom of the will (33:2). Human beings can exercise freedom of the will because they possess the rational faculty, which is what distinguishes them from all other creatures (2:30-34). Although human beings can become "the lowest of the low," the Qur'an declares that they have been made "in the best of moulds" (95:4-6), having the ability to think, to have knowledge of right and wrong, to do the good and to avoid the evil. Thus, on account of the promise that is contained in being human, namely, the potential to be God's vicegerent on earth, the humanness of all human beings is to be respected and considered an end in itself. Flowing from this primary right is the right to be treated with justice and equity. The Qur'an puts great emphasis on the right to seek justice and the duty to do justice. Justice encompasses both the concept that all are equal and recognition of the need to help equalize those suffering from a deficiency or loss.

Yet justice is not absolute equality of treatment, since human beings are not equal as far as their human potential or their human situation is concerned. While each person's humanness commands respect, the Qur'an also establishes the right to recognition of individual merit. Merit depends not on gender or any other characteristic, but only on righteousness. Righteousness consists of just belief plus just action, including faith, prayer, wealth-sharing, equitable and compassionate behavior, and patience in the face of hardship or difficulty (2:177). Additionally, with great implications for the status of Muslim women, human beings possess the right to work, to earn, and to own property. This right is not the monopoly of men. In Islam, everything belongs to God, not to any person, and so every human being has the right to a means of living. Given the recognition of women as persons in their own right and not as adjuncts to men, the right to earn a living is of great importance to women, and the Qur'an entitles both women and men to the fruits of their labors.[5]

Islam presents the roles of men and women as complementary roles and not contradictory or conflicting roles; the roles of partners with a common set of goals and objectives and not roles that conflict with each other, with each of them having the objective of the civilizations and societies that for centuries refused to consider women as human beings, or to give them any rights, have now gone from one extreme to another. Islam has never had anything to do with such nonsense. When women had no rights in the world it declared: "And women shall have rights, similar to the rights against them, according to what is equitable" (2:228). Verse 33:35, not only enumerate the responsibilities and rewards of men and women, it clearly proves that there is no superior gender, and the general rules apply on both. The Scripture regards men and women as complementary to each other, one sex making up what the other lacks.[6] Islam does not consider a woman a mere shadow or an extension of a man, always following him or obeying him. She has her full individual freedom and responsibility to the belief in the message of God and in practicing its obligations.

Islam recognizes woman as equal partner in the procreation of humankind. Man is the father, woman is the mother, and both are essential for life. By this partnership, woman has an equal share in every aspect; she is entitled to equal rights; she undertakes equal responsibilities, and she has as many qualities and as much humanity as her partner. So, fourteen centuries ago, Islam made men and women equally accountable to God in glorifying and worshiping Him without setting any limits on her spiritual progress. The Qur'an says: "O mankind! Be careful of your duty to your Lord Who created you from a single soul and from it its mate and from them both have spread abroad a multitude of men and women. Be careful of your duty toward God in Whom you claim (your rights) of one another, and towards the wombs (that bore you). Lo! God has been a Watcher over you." (4:1). "And among His signs is that He created for you mates from among yourselves that you may live in tranquility with them, and He had put love and mercy between you; Verily, in that are signs for people who reflect" (30:21).

Marriage, therefore, is not just a physical or emotional necessity, but in fact, a sign from God! It is a relationship of mutual rights and obligations based on divine guidance. God created men and women with complimentary natures, and Qur'an laid out a system of laws to support harmonious interaction between the sexes: "They are your garments and you are their garments" (2:187). Clothing provides physical protection and covers the beauty and faults of the body. A spouse is viewed similarly. Each protects the other, hides the faults and compliments the characteristics of the spouse. And again in the Qur'an we read: "O mankind! Verily we have created you from a single (pair) of a male and female, and made you into nations and tribes that you may know each other" (49:13). "Whoever performs good deeds, whether male or female and is a believer, We shall surely make him live a good life and We will certainly reward them for the best of what they did" (16:97). The Qur'an reproached those who believed woman to be inferior to men (16:57-59) and repeatedly gives expression to the need for treating men and women with equity (2:228, 231; 4:19). If she commits any civil offense, her penalty is no less or no more than a man's in a similar case (5:83, 24:2). If she is wronged or harmed, she is entitled to compensation just like a man (4:92-93). Therefore, if Muslim women experience discrimination in any place or time, they do not and should not lay the blame on Islam, but on the un-Islamic nature of their societies and the failure of Muslims to fulfill its directives. Man and woman are equal partners to work as a team in running the home. Neither of them should try to dominate and exploit the other. Woman's rights are to be respected as much as man's. The husband cannot encroach on the rights of his wife: "Women have rights against men like as men have rights against them in reason and law" (2:228). Islam emphasizes the importance of taking counsel and mutual agreement in family decisions. It gives us an example: "If they (husband and his wife) desire to wean the child by mutual consent and (after) consultation, there is no blame on them" (2:233). Islam introduces the gender relation concept with the objective that is manifesting the justice and righteousness (16:90), security and peace (4:58), and in the call to righteousness and the prevention of evil (3:104). These are some of the verses that can be used as a framework for analyzing gender relations in the Qur'an.

The idea about women's role being limited to housework is, however, a creation of our own minds and is not based on what God and His Messenger have given us. Thus, for example, mosques are meant to be the centres of Muslim participation and even though some Muslims oppose women going to the mosques, the Qur'an and Hadith leave no doubt that it is as desirable for women to visit the house of God and pray there in congregation as it is for men. One of the Qur'anic verses where reference is made to congregational prayers reads: "And establish regular prayer and practice regular charity and bow down with those who bow down" (2:43). A further proof of this is found in 3:43 where one of the most saintly women of all human history is told: "O Mary! Worship your Lord devoutly; prostrate yourself and bow down with those who bow down." Here the verb "bow down" (*'arka'u*) is in the masculine plural, but it is a well-known rule of Qur'anic interpretation that unless otherwise indicated all recommendations, commandments, etc. delivered in the masculine plural are applicable to both men and women. In this verse there is no indication of any kind that women are excluded: just as the words "establish regular prayer", "practice regular charity" are meant for both men and women, so also the words "bow down with those who bow down" (i.e., pray in congregation) are addressed to both. Interesting to note that God does not command Mary to "bow down with those women who bow down" but rather uses the masculine plural, which, as pointed out earlier, includes both men and women. God's command to Mary thus means: "bow down (in prayer) with those fellow human beings, men and women, who bow down." Nothing that the Qur'an says about earlier men and women is without relevance for us, for the Qur'an does not relate the stories of earlier people just for our amusement. In the original Prophet's Mosque in Madinah, the women and men all prayed in one open space, with no sexual apartheid. There is no separate entry for women at the Hajj pilgrimage, as is the practice in mosques across the world, including the Prophets mosque in Madinah. Nor was there a curtain or a screen to divide the men and women at the prayer.

In Qur'an 27:42-44, we read one of the first Muslim women in charge of a nation, ruling them as a queen of Sheba. We should learn a lesson from this Qur'anic portrayal of a historical incident. The lesson is that, God in the Qur'an never put restrictions on a woman in a ruling position. Contrary to what the traditional Muslim scholars teach, a woman in a leading political position is not against God's system or against the Qur'an. Ayesha, Mother of Believers, who taught hadith, is as always, the indispensable paradigm for Muslim woman: lively, intelligent, devout, and humbling to all subsequent memory. Women's position is determined not so much by the principles of Islam as by social practices. It is well known that women like Aisha, Umm Salamah, Laila bint Qasim, Asma bint Abu Bakr, Kaula bint Umm Darda, and many others, were trusted with preserving and teaching religion. Any discrimination based on gender is a grave offense and against the teachings of the Qur'an. Muslim women have for long periods of history left their homes to become scholars. A hundred years ago the Orientalist Ignaz Goldziher showed that perhaps fifteen percent of medieval hadith scholars were women, teaching in the mosques and universally admired for their integrity. Colleges such as the 'Saqlatuniya Madrasa' in Cairo were funded and staffed entirely by women.

Acquiring knowledge is a prerequisite for evaluating the conditions of life and working toward the creation of a just world. Denied knowledge, Muslim women are denied justice. Fortunately, there is an emerging trend for the betterment of our understanding of gender equity, based on the Qur'an and Hadith, not on alien and imported un-Islamic or non-Islamic values and not on the basis of the existing oppressive and unjust status quo in many parts of the Muslim world. It is not the revelatory Qur'an and the Sunnah that need any editing or revision. What need to be reexamined are fallible human interpretations and practices.

Hasan Turabi, a Sudanese scholar who was a leading power in Sudan, wrote a booklet, 'Women in Islam and Muslim Society', because women were not joining the Islamic movement and he wanted to convince them that: "the limitations on women's freedom in traditional society had nothing to do with Islam."[7] He further states: "Islam does not call for segregation between men and women."[8] "Whenever weakness creeps into the faith of Muslim men they tend to treat women oppressively and seek to exploit them."[9] "The male tendencies and the appending customs and ways are manifest in many societies where male arbitrariness runs amok with no religious or human limitation...Take, for instance, the Arab, Persian and Indian societies. Although the message of Islam has spread in these societies from early times, the teaching and inculcation of Islamic cultural values was not coextensive with the horizontal expansion. Consequently some pre-Islamic values and prejudices have continued to persist despite the domination of Islamic forms. In some cases there was manifest historical religious decline and relapse to the earlier social ethos and mores... This phenomenon has sometimes occasioned an even more serious development. New or degenerate Muslim societies would sometimes, out of ignorance, attribute their un-Islamic legacy or custom to Islam itself. By attaching an Islamic value to these practices they seek to give them legitimacy and sanctity, the values of Islam being accepted as sacred and supreme. This explains the unabated influence on the minds of many otherwise good Muslims of attitudes abhorrent to Islam, especially in the sensitive areas of sex relations where passion is strong and custom is sacrosanct"[10] Akbar S. Ahmed, an Islamic scholar, concurs with the view: "The position of women in Islamic society mirrors the destiny of Islam: When Islam is secure and confident so are its women; when Islam is threatened and under pressure, so too, are they."[11]

Islam would say that there are in fact three discourses: male, female, and God. Tawhid, as we have seen, refuses to a gendered God; and the Qur'anic text is hence a gender-neutral document. It is read by men and by women, and hence, often, imported and internalized in gender-specific ways. If the Creator is Eternal and Everlasting, then His attributes must also be eternal and everlasting. He should not lose any of His attributes nor acquire new ones. If this is so, than His attributes are absolute. Can there be more than one creator with such absolute attributes? Can there be, for example, two absolutely powerful Creators? A moment's thought shows that this is not feasible. The Qur'an summarizes this argument in the following verses: "God has not taken to Himself any son, nor is there any god with Him: For then each god would have taken of that which he created and some of them would have risen up over others" (23:91). "And why, were there gods in earth and heaven other than God, they (heaven and earth) would surely go to ruin" (21:22).

The Challenge Before a Muslim Scholar

In Islamic legal discourse, on women's issues, there is a blatant absence of female voice. It is remarkable that even when women transmitters of *hadith* were admitted in the 'ilm al-rijal' ("science dealing with the scrutiny of the reporters") dealing with source criticism to authenticate ahadith reports in the Sunnah, and even when their narratives were recognized as valid documentation for deducing various rulings, they were not participants in the intellectual process that produced the prejudicial rulings encroaching upon the personal status of women. More importantly, the revelational text, regardless of its being extracted from the Qur'an or the *Sunnah*, was casuistically extrapolated in order to disprove a woman's intellectual and emotional capacities to formulate independent decisions that would have been more sensitive and more accurate in estimating her radically different life experience. The demand today for new and expanded methodology of 'usul al-fiqh' among the Muslim fundamentalist leaders, clearly shows the crisis that faces male-dominated epistemology in coming to terms with the demands about the recognition of the women's personal status and the substantive-cognitive role of their reason in reversing prejudicial decisions that deny her dignity as a full person. Muslim men are Islamically duty-bound to bring about a substantial change in the families and societies. They should listen carefully to the voices of women, to see the tears and listen the sighs of the granddaughters of Mary, Asiya and Khadija. They should formulate Qur'anically satisfying solutions to the contemporary problems, for the salvation of Muslim men and women, which are inextricably intertwined. They should be aware that this effort is only a re-introduction of their own heritage of fundamental Qur'anic principles of fairness and justice (5:8, 4:135).

Respect for common humanness, is a theme that as we all know is reiterated throughout the Qur'an,[12] is rarely allowed by interpreters and religious scholars to be a governing principle in constructing gender relations. In seeking to bridge the gap between theory and practice in this area, one can never overemphasize the difference between the basic equitable religious principles of the Qur'an and the authenticated *Sunnah* as referential framework, on one hand, and culture or cultural trappings on the other hand. These constitute the inherited cultural concepts and notions about gender distinctions and women, practices that have developed historically as a result of a very complicated process of acculturation or, sometimes, pre-Islamic ideas that heavily influenced religious thought and were thus incorporated and canonized. Eventually, these notions have become part of the popular understanding and practice of religion. This is where the crux of the problem lies: working up the care and patience to sift, the real Qur'anic ideal, through all of these entanglement and specifically trace the cultural history of Muslim society so as to develop a theology viable for gender justice.

End Notes

1. Sachiko Murata, *The Tao of Islam: A Sourcebook on Gender Relationships in Islamic Thought*, State University of New York Press: Albany, 1992.
2. Qur'an 6:74, 37:102-107.
3. Genesis 2:2-3, Hebrews 4: 10; Compare with Qur'an 50:38.
4. Genesis 11:1-9; Compare with Qur'an 9:11.
5. Qur'an 4:124,16:97.
6. Qur'an 66:19-21, 9: 71, 3:195.
7. Hasan Turabi, *Women in Islam and Muslim Society*, Milestones Publishers: London, 1991, p. 3.
8. Hasan Turabi, *Ibid*, p. 25.
9. Hasan Turabi, *Ibid*, p. 38.
10. Hasan Turabi, *Ibid*, p. 37.
11. Jan Goodwin, *Price of Honor: Muslim Women Lift the Veil of Silence on the Islamic World*, Little Brown & Co: New York, 1994, p. 47.
12. Qur'an 49:13, 17:70, 30:30, 7:172, 3:103, 4:58.

6

Who is an Ideal Muslim Woman?

The diversity of Muslim societies shows that Islam does not have a static or monolithic tradition. It has absorbed not only the practices and traditions of the two other monotheistic religions-Judaism and Christianity-from the region of its birth, but also other pre-Islamic practices and traditions from the geographic location in which it strove to survive and gain power as a cultural and political system. Thus, it is very difficult to define what is intrinsic to Islam in shaping sexual behavior. The issue becomes even more complicated when we attempt to analyze its interaction with various socioeconomic and political systems. Within hundred years after the beginning of the Islamic calendar woman almost lost all her Qur'anic rights. Qur'an recognized her as legal entity and gave her all rights including contracting marriage, divorce, right to inherit, to have her own property, to earn and have her own income and to own her own business. But by the time the Umayyads consolidated their rule, all pre-Islamic traditions and customs were revised and also feudal traditions added to them thus completely subjugating women. Muslims also picked up some of the Christian misogyny and reduced women to the rank of second-class citizens even though the ideal of the equality of all believers was crucial to the Qur'anic message. Another reason offered is that with the spread of Islam to areas of the Byzantine Empire, there were encounters with societies where women were more restricted in their roles and rights. It was in societies such as Syria, Iraq, and Persia that the upper-class women in particular were veiled (similarly to Greek and Roman women), a custom which Muslims adopted. It is the issue of the veil today which has become, (unfortunately), the principal focus of discussion of the Western preoccupation with the oppression of Muslim women. Muslim men, always, seek to provide sanction for unrestrained polygamy, child marriages, arbitrary divorce and the denial of women the right to education by claiming that all this is somehow sanctioned in Islam. What we try to do is to offer alternate interpretations of Islam that can challenge these sorts of arguments and claims.

We discover the immense diversity among Muslims and, of course, the multiple interpretations of Islam, although the Qur'an functions as a sort of common thread for all Muslims. The ways in which Islam and the *shari'ah* are understood vary across countries, classes and ethnic groups, so there is this inherent possibility of reinterpretation to promote more women's-friendly or gender-just interpretations. So, for instance, in some Muslim communities female genital mutilation is sought to be justified as 'Islamic', while in others it is completely unknown. The *Sunnis* split inheritance in a way the *Shias* believe is unjust to women. If a *Sunni* father dies leaving no sons, the daughters still inherit only part of the estate; the rest goes to the nearest male relative. If there are no sons, *Shia* law gives daughters all of the father's estate. The interpretation of the concept of 'ma'ruf' (equity) (2:228) changes between earlier and latter exegetes, with negative implications for gender-role division. Whereas Tabari (10th century exegete) treats it as the balancing of rights and duties among men and women through kindness and goodness, Zamakhshari (12th century) and much later Muhammad Abdu (20th century) define it as adhering to people's established customs concerning gender roles and duties. Muhammad Abdu at one point contests the very early commentaries that a wife has no specific domestic responsibilities-since no Qur'anic text enjoins it-and insists that this would be relieving women of their necessary and established duties as wives. Al-Qurtubi (end of 13th century) in his commentary states that men are preferred over women in their ability to "enjoin what is righteous and admonish what is unlawful," in complete contradiction to another verse that clearly and directly states that believers, men and women, are supporters of each other in "enjoining that which is righteous and admonishing that which is unlawful" (9:71).

We have been used to thinking that women have been created for the family life and for raising children, and thus their natural place is in their homes. Nothing in the Qur'an or *Sunnah* clearly supports such a view or assumption. Such a division of labor between the husband who earns the living of the family and the wife who stays at home doing housework is a societal experience, which has occurred for a very long time throughout history in so many societies, including the Arab society at the time of Islam, and the subsequent Muslim as well as other societies until recent times when change has come out. Women learn and work equally to men, and the family responsibilities are requiring more financial resources. Caring about the home has to be reviewed, and the Prophet's traditions indicate his assistance to his wives.

Should An Ideal Woman Bear Many Children?

Despite an incentive to have a family, neither marriage nor children are considered obligatory in the life of a Muslim man or woman. In fact the Qur'an also warn the believer that if she or he does not approach marriage and parenting with the right attitude and awareness, these too can have a negative impact in one's life; and if one fears such a possibility and does not have wherewithal for marriage, the Qur'an even permits one to remain unmarried (24:33). Opponents of family planning often base their rejection of both contraception and abortion on their reading of the verse 6:151. This verse was, actually, a response to the pre-Islamic Arab custom of burying female children alive. It was therefore a condemnation of infanticide and of the deep misogyny of that culture. Mullahs' argument that these Qur'anic verses prohibit all family planning initiatives is therefore a misreading of the text. Furthermore, their resistance to it on the basis that it constitutes a lack of trust in God and in God's sustenance and that it is an assertion of ones own will vis-à-vis God's will. The verses that they use to support this position are the following Qur'anic verses: 'There is no creature on earth, but its sustenance depends on God. He knows its habitation and its preservation' (11:6). 'And whosoever is conscious of God, He will find a way out (of difficulty) for him, and He will provide for him in a manner beyond all expectations, and for every one that places their trust in God, He alone is sufficient' (65:2-3).

Indeed trust in God and in God's sustenance is an integral dimension of Islam. These verses speak to the reality that in Islam ultimately the outcome of all things resides with God, for God is without doubt, the Sustainer, the all-Powerful. This does not, however, absolves human being from any responsibility for agency in the world. On the contrary this type of reasoning is contrary to the very fundamental Islamic notion of human vicegerency (2:30). Caliphate implies that humanity is entrusted with moral agency which demands a God-conscious, active and responsible attitude to oneself, to fellow human beings and to the world. It includes using the faculties of reason, judgment and God-consciousness that are part of our pure nature ('fitrah'), to plan one's life, to seek out sustenance, and to strive actively for the well being of self and society in relation to the challenges of our age. In the current context of living in world, while a believer trust that ultimately all lies within the power of God, human agency is intrinsic to the Qur'anic worldview and the prophetic teachings. The Qur'anic narrative of Joseph's planning and preservation of food in anticipation of the famine is an act of agency that does not demonstrate a lack of trust in Gods sustenance (see Qur'an 12:43-56). Similarly there are prophetic traditions that address the combination of human agency with trust in God as is reflected in the Prophet's advice to a man to tie up his camel and then trust in God; or the caliph Umar's statement that reliance on God means to plant the seeds in the earth, then trust in God for a good crop. Family planning including contraceptive usage may be seen as extension of the human capacity to plan, to respond to and to actively make choices in terms of contextual needs and emerging realities. Early Muslim jurists, even, considered abortion lawful for a variety of reasons until 40-120 days after conception (first trimester). This was based on interpretation of Qur'an (22:4 and 23:12-14) and hadith that implied that ensoulment or "life" did not exist until after that time.[1]

The scholar Hamid Al-Ghazzali (d. 1111) supported the use of contraceptive practice for a number of different reasons including economic factors where a large number of dependents would impose financial and psychological hardship on the family. He reasoned that a large family might cause one to resort to unlawful means to support these excessive responsibilities. Fewer material burdens, he adds, are an aid to religion. He also supported the decision to use contraception in order to protect the life of the wife, given the possible physical dangers that childbirth posed to the life of the mother. In addition, he considered the need for the wife to preserve her beauty and attractiveness for the enjoyment of the marriage as a reasonable justification for contraception. While the last mentioned rationale might characterize a patriarchal emphasis on the primacy of the wife's appearance to the enjoyment of the marriage, it nonetheless simultaneously illustrates the high levels of tolerance for contraceptive practices in the Islamic legacy. This is reflected in the fact that there are many other influential jurists and theologians in different historical periods who discussed the permissibility of contraception ('azl') for similar and additional reasons.

Is Gender Inequality Ingrained In Islam?

The Qur'an has made several references to women who disobey their husbands, whether out of faith, such as Asiya the wife of Pharaoh, proposed as a model for believing women, who defied her husband by believing in the Prophet Moses; or out of disbelief such as the wives of Noah and Lot. The Qur'an also states the rights of believer women who have chosen faith in defiance to their family and tribe, thus demonstrating their rights to make independent decisions for themselves (60:1O, 3:193). Throughout the Qur'an, human beings, regardless of sex, are evaluated on the basis of their spiritual merits, ethical qualities and the achievements they have made during their life (33:35, 4:24). Human beings are each personally responsible for their actions and no one person can accept the burden of another's actions. This concept of the Qur'an, which is in clear contradiction of any form of absolute obeisance to another person, has been repeatedly mentioned in several instances (17:13-15).

There are certain verses in the Qur'an, which apparently reflects patriarchal situation. This was mainly because the Qur'an was revealed in a particular historic circumstance. At any rate, these verses of the Qur'an were so understood as fixed according to certain cultural milieu, interpreted and constructed, and their teaching incorporated in 'fiqh', or Islamic jurisprudence, and the codifications of the Shari'ah, or Islamic law, and implemented in real life that, in sum and substance, not equality in any sense of the word, but the inequality of men and women became the stock tradition and the general rule of Muslim life and living, and the transcendental organizational principle of the Islamic social order. Consequently, not only inequality of the sexes, but also the inequality of the sexualities of men and women, became the accompaniment and the outcome of this centuries old trend in the intellectual, cultural, and social history of Islamic civilization. Although all sectors, sections, and segments of Muslim society have been a party to this transformation, in my opinion the guiltiest party has been the 'ulema' (religious scholars), 'fuqaha' (Shari'ah jurists), and 'Imams' (professional prayer leaders), because it is they who acted as the professional interpreters of Islam. In collaborating opportunistically with the holders of political power-the Caliphs, Sultans (Kings), and military rulers of Muslims-they not only devalued and denied equality and dignity to Muslim women but also the social and cultural evolution of the religious, social, political, and cultural life of the ummah, i.e., the Muslim community as a whole.

'Taqlid', or the unthinking, virtually blind, imitation or following of the religious pronouncements of past Imams, religious scholars, and jurists and the categorical rejection of fresh thinking and conceptual breakthroughs or any sort of innovation in Muslim life and living and the reorganization of the social, political, and economic institutions became their sole public theology, with disastrous results for Muslim society and the fortunes of Muslims in the modern world. Under the influence of the ulema, 'fuqaha', and imams, religion, state, rulers, military, feudal lords, merchants, and masses were all turned into the internal enemies of the social, political, economic, cultural, intellectual, religious, moral, and civilizational progress of Muslim society and culture.

Qur'an says: "Verily, Muslims, men and women, believers, men and women, obedient men and women, truthful men and women, patient men and women, humble men and women, charitable men and women, fasting men and women, chaste men and women, those who mention and remember God-men and women-, for all those God has prepared forgiveness and a great reward" (35:33). "Whoever performs good deeds, whether male or female and is a believer, We shall surely make him live a good life and We will certainly reward them for the best of what they did" (16:97). What is the significance of these narratives? (a) They demonstrate the concern on the part of the women for being included in the public affairs of the community or the Divine address itself, and to be a visible part of Muslim life-its public aspect as well as its religious aspect. (b) They reflect concern for the recognition and acknowledgement of what women do and participate in, so as not to be excluded, ignored, or marginalized. (c) Such narratives also show observing the necessity of a certain balance between the two groups of the community; in other words, a gendered view that is also holistic and seeking equity. This view, or the expression of this view, underscores a woman's perspective, initiative, and agency in questioning and debating. (d) A final important point here is that God "responded" (the Qur'anic word) to the questioning by a revelation that inscribes and hence validates women's right to voice concerns and questions. If God Himself and the Prophet gave ear to Muslim women's queries then why not reproduce the same situation if there is need for it at another point of our history or in a particular Muslim community, depending on the issues needed to be addressed?

That is the real Islam: tolerant, adaptive, enriching, empowering, laden with aesthetical and ethical values. These are the strengths of Islam; which are now at stake because of the way its followers practice the religion. In terms of gender relations, Islam is clear in its principles of gender justice and equality. History notes the social transformation Islam played in the Arabian Peninsula in terms of women's status fourteen centuries ago. Women were uplifted from being 'inhuman' or 'half-human' into 'full-human beings'. Women's status was shifted from being inherited into a human with the right to inherit. Women were transformed from a worthless creature, into a respectful creature, absolutely equal to men in their humanity. Islam is an invitation to all human beings to liberate themselves. Throughout the Qur'an, women and men have been addressed in equal terms. In not a single case are the criteria for women differentiated from that for men. Prophet Muhammad is the greatest feminist the world has ever known. From the lowest degradation, he uplifted women to a position beyond which they can only go in theory. The Arabs of his day held woman in supreme contempt, ill-treated and defrauded them habitually, and even hated them (see Qur'an 4:19).

The Qur'an had just required her to dress in dignified manner and conceal her sexual charms; the Muslim society put her under veil requiring concealing her face completely (24:30). She could only peep though her two holes provided in the veil. This is nowhere the intention of the Qur'an yet this form of veiling is practiced in many Muslim countries today. She was confined to her house whereas during the Prophet's time and for quite some time thereafter she even took part in battles. It is not without reason that women flourished with the coming of the Prophet Muhammad, in an era when slavery and patriarchal tribal societies were intertwined. Distinction, discrimination and inequality are alien to the spirit of the Qur'an and *Tawhid*. The first believer in Islam was a woman, Khadijah, the Prophet's wife, who devoted all her wealth and her entire life to Islam. Her effective support played a prominent role in the advancement of the religion. The first martyr to the cause of Islam was also a woman, Sumaya, wife of Yassir and the mother of Ammar, one of the Prophet's great disciples. It was Umm Ammarah who saved the Prophet's life in the Battle of Uhud. As for the exclusion or segregation of women, there is no precedent for this during Prophet Muhammad's life. During the time of Abu Bakr and Umar, a lady called Ayesha (wife of Prophet Muhammad) gave rulings and her 'fatwas' were instrumental in changing certain minds of men. We do not see women 'muftis', religious rulers as we did in earlier periods during the Prophet's time, for instance. We are all aware that even early in the history of Islam, it was the strict Umar who corrected himself when a woman stood up in a Friday speech ('khutba'), and told him that he was wrong in his opinion. We do not see women military rulers. We do not see women forming groups going to their leaders and demanding that God-given rights are implemented through the state or through scholarship.

Women used to fight in battles alongside men. Women and men attended classes together taught by the Prophet where women asked the Prophet questions and had the opportunity to interact with him and educate themselves. Women did not even pray behind a curtain or physical barrier of any sort. However, from Umayyad period onwards she was not even allowed to go out of home without her husband's permission after marriage and with father's permission before that and that too accompanied by some male relative called 'mahram' (a blood relation with whom marriage is not permissible like brother, uncle etc.)

If the Prophet Muhammad is cited as gentle, tender, caring, and loving to women, then why do the clerics cite misogynistic *ahadith* to sustain their patriarchal attitudes? There are numerous other questions that can be asked to inquire why there is a big gap between Islamic teachings on women and their realization among Muslim communities. Although the Qur'an views women and men to be equal in human dignity, this spiritual or ethical equality has not been reflected in most Muslim laws. For example, women do not have equal rights to make independent decisions in relation to choice of (marriage) partner, obtaining a divorce and custody of their children. Whereas we want to bridge the gap between theory and practice in this area, we can never emphasize too much the difference between the basic equitable religious principles of the Qur'an and the authenticated *Sunnah*-acting as referential framework-and culture or cultural trappings. These constitute the inherited cultural concepts and notions about gender distinctions and women, practices that have developed historically as a result of a very complicated process of acculturation, or sometimes pre-Islamic ideas that heavily influenced religious thought and were thus incorporated and canonized. Eventually these notions have become part of the popular understanding and practice of religion. This is where the hard part lies: working up with the care and patience to sift through all of this entanglement and specifically tracing the cultural history of Muslim societies. This contradiction is most evident in the rules that classical jurists devised for regulating the formation and the termination of the marriage contract-a product of tension in which the voice of the patriarchal social order outweighs the egalitarian voice of the revelation (*wahy*). Take the case of 'diya' (amount of compensation payable for inadvertent killing). Despite having no evidence either in Qur'an (see 4:92) or in the authentic Hadith literature, the amount of 'diya' fixed for female is half that of male, in almost whole of the Muslim nations where shari'ah is in practice. More than that consensus of the 'ulema' supports gender discrimination even in valuing life!

All religions can be read for the sinfulness of women, the contamination of their blood, their lust, and the need for their seclusion. The Qur'an, which is the text for Islamic practice, has multiple interpretations and interpreters. Much of the interpretation is done within and through a misogynist rendering of patriarchal privileges. Women are then read as less than, different from, in need of protection, to be veiled and hidden away. This patriarchal reading matches similar readings in fundamentalist and orthodox Judaism and Christianity. There is no clear divide between West and non-West when it comes to misogynist fundamentalism and patriarchal privilege. The Taliban took this fear and rage towards women to a horrific extreme but this should not occlude the recognition of the universalizing practices of masculinist privilege. A problem with calling the Taliban fundamentalist is that it makes it seem as though they actually do not know the authentic fundamentals of Islam. Instead there are many Muslim scholars who argue that the Qur'an is potentially as democratic for women. The text itself has democratic capabilities. Most of the Muslim women are not guilty of following 'Western feminism' but are agitating for gaining their Islamic rights. The Taliban regime was the worst offenders in this respect. The Qur'an is filled with open meanings for what equivalence can and should mean for women and men. The Taliban sought to ban women's education, while Islam actually insists on equal opportunities for education for males and females. Their whole project of forcibly imposing their version of the *shari'ah* was doomed to failure from the very outset. It made a complete mockery of Islam's liberating and emanicipatory message.

As far as Muslim women are concerned, the source of any difficulties experienced today is not Islam and its traditions, but certain alien ideological intrusions on our societies, ignorance, and distortion of the true Islam, or exploitation by individuals within the society. One approach would be to examine the historicity and development-or devolution-of some of these cultural constructions that proved unfair to women, promoted illogical assumptions about gender differences, and were so oblivious of the higher Qur'anic paradigm of moral, ethical, and religious egalitarianism, as well as the sheer compassion and humanity of the Prophet himself in his treatment to the women around him. Through that, many cultural norms became to be considered by societies as being Islamic, but they're really cultural. So in matriarchal societies, which you will see some matriarchal societies like in West Africa or in Egypt, one will find women very, very influential. Women hold the purse strings; women determine a lot of what happens, because ancient Egypt had a tradition of having women kings, women queens. Whereas in some societies, which tended to be nomadic, it was very much more male-oriented, and the patriarchal and very strong male orientation became predominant. So as one goes across much of the Muslim world, he or she will see this diversity, which really entered into Muslim life through custom, and not through the Qur'an and the *hadith* itself.

Mutuality in Sexuality

In English, the verb form "to husband" denotes the mastery and management of the house, and "husbandry" may mean the control of resources and careful management or the production of plants and animals. The word "groom"-used in bridegroom-is related to feeding. This may merely reflect a societal tradition that has existed throughout history. The Arabic language, however, differently uses the same word "zawj" meaning mate or companion of the other, for both husband and wife. Some may add the feminine suffix "h" to "zawj" to indicate that the word in a particular context means wife, but this is not a linguistic rule or obligation, and the Qur'an uses the word "zawj" and its plural "azwaj" to mean wife and wives respectively.[2]

Different social orders have integrated the tensions between religion and sexuality in different ways. The

Christian Church attacks sexuality in itself. Sexuality is reduced to something "profane and sinful"; it signifies the division of human beings into body and soul. Civilization represents the soul's victory over the body, spirit over the flesh, and diligence over lust. Islam takes a different approach. It never repudiates sexuality as such. In fact sex is a taste of paradise. In the Western Christian experience sexuality itself is attacked, degraded as animality and condemned as anti-civilization. The individual is split into two antithetical selves: the spirit and the flesh, the 'ego' and the 'id'. The triumph of civilization implied the triumph of soul over flesh, of 'ego' over 'id', of the controlled over the uncontrolled, of spirit over sex. Islam took a substantially different path.

In Islam, sex within the bounds of marriage is to be enjoyed as one of the pleasures of this world, a view closer to Judaism than to Christianity. In contrast, Christians have always celebrated the elevation of the spirit and the suppression of the flesh. Islam has recognized that both women and men have sex drives and the right to sexual fulfillment and has also acknowledged that women, like men, experience orgasms. The Islamic view of love and sexuality-in which pleasure and responsibility are coexistent-removes any guilt from the sexes. Marital intercourse does not need the justification of reproduction and is based on the right to sexual fulfillment; contraception is permitted and abortion, in some cases, tolerated. Women's ejaculation was recognized in the *hadith*, the traditional body and texts of knowledge and memories about the Prophet's life, his custom and his words, where female sexuality is regarded as active, like male sexuality. Marriage is a highly recommended deed. Qur'an says, "Marry the spouseless among you...if they are poor, God will enrich them of His bounty" (24:32). Sex has been openly recommended in the Qur'an: "When they [i.e., the wives] have cleansed themselves [after menstruation], you go into them as God has commanded" (2:222). Marriage and sex are among the signs of God's power and blessings. The

Qur'an informs: "And among His signs is that He has created for you spouses from among yourselves so that you may live in tranquility with them; and He has created love and mercy between you. Verily, in that are signs for those who reflect" (30:21).

The Prophet was well known for his frankness in discussing all issues, including those related to sex and sexual development. In one hadith, a woman asks him if, when a woman has an orgasm while asleep (during dreaming), does she have to perform complete ablution ('ghusl') prior to doing her prayers. The Prophet answered that she does because such an experience is akin to the nocturnal emissions of men, which require ablution (*Muslim*, Nos. 607-613). This well-known hadith, shows that the early Muslims felt no inhibition about addressing the Prophet about sensitive issues such as female orgasm (see also *Muslim*, No. 649). Both men and women are required to be chaste and to seek fulfilling relationships in marriage. Consequently, pre-and extra-marital relations are prohibited (17:32, 24:26, 25:68). Based on Qur'an 2:222-223, Muslim couples are encouraged to enjoy sexual relations in any manner the two would prefer. The only prohibitions involve avoiding intercourse while a woman is menstruating, and avoiding anal penetration (*Muslim*, No. 3365).

While Islam stresses the importance of mutual sexual satisfaction between marriage partners, negative cultural factors can prevent such an outcome. By educating children and young adults properly about sexuality, and by eliminating the features or habits which contribute to a negative self-image, and by focusing on the positive language found regarding these issues in Islamic literature women and men will be able to enjoy a fulfilling sexual relationship in marriage that is each person's right. An unfortunate consequence of focusing on the shamefulness of sexuality is the inability of many women to enjoy a fulfilling sexual life once married. If a woman is taught from childhood that her genitals are unclean, untouchable, and basically an area off limits, and if inadequate discussion takes place to prepare her for her first sexual experience, then naturally she would be horrified to imagine the penetration of that area by her husband. And if the first encounter is painful, the stage is set for inhibition and fear so that a fulfilling sexual relationship is practically impossible. Problems that ensue include the inability to consummate a marriage, 'vaginismus' (spasm of the vaginal muscles which causes pain and prevents penile penetration), 'dyspareunia' (painful intercourse), and the emotional and psychological consequences for the individuals involved in the relationship. Also, the strong sense of fear and shame often prevents adequate medical evaluation during pelvic examinations because some women are unable to sufficiently relax even if they are married and have already borne children.

Both Qur'an and hadith allude to the nature of sexual relations as a means of attaining mutual satisfaction, closeness and compassion between a wife and husband. "Permitted to you on the night of the Fasts is the approach to your wives. They are your garments and you are their garments" (2:187) Also, Muslims are advised to avoid sexual intercourse during menses so as not to cause discomfort to the woman (2:222). The goal of marriage is to create tenderness between two individuals and satisfy the very basic human need for companionship (30:21). Marital sexuality is meant as healthy way of human reproduction, releasing tensions, fulfilling natural and biological needs, and strengthening the marriage ties between the spouses. The ideal sexual relations in Islam are depicted in the verse "Your wives are a garment for you and you are a garment for them" (2:187). Annemarie Schimmel, the great German Orientalist, posits that the term "garment," according to ancient religious ideas, is a reference to the alter ego of a human being. The garment can function as a substitute for the person, and with a new garment one gains as if it were a new personality. Furthermore, it hides the body, blocks private parts from the eye, and protects the wearer. Husband and wife is, according to this interpretation, so to speak, each other's alter ego, and each of them protects the partner's honor. The husband and wife are equal and complement each other in their perfect togetherness.

Islam looks definitely disapprovingly upon celibacy, because it is considered both unnatural and undesirable. Muslims also regard it as impossible to practice, which is so very evident by the publicly known practice of homosexuality in the religions, which pretend to uphold priestly celibacy as a requirement for priesthood. In this regard, Islam has a highly normal and reasonable doctrine of human sexuality. Bouhdiba writes about Islam's view of sexuality: 'Islam in no way tries to depreciate, still less to deny the sexual and invests it with such a transcendental significance that any trace of guilt is removed form it. Taken up this way sexuality is full of positivistic. Islamic life becomes an alternation and complementarity of the invocation of the divine Word and the exercise of physical love. The dialogue with Being and the dialogue of the sexes punctuate our daily lives'[3]. In the early sixteenth century, the grand vizier of Tunis commissioned a study to be made of how men could best satisfy their sexuality. A man named Sheikh Nefzawi, with the reputation of being greatly informed and knowledgeable about human sexuality, was retained under a royal grant to compose a treatise on the subject. The document that he authored, not only pleased his royal patron, but also became a best seller of the time and has remained so in the Arab world and is probably the greatest classic on the subject in Arabic literature. In our own time, it was translated into English by Sir Richard Burton under the title of 'The Perfumed Garden' in the late nineteenth century and has been published many times since.

There are a number of *ahadith* which feature the positive side, pleasures, and reciprocity of sexuality, among others as follows: 'If one of you are in the company of your wife, do pay attention to her needs; if the husband has fulfilled his desires [reached orgasm] before his wife, he should not leave her in haste but stay until she reaches her orgasm'. Still, in order to ensure the wife's pleasure, which is often denied her because of her husband's premature ejaculation, the Prophet forbade the practice of coitus interruptus (*'al-'azl'*) without the wife's consent. Among the five major traditional Islamic schools of thought, the majority of Hanafis, Malikis, Ja'faris (Imamis) and Hanbalis permitted the practice of 'al-'azl', subject to the wife's consent. The importance of mutual pleasures for both partners is illustrated in the following hadith: 'If one of you would like to have sexual relations with your wife, do not do it as two camels or donkeys would; instead, be with her, whispering sweet nothings and showering her with kisses' (*Bukhari*). In Islam, contrary to Christianity, marriage and sex are not antipathetic to the love for and worship of God. Instead of an obstacle, marriage is regarded as an asset in acquiring spiritual perfection. Neither is there any Qur'anic verse or *hadith* against birth control, nor is it 'wajib' (compulsory) to have children in marriage. So basically, birth control would come under the category of 'ja'iz', or lawful acts. Moreover, we have some *ahadith* (especially on the issue of *'azl'*, coitus interruptus), which categorically prove that birth control is permissible.

A woman's satisfaction is particularly referred to in the interpretation of the hadith, which discuss penile withdrawal as a method of contraception. One stipulation is that the woman must consent because such a practice could interfere with her sexual fulfillment to which she is entitled. Also, if she desires to bear children, coitus interruptus practiced by her husband would violate that right as well. This viewpoint is based on a hadith transmitted by Umar ibn-al-Khattab who said that the Prophet forbade the practice of coitus interruptus with a woman except with her permission. In several ahadith, Prophet Muhammad speaks about the importance of foreplay and speaking in loving terms during sexual relations. Again, the concept of mutual satisfaction is elucidated in a hadith, which advises husbands to engage in acts that enable a woman to achieve orgasm first. Sexual dissatisfaction is considered legitimate grounds for divorce on the part of either wife or husband. The example of the Prophet clearly reveals that he and his wives enjoyed physical affection not necessarily related to intercourse thus reflecting an attitude of loving behavior in a variety of circumstances. Based on the hadith transmitted by his wives (particularly regarding physical intimacy while they were menstruating), this behavior included kissing, caressing, embracing and bathing together (*Abu Dawud,* Nos. 267-273, 2376-2379; *Muslim*, Nos: 577-586, 629).

Here is the hadith, which beautifully illustrates the ideal wife-husband relations in the marriage: "When a husband and his wife look at each other lovingly, God will look at them with His merciful eye. When they hold hands, their sins will fall away from between their fingers. When they engage in coitus prayerful angels will surround them. For every sensation of their delight there is a counterpart of reward for them in paradise as huge as a mountain. If the wife conceives, she will have the rewards of a worshipper who is constantly engaged in prayers, fasting and in the struggle in the way of God. When she delivers a child, only God knows the magnitude of the rewards for the parents in paradise." Once a companion having heard the Prophet praising coitus with one's wife as a charitable act for which a Divine reward was to be awaited, retorted: "O you, the Messenger of God. Would a person satisfy his lust and anticipate Divine reward for it?" The Prophet said, "Would he be punished if he (or she) does so with the wrong partner? In the same way, fulfillment of sensual satisfaction in the legitimate way shall be rewarded" (*Bukhari*). In another ahadith men are advised that meeting the needs of their wives takes precedence over voluntary worship: "Prophet Muhammad said, "O Abdullah! I have been informed that you fast all the day and stand in prayer all night?" I said, 'Yes, O God's Apostle!' He said, "Do not do that! Observe the fast sometimes and also leave them at other times, stand up for the prayer at night and also sleep at night. Your body has a right over you and your wife has a right over you" (*Bukhari*).

The Prophet has defined an ideal Muslim male in these words: "The best among you are those who are best towards their wives" (Ibn Majah). He added, "and I am the best among you in that respect." Couples should strive to satisfy one another's sexual needs as much as possible. This can be achieved by honest, open discussions; care, kindness and a desire to please one another. Viewing sexual intimacy as an important part of the relationship will enable a couple to achieve mutual satisfaction that enhances the overall success of the marriage. Clearly, bullying and lack of consideration for one's spouse's feelings will result in tension that can have negative effects on the rest of the relationship. Unfortunately, if women were raised to detest and worry any matters related to sex, then in most instances of sexual contact she would be a passive and perhaps unwilling participant, and definitely not one who derives pleasure from sex.

Subversion of the Qur'anic Ethos

In the currently fast changing world characterized by prevailing violence, social conflicts, and social injustices, there needs to build a moral force which will be able to take human beings out of the problems posed to them. The question that will immediately emerge is, "Where is the place of religion amidst the surge of such injustices and oppression?" Thousands people claim to be religious but they do not show any concerns about other people's problems; thousands of them claim to be practicing religious rituals, but they transgress others' rights; thousands of them claim to be religiously devout, but they abuse their own wives and children. On the one hand, religion is believed to be the source of ethical values and norms; but on the other, religion is also believed to be the source of violence, be in the public sphere or in the domestic one. The challenge to religion is clear: at the empirical level, religion is facing a dynamic contestation, requiring it to be open to contemporary human problems. But the practice of many of its followers has been such that makes it difficult for religion to mingle freely at the profane level. Religion is, thus, cast away from the human daily life and is put in a sacred place, an ivory tower, and untouchable by most, especially women.

The Qur'an's is constructive, flexible, and humane guidance for all aspects of family life that reflects consistency and wisdom, which are not seen elsewhere. There we can see a fresh, unique approach to the most critical of human relationships. The Scripture says: "Seek, among that which God has given to you, the hereafter, but do not forget your portion of this world either" (28:77). "And when the prayer has ended, spread out in the world and seek the blessings of God and remember Him often, haply you will succeed" (62:10). If a person misuses or abuses his body, then he is guilty of infringing the rights of his own body and also the rights of God who has given the body as a trust to us. The Qur'an says, "The believers are...those who protect their sexual organs except from their spouses. Therefore, whosoever seeks more beyond that (in sexual gratification), then they are the transgressors" (23:5-6). This is the strongest of bonds, in which God unites the two Muslim partners, who come together on the basis of love, understanding, co-operation and mutual advice, and establish a Muslim family in which children will live and grow up, and they will develop the good character and behavior taught by Islam. The Muslim family is the strongest component of a Muslim society when its members are productive and constructive, helping and encouraging one another to be good and righteous, and competing with one another in good works. A true Muslim should respect his or her spouse, and seriously avoid all insults and humiliation. Spouses will treat each other in a manner in which he or she would like to be treated.

Human dignity does not allow that any one person has the right to own, mind/body/soul, another human being... and Islam demands that all human beings respect the humanity of everyone. Qur'an 49:11-12 points out categorically that emotionally abusive language and behavior is not acceptable: "You who believe do not let one (set of) people make fun of another set. Do not defame one another. Do not insult by using nicknames. And do not backbite or speak ill of one another." In Islam, an individual's rights are not limited only by rights of the society but also by those of his own body and God. The justification for this is very simple: Islam does not allow a person to harm or destroy himself; and sin or immorality is a means of perdition. This limitation is based on the love and concern, which the Merciful God has for us. "God does not desire to make any impediment for you, but He desires to purify you and to complete His blessings upon you" (5:6). In Islam, marriage is a blessed contract between a man and a woman, in which each becomes "permitted" to the other, and they begin the long journey of life in a spirit of love, co-operation, harmony and tolerance, where each feels at ease with the other, and finds tranquility, contentment and comfort in the company of the other. The Qur'an has described this relationship between men and women, which brings love, harmony, trust and compassion, in the most moving and eloquent terms (30:21). It further says: " O ye who believe, you are forbidden to inherit women against their will" (4:10). And the word "inherit" includes marital rape. The common notion that women are duty-bound to submit sexually to their husband's will comes from the *hadith,* it is not mentioned anywhere in the Qur'an. As expectable from any patriarchal system, most male sexual behavior is savage, insensitive, inhuman, exploitative, oppressive, and humiliating. These harsh adjectives indicate deep feelings of oppression and humiliation among their female spouses. We should develop a religious worldview on women and gender relations that is empowering, emancipating, and liberating.

There is an interpretation of Qur'anic verse 4:34, which is often cited to justify husband's authority in dictating his sexual desires. The Qur'an is internally consistent because it is a Divine revelation. It repeatedly describes the relationship between husband and wife as one of tranquility, affection, and mercy (30:21). Domestic violence is diametrically opposed to each of these Qur'anic views and ideals expressed in the various verses. Because of its internal consistency, the Qur'an could not be exhorting one ideal and enjoining the related conduct in some passages, and their opposite in another one. Consequently, an interpretation of one of the elements involved in this apparent inconsistency is wrong. For example, a verse may be interpreted too broadly when it is specific or conditional, thus distorting its true meaning. In this case, the repeated Qur'anic statements about tranquil marital relations are both unconditional and grammatically simple; this suggests a general rule. On the other hand, the structure of the verse speaking about "hitting" one's wife is both conditional and structurally complex, leaving room for erroneous, culturally skewed, or subjective interpretations. Therefore, the most likely scenario is that the interpretation of this single verse is responsible for creating the apparent inconsistency, and needs to be revisited or reread.

The hegemonic version of interpretation of the text, reaffirmed by among others the following quoting from a highly renowned scholar such as Abu Hamid Al-Ghazali (1057–1111), will unsurprisingly shape misogynistic views among Muslim societies. In his Book of Counsel for King, Ghazali devotes chapter 7 to "Describing Women and Their Good and Bad Points", wherein he states: 'A wife will become dear to her husband and gain his affection, firstly by honoring him; secondly by obeying him when they are alone together; and (further) by bearing in mind his advantages and disadvantages, adorning herself (for him only), keeping herself concealed (from other men) and secluding herself in the house; by coming to him tidy and pleasantly perfumed, having meals ready (for him) at the (proper) times and cheerfully preparing whatever he desires; by not making impossible demands, not nagging; keeping her nakedness covered at bedtime, and keeping her husband's secrets during his absence and in his presence.' The above citation is part of Al-Ghazali's magnum opus, 'Ihya Ulumuddin', a widely circulated prestigious series of classical books, which have inspired subsequent writings on similar themes and topics for more than years.

Many Qur'anic verses and *ahadith* have been used to legitimize gender inequalities, which give rise to the misbelieve that women are theologically dependant on men. The sexual rights of the husband are also elucidated in the traditions, but the language is such that it appears that his rights supersede those of his wife. A *hadith,* which often brings repercussions to the life of Muslim women, is the one, which is retold by Bukhari and Muslim, two most reliable 'rawi' (transmitter), as follows. 'If a husband wants to have sex with his wife and the wife refuses him and the husband is angry, the angels will curse her till morning'. Such teachings as the *hadith* socialized to Muslim youths, will unsurprisingly shape gender-biased views among Muslim societies; and the beautiful and noble mission of the Qur'an and the Prophet to uplift the status of women will be useless. In patriarchal societies, sexual violence or rape within marriage is not considered a crime against women. And women are never supposed to refuse their husbands' sexual demands even if she is disinterested. The normative force of natural behavior cannot and should not be ignored. The concept of unnatural behavior throughout the history of humankind has been used to justify and legitimize various forms of social oppression. An example of this is the way in which belief about the nature of women has been used to justify their social standing. Usage of the concept of 'irrationality' or 'emotionality' of women as a justification for discrimination in employment, in political and economic participation is universal. Pregnancy, the menstrual cycle and post-natal depression serve as reasons to perpetuate patriarchy. These are used as obstacles against increased access to employment for women. Emotionality has been used as a key factor in excluding women historically across culture and across religions from the public sphere. Women are denied jobs and economic opportunities because of their childbearing role, and national policies maintain by-and-large that the work place and the home are incompatible.

According to traditionalists, the ideal Muslim woman devotes herself to taking care of her house and husband.

She knows her husband's rights over her, and how great they are, as was confirmed by the words attributed to Prophet Muhammad: 'No human being is permitted to prostrate to another, but if this were permitted I would have ordered wives to prostrate to their husbands, because of the greatness of the rights they have over them.'[4] 'Any woman who dies, and her husband is pleased with her, will enter Paradise.'[5] Islam holds every individual, whether male or female, directly responsible for his own actions towards God (6:164). The above *hadith* appears to negate the independent spirituality of women by making them dependent on men. Man is seen as the mediator between women and God. A woman is denied her own spiritual autonomy, which is so explicitly stated in the Qur'an (33:35).

Some *ahadith* give a clear preference to male sexuality: 'By the One in Whose hand is my soul, there is no man who calls his wife to his bed, and she refuses him, but the One Who is in heaven will be angry with her, until the husband is pleased with her once more.'[6] 'If a man calls his wife to his bed, let her respond, even if she is riding her camel [i.e., very busy].'[7]Another tradition reads thus: The Prophet draw a clear and delightful picture of the well-behaved, easy-going, loving, righteous Muslim wife, one who will be happy in this world and the next: "Shall I not tell you about your wives in Paradise?" We said, "Of course, O Messenger of God." He said, "They are fertile and loving. If she becomes angry or is mistreated, or her husband becomes angry, she says, 'My hand is in your hand; I shall never sleep until you are pleased with me.'[8]

In another *hadith*, which is said to have narrated by Ayesha we read, "I asked the Prophet, 'Who among people has the greatest right over the woman?' He answered, 'Her husband.' I asked, 'Who has the greatest right over the man?' He answered, 'His mother". (*Nasai*). In 'Ihya' 'ulum al-din', one can see this passage of quotation of another week *hadith*: "There was once a certain man who set out on a journey after having covenanted with his wife that she should not come down from upstairs to downstairs. Her father was downstairs. When he fell ill, the woman sent for the Messenger of God asking his permission to go down to see her father. The Messenger of God said, 'Obey your husband.' The father died. She tried again to get permission from him to see her father, but he said again, 'Obey your husband.' Her father was buried. The Messenger of God sent a message to her that her father was forgiven on account of her obedience to her husband" (4:746). In Ghazali's opinion, the obedience of the wife to her husband is one of the pillars of faith. Imam Ghazali attributes this narrative to Prophet Muhammad: 'Ayesha said, "A girl asked the Messenger of God, 'What right does a husband have over his wife?' He said, 'If he was covered from the parting [of his hair] to the bottom of his feet with matter [or pus], and she licked him, she still has not thanked him enough'" (*Ibid* 4:747). In a weak tradition, Prophet Muhammad is said to have stated, "The woman is nearest to her Lord's Face when she is in the innermost part of her home. Her prayer in the courtyard of her house is better than her prayer in the mosque, and her prayer in her home is better than her prayer in the courtyard of her house, and her prayer in her chamber is even better than her prayer in her home" (*Ibid*). Perhaps this stress on keeping the woman confined to her chamber stems from the statement ascribed to the Prophet: "The woman has ten nakedness; when she marries the husband covers one nakedness, and when she dies the grave covers all ten of them" (*Ibid*).

The same tendency is reflected in a famous medieval text while it depicts the concept of an ideal woman prevailing in that society. "An ideal women", according to Shaykh Nefzawi, "speaks and laughs rarely and never without a reason. She never leaves the hose, even to see neighbors or her acquaintance. She has no women friends, gives her confidence to nobody, and her husband is her sole reliance. She accepts nothing from anyone, excepting her husband and her parents. If she sees her relatives she does not meddle in their affairs. She is not treacherous and has no faults to hide, nor bad reasons to proffer. She does not try to entice people. If her husband shows his intention to performing the conjugal rites, she agrees to satisfy his desire and occasionally provokes it. She assists him always in his affairs, and is sparing in complaints and tears; she does not laugh or rejoice when she sees her husband moody or sorrowful but shares his troubles, and wheedles him into good humor till he is quite content again. She does not surrender herself to anybody but her husband, even if abstinence would kill her. Such a woman is cherished by everyone."[9] This is how a Muslim woman was pictured in medieval ages and ever since.

Inherit the Wind

The inequality of the sexes in Muslim society had consequences not only for Muslim women, but also for Muslims as a people, as an 'ummah', or a community, and as nations and states. The institutionalization of sexual and gender inequality in the family has systematically produced universal institutionalization of human inequality in all the social, political, and cultural institutions of the Muslim society as a whole, which is why no Muslim country can establish and sustain democracy in our time. To continue this will be the greatest folly of Muslims of all time. The time has come when we must accept that human beings, people, even Muslims, come in two sexes and / or genders and that the two are still equally deserving of having their humanness recognized equally-religiously, spiritually, morally, socially, politically, economically, psychologically, and culturally. And if the old, familiar Islam cannot handle it, we shall have to reinvent a new Islam that can.

The concept of the ideal Muslim women encouraged by orthodox groups was used as arguments for denying women the right to vote by the opposition. Being ignorant of the requirement to read the Holy text based on equity and fairness, they attribute passiveness in the female gender. They are also unaware of the fact that Islam, as an ideology, is adamantly opposed to the subjection of one human being by another. Any discrimination against any individual or group about their basic rights as members of humanity is a challenge to the faith of believers, since for any human to claim superiority based on origin or power is contradictory to the belief in the One Ultimate Supreme Being (21:22-23). Any discrimination between men and women in rights or responsibilities is forbidden according to the divine justice- the same as any other discrimination (9:71). Qur'an insists that men and women were created in God's image and both sexes have equal rights and responsibilities before God. An ideal Muslim woman realizes that she has similar rights just like man (2:228), the right for bridal gift (4:4), economic and possession rights (4:7, 4:32), rights of inheritance (4:7), right to participate in the political (60:10-12, 58:1) and public life (9:71-72, 3:195, 24:30-31). She is aware that the Qur'an views 'Justice' in terms of absoluteness as an imperative which is unconditionally, universally and absolutely binding-binding on everyone, under all circumstances, and in all situations, binding without considerations of sex, caste, tribe, or race, binding without regard to the distinction of Muslim and non-Muslim, or of the ruler and the ruled, or of the rich and the poor, binding even if it hurts one's personal interests (4:135, 5:8, 6:152). Doctrinally Islam carries comprehensive projects and destination for the achievement of gender justice (2:187, 7:189, 3:195, 4:19, 24:2, 60:12, 4:124). As such, she will be committed to strive to build a society where justice prevails everywhere. She is aware that she has the right to give political asylum (9:6), and, even, in the participation of war (3:195). She knows very well that she has the right to divorce (2:229), to remarriage (2:234) and, has, more right over her children (31:14). She understands that her religious duties are almost similar to man (2:286, 4:97-100, 74:38, 6:164). She will be a participant in the decision-making discussion with her spouse (2:233, 7:189). She will dare to disobey tyrants just like the wife of Pharaoh (66:11-12). She will show diplomatic acumen and sagacity just like the Queen of Sheba (27:27-44).

The Prophet himself used to help with the domestic work, and mended his own shoes. Women are not even obliged in all cases to suckle their own children. If a divorcing couple mutually agree, they can send the baby to a wet-nurse and the husband must pay for the suckling. If the mother decides to keep the baby and suckle it herself, he must pay her for her trouble! This is laid down in the Qur'an itself (2:233). Married couples are urged in the Qur'an to deal with one another in a spirit of mutual consultation and agreement, even when contemplating divorce and the custody of children: 'If they both decide on weaning, by mutual consent, and after due consultation, there is no blame on them' (2:233). The family life of Prophet Muhammad reflects clear testimony of the freedom that the women related to him enjoyed. When Umar ibn-al Khattab found out that his daughter Hafsa, who was married to Prophet Muhammad, used to argue with him all day, he could not contain himself and decided to go and chastise his daughter. Hafsa was never at a loss for words and the Prophet welcomed this. He enjoyed the challenges presented to him by his wives. When he learnt of Umar's intentions he did not allow Umar to stop his daughter. Umar then went to seek audience with Umm Salama, also a wife of the Prophet. Umm Salama was an intelligent and forthright woman. Prophet Muhammad held her in high esteem and used to consult her on many complicated issues regarding the governance of society. To Umar's chauvinist remarks, she replied, "I wonder at you, Ibn Khattab. You interfere in everything. Will you now interfere between the Messenger of Allah and his wives?"

A common view of sex was that the stronger sexual urges of men (compared to women) could be controlled only to a certain extent. Also, the same argument is made to justify forcing wife to have sex against their will, as they are forbidden to refuse to have sexual relations. Since the male's urges are so strong, and to prevent him from acting out on them illicitly, a wife's duty therefore is to submit in order to preserve the marriage. Yet, human beings are endowed with self-control not seen in any other species, such that we do not act on every instinctual impulse because of some uncontrollable force. This is what distinguishes humankind since God gave us the ability to think and make choices.

Clearly, Islamic literature stresses the importance of the sexual relationship between a husband and wife, but some traditions (as quoted above) seem to show that the husband's right to have sex is more important than the wife's right of refusal if she is not willing for whatever reason. The only time she can refuse intercourse, then, is during menstruation.

However, the verse 2:222 commands Muslims to avoid sex during that time because it may be associated with uneasiness on the part of the woman. A logical conclusion would be that sexual relations are better avoided for any circumstances (physical or otherwise) that would lead to distress. In a marriage abusive or forced sexual activity cannot be justified in any way. Rape is defined as unwanted, violent and forced sex, whether this occurs in a marital context or outside it. The definition of rape does not change because of the relationship. It is important to not confuse the issue of mutual rights that a couple has on each other with the misguided, distorted and misogynist assumption that women become a husband's property. Islam does not allow for or tolerate ownership of human beings. Human dignity does not allow that any one person has the right to own, mind/body/soul, another human being and Islam demands that all human beings respect the humanity of everyone. Historically, Islam has addressed serious issues openly and sought to correct actions that constitute harm or 'zulm' (i.e., cruelty and abuse) to the dignity of humankind. Human life and respect for it has been stressed unstintingly, regardless of age or gender. According to the Qur'an, men and women have the same human spiritual nature (4:1, 7:189, 42:11, 32:9, 15:29, 17:70). Each human being shall face the consequences of his or her deeds (4:124, 33:35, 57:12). Islam views human life as a sacred gift from God (6.151, 17.33, 5.32). As a general rule, Qur'an forbids all 'zulm', be it physical, mental, emotional or spiritual (6.120, 22:53, 22:60). The verse 49:11-12 points out categorically that emotionally abusive language and behavior is not acceptable. Qur'an constantly warns husbands not to use injurious statements against their wives (58:2-4). The Scripture is very clear that the basis of a marital relationship is love and affection between the spouses, not power or control. Rape is unacceptable in such a relationship: "And consort with your wives in a goodly manner, for if you dislike them, it may well be that you dislike something which God might yet make a source of abundant good" (4:19). Therefore, there is no justification for forcing women to have sex against their will, even in marriage. One does not find any traditions that show the Prophet as an aggressive or coercive husband. Similarly, behavior involving coercion and force goes against the philosophy of mutual satisfaction outlined in the Qur'an (2:222-3, 30:21, 2:187) and against the hadith which states that the best among Muslims are those who are best towards their wives (*Riyadh-us-Salaheen*, No. 278). Also, the Prophet Muhammad expressed his strong disapproval of those who physically beat their wives and then had sexual relations at night (*Bukhari*, *Riyadh us-Salaheen*, No. 274).

In this connection it must, first of all, be clearly understood by all Muslims that the Qur'an unequivocally prohibits keeping women in wedlock against their will. In 2:231, it is said: "And do not retain them (i.e., women) in wedlock against their will in order to hurt them. He who does such a thing indeed sins against himself. And do not take the signs of God lightly." Within the context of a husband-wife relationship, authoritarianism and dictatorship should be replaced with the ideal and equal partnership advocated by the Qur'an; the husband should not assume the role of ruler, superior, controller, oppressor and master, while the wife, on the other hand, is reduced to a slave, a captive, a low, inferior and submissive person. As for "marital rape", Islam teaches both husband and wife the understanding of having to minimize the times when they are reluctant to respond to their spouses' sexual demand. Unless there are really serious reasons concerning, for example, health or mental difficulties, they should not refuse such a demand. This is not because any side is a "property" of the other or because Islam approves what is called "marital rape". On the contrary, this is because Islam prohibits adultery and marital infidelity. This, in fact, is prohibited for both parties. Therefore, Islam urges both parties to be always welcoming to meet the other party's sexual demands and needs. Both parties are also obliged to make sure that this affair has ended with full satisfaction for ones' partner.

Strong and resourceful women have played a key role in history and yet Muslim society, at a later time in their societal development, has pushed women into an inferior and marginal position, excluding them from full participation in the social, cultural and religious life of the community. She has many outstanding women, in the Islamic history, as role models. Many great women contributed to the history of Islam, fighting alongside the Prophet and engaging in debates and discussions. The relationship that the Prophet had with his wives, who were not afraid to rebuke or oppose him, is another example of the relatively equal status women occupied. Women in the early Islamic period continued to be independent and were not subject to the restrictions later introduced. One famous case that of Thabit Bin Qais whose wife complained to the Prophet about his appearance saying "O messenger of God, as for Bin Qais, I do not blame him for his character and piety, but I dislike infidelity in Islam." The Prophet asked her husband to divorce her upon the condition that she give back an Orchard given to her for her dowry, which she did and was hence divorced. Even during the Caliph Umar's time we see that women were not compelled to remain married to husbands they could not stand. Even such things as remarriage after divorce or widowhood were not a stigma and many married as much as four to five times such as Umm Kulthum and Atika Bint Zaid. The fact that women could divorce their husbands at will shows that women in the early Islamic era possessed a substantial independence and self determination] which was later restricted in the second century of Islam. The lady who altercated with Prophet Muhammad is, also, included in her many role models (58:1-4).

As in other monotheistic religions, the classical 'fiqh' texts-that is, texts of early Islamic legal jurisprudence-ignored gender equality as it was presented in the Qur'an and introduced interpretations in line with the then patriarchal social order. Thus, one can find several logical contradictions in the classical 'fiqh' texts since they reflect two dissenting voices: an egalitarian voice inspired by the revelation (*wahy*), and a patriarchal voice incorporating the social order and social, cultural and political pragmatisms of the time and place where Islam was trying to ensure its survival. An analysis of discourses based on the Qur'an and the early literature of Islamic legal jurisprudence leads to contradictory conclusions about the construction of women's sexuality in Islam.

A well known *hadith* which leads to the conclusion that menstruating women neither prayed nor fasted is found in Bukhari with several versions: The Prophet is reported to have said, "Isn't it true that a woman does not pray and does not fast on menstruating? And that is the defect in her religion." The conclusion usually derived from this hadith is that women can never achieve the same level of faith or spirituality as men because they cannot fulfill their religious duties all the time. The weakness in this argument and therefore in the hadith is that it contradicts the undisputed image expressed in the Qur'an of women and men as equal in terms of their duties and expectations as servants of God (3:195, 16:97, 33:35). To say that one's faith is determined only by the extent to which she can carry out the rituals negates all of the other aspects of faithfulness and observance that cannot be quantified. God rewards or punishes according to deeds and intentions (6:152, 23:62, 7:142); how, then, can something that is biologically determined, not chosen or willed by the individual, serve as a measure of faith? Would God penalize women for something that He created? Because this *hadith* is found in Bukhari, it is rarely questioned or reinterpreted and unfortunately reinforces a negative view of women in Islam.

The theology of woman implicit in certain *ahadith* is based upon generalizations about female ontology, biology, and psychology that are contrary to the letter and spirit of the Qur'an. These *ahadith* ought to be rejected on the basis of their content alone. However, textual ('matn') analysis, (which was strongly urged by Ibn Khaldun, 1332-1406) has received inadequate attention in the work of many Muslim scholars who insist that an ahadith is to be judged primarily on the basis of its 'isnad' (chain of narrators). The test of any *hadith*, according to the Prophet himself, is that if there is anything in the *hadith* that contradicts what are in the Qur'an you must reject it because the Qur'an is always supreme. Furthermore there are more laws in the Qur'an governing the relationship between a husband and wife than on any other subject. And at that time when women were socially disadvantaged, the Qur'an reiterated that the more powerful, which were the men, must treat women justly and kindly.

It is unfortunate that after 11th century AD, the *ulema* began to frown upon *Ijtihad* for various reasons. Muslims ignored the dynamics of the Qur'an, which treats all humans as trustees (2:30). Such misinterpretations continue to haunt Muslims, to the point of separating the political and the religious from the intellectual in interpreting the governing principle of mutual consultation or 'Shura' as directed by the Qur'an (42:38). As this latter principle applies to both domestic and community relations, by limiting the consultative power to males in communal leadership, Muslims ended-up with another state of confusion, creating another rift within, and between the domestic and the communal. This misinterpretation still dominates Muslims' behavior, resulting in partial solutions to domestic issues and inviting the interference of Occidentals and Western government bureaucrats who think that democratization of the Muslim world is the one that separates the religious and the secular.

Examples of issues being debated that might have positive implications for Muslim women are: a return to a more direct examination of the Qur'anic text and message; exaggerated gender distinctions should be superseded by the Qur'anic egalitarian worldview and repeated emphasis on ethico-moral religious equality (i.e., regarding distinctions are strictly legal and functional and not inherent); the higher paradigm of egalitarian values should be made to prevail, thus focusing on the general 'just' intent and purpose of the Divine message; consideration of inner-Qur'anic references to view the overall picture of certain themes and issues; considering seriously the Qur'anic view on women's integration to the public sphere and the evolving problematic of the private-public dichotomy (i.e., how much of it is actually Qur'anic and how much is cultural and historical); studies on the formation of the legal tradition of Islam ('fiqh') incorporating non-Qur'anic cultural pre-suppositions (derived from the wider region of the pre-Islamic middle east) etc.

Islam is standing clearly and unequivocally for the support of male-female equity. The verse 57:25 describes the aim of social development in Islam as the establishment of 'quist' or justice: "Indeed, We sent our Messengers with the clear signs, and We sent down with them the Book and the Balance so that human beings might uphold justice." Within society, *Tawhid* means establishing social justice. The notion that God's unity is reflected in the equality and unity of human kind provides a basis for a strong critique of sexism and gender hierarchy. The Qur'an explicitly asserts the fundamental equal worth of male and female believers as well as the fact that gender relations are intended to be cooperative and mutually enriching. This ethos of reciprocity between women and men is further reinforced in the Islamic understanding of marital relationships (30:21). In terms of human relationships, it means equality, including between women and men. Women's legal and religious rights in Islam are well known and are unquestionable. A Prenuptial Agreement can guarantee a woman many of her Islamic rights, which can be enforceable by law. For example, if a woman does not feel that she could allow her husband to marry more than one woman at the same time, then Islam allows her the right to refuse him permission to do this at the outset of their marriage.

They just need to be more defined in terms of actuality. Women are as much human beings as men and today women's rights are part of human rights. Every man has the right to be an equal partner in his marriage; however, men should always be very careful to observe where to draw the line, and never hurt their wives. It is not safe to assume that when your wife says 'No' she really means 'Yes'. There is always a difference between fun and cruelty, and Islam has no place for torture and abuse. Unless there is a genuine and legitimate reason, the refusal of the partner's advances is forbidden in Islam. It is a hurtful rejection. Men and women should realize that sometimes the partner has a very strong urge, which may prevent sleep, and should be kind. The texts of Qur'an affirm that the wife, too, has the right to sex. If either partner is 'not in the mood', or perhaps is in deep sleep when the other partner feels amorous, it is un-Islamic and bad manners to bluntly reject the other. Men, because of the very obvious physical nature of their arousal, often find it hard to understand a woman's needs, which do not show themselves so conspicuously; they should bear in mind that the urge can be just as overwhelming and just as frustrating if not fulfilled.

Women have every right to take part in all social, cultural and political movements. They should not be debarred from any arena. There is no sphere of activity in which women have not excelled men. Muslim countries while prohibiting and restricting her from taking part in public sphere are acting against Qur'anic norms. Crucial key words are women's empowerment and persevering struggles and paradigm shift among *ulemas* and other power holders in the society that will enable transformation from within, from women-oppressing interpretation of religious texts into women-liberating and empowering one. The need of the hour is that all laws that attempt to dominate women by denying them equal rights must be revised to reflect the fundamental

Qur'anic principle of human equality. By questioning underlying presumptions and conclusions, enlightened Muslims are creating a space in which to think about gender. Drawing upon enduring principles of human rights, enshrined in the Qur'anic text, they should extract meanings that can interact with the changing moral and intellectual circumstances.

End Notes

1. See B.F. Musallam, 'Sex and Society in Islam, Cambridge University Press: Cambridge, 1983.
2. See Qur'an 2:35, 102, 232, 234, 240, 4:12, 20, 6:139, 7:19, 13:38, 20:117, 21:90, 23:6, 24:6, 26:166, 33:4, 6, 28, 37, 25, 50, 53, 59, 60:11, 66:1, 3, 5, 70:31, 2:230, 58:1.
3. Abedlwahab Bouhdiba, *Sexuality in Islam*, Routledge & Kegan Paul: London, 1985, p. viii.
4. Reported by Ahmad and al-Bazzar. See: *Majma' al-Zawa'id*, 9/4, Bab haqq al-zawj 'ala'l-mar'ah.
5. Ibn Majah, 1/595.
8. Sahih Muslim, 10/7.
7. Reported by al-Bazzar. See: *Majma' al-Zawa'id*, 4/312.
8. Reported by al-Tabarani. See: *Majma' al-Zawa'id*, 4/312.
9. Shaykh Nefzawi, *The Perfumed Garden* (Tr. Sir Richard Francis Burton), Signet Classics: New York, 1964, p. 97.

7

The Ontological Devaluation of Woman: The Case of Blood Money

Throughout the world, women still suffer discrimination and oppression, for no reason other than their gender. The condition of women in the Muslim world is not much different. History is replete with examples of traditional societies where women have typically been subject to more restrictions than men, exemplified by lack of opportunities (being able to work or vote) or immobility (needing permission from a male relative to travel or not being able to drive), etc. Although it is mistakenly argued Islam has played a strong role in restricting the freedom of women in Muslim societies, these restrictions are not inherent in the religion of Islam, but rather stem from cultural interpretations. We can study this thesis with an inquiry into the application of law of blood money in the Muslim world. There are about 450 million women living in Muslim countries or communities. They are spread throughout the continents, but the majority live in Asia, with Africa next. Is Islam opposed to women's rights? Why is Islam stereotyped as inherently and irredeemably hostile to women? At the moment, and except in the West where a civil code generally governs all citizens, most Muslim communities have specific laws allegedly transposed from Shari'ah. These laws, as well as the influence of Muslim conservatives over their evolution and application, are increasingly affecting women's lives, their legal rights and traditional practices as well as limiting women's organizations, defining the parameters of their struggles and their strategies.

Blood money ('Diya') is intended as compensation for the unintentional damage caused to the victim's family; it is confined to the cases of killing by mistake, in which premeditation of murder has no room absolutely. 'Diya' is basically a compensation for the financial harm caused to the family of the victim. And since the accidental killer is the one who caused the family that harm, he or she is to pay them that compensation, even though he or she had not intended to kill the victim. Compensation is a principle applied by all civilized systems in the world with regard to casualties, injuries, damages that are caused by unintentional mistake. The criminal in such cases is to be sentenced to death whether the victim is a man or a woman, young or old. We have realized from the former chapters that what is commonly understood today about women's status in Islam is the product of biased interpretation and selective acknowledgment of textual sources from which rights have been derived. This chapter seeks to illustrate specifically the ways in which traditional Islamic jurists have interpreted and formulated rights based on cultural definitions of "man" and "woman" and "male" and "female." We will also explore the ways in which traditional scholars have given greater weight to textual sources that appear to substantiate such definitions, ignoring other textual sources that are inconsistent with such definitions.

Qur'an is divinely inspired and that the law and religious values embodied in the letter and spirit of the Qur'an constitute the command of God to humankind. Sunnah of the Prophet Muhammad is a guide to Muslims and an essential tool in the formulation of laws. The Shari'ah is traditionally understood by Muslims to be a comprehensive code for daily life. However, the question of what is a legal and/or an ethical obligation is complicated, hence the use of methods for the explanation of how the Shari'ah is to be understood and applied. Traditional Islamic scholars developed 'usul al-fiqh'—a "science" of jurisprudence for the investigation of legal questions. According to traditional jurisprudence, Islamic law is expressly devised by God and revealed by him in the Qur'an, containing the express laws of God, and the Sunnah. Traditional theory is that the Sunnah confirms the Qur'an, assists in its interpretation, or fills lacunae. However, there is considerable controversy surrounding the authenticity of many reports that are attributed to the Prophet. There is considerable controversy surrounding the authenticity of the thousands of ahadith that have been collected and recorded. There is also controversy surrounding how to interpret ahadith, the weight that is given to any particular hadith as against a Qur'anic prescription and how to deal with contradictions between many ahadith. In order to interpret and formulate rules, traditional jurists relied on "the four proofs": the Qur'an, the Sunnah, 'ijma', and 'qiyas'. As far as the Qur'an is concerned, its authenticity is unquestioned. What is expressed in the Qur'an is the expression of the absolute authority of God. Some ahadith simply refer to the acts of the Prophet and concern his own conduct exclusively, as opposed to being normative. Also, the Sunnah came to incorporate reports of the practices of the first generations of Muslims, and therefore not simply the Prophet. Some schools in Islamic jurisprudence, or 'madhahib', relied upon the Sunnah of the companions of the Prophet, or the first communities of Islam. Because the written record was delayed and because of the fabrication of many ahadith, various traditions developed among different communities.

The Sources of Islamic Jurisprudence

What is Shari'ah? In Arabic the word means a path through running water for people and animals to be able to drink in safety. There can be nothing more fluid than running water and there is a connotation of safety. Shari'ah is really an umbrella concept. 'Shari'ah' is not a term that has a rigid or fixed connotation or context. The mission of Islam that is most important now is how to erect justice on the face of the earth, especially in the political and economic fields (also, of course, the cultural). The present efforts to implement Islamic (Shari'ah) law are, really, a demonstration of the incapacity of the Muslim 'ummah' to face up to the problems that are pressing on them and deal with them in a rational manner. The 'ummah' take the view that all problems will automatically be solved as soon as the Shari'ah, in its most traditional and dogmatic form, is applied on the earth. The conservatives claim not to limit their quest for Islamic identity to a rejection of Western values, they pretend to restore identity by an alternative model which should innovate in all domains: economic, political and social relations. In fact their activities directly and primarily affect women and the private sphere. We do not know of examples of Muslim specificity in the political or economic domains. But family codes or personal status laws which rule personal life, in matters of marriage, divorce, guardianship and child custody, polygamy, inheritance, standards of behaviour, clothing and so on... constitute the sphere of orthodox predilection.

The sources of Islamic jurisprudence are of two kinds. The first is drawn directly from the primary sources of the Qur'an and the Traditions. The other is secondary and includes 'ijma' or consensus of opinion of jurists by analogy drawn from precedent. To this may be added the source of equity and custom, which was the basis of the Hanafi and the Maliki schools. The study of these sources was the subject of a special science called 'Ilm al-Usul'. It gave rise to what is called 'Ijtihad', i.e., the effort or endeavour to interpret legal sources and to discover proper solutions for religious and legal cases. 'Ijtihad' was thus—an important factor in Islamic legal history, in adapting rules to the need of civilization, and was one of the causes of the florescence of Islamic jurisprudence in the Abbasid period. But after the fall of Baghdad in the 13th century, Muslim civilization began to fade, and orthodox or Sunni jurists agreed that the four well-known Sunni schools, i.e., the Hanafi, Maliki, Shafi and Hanbali were sufficient. They thus agreed upon the closing of the door of 'Ijtihad'. As a result, new interpretations were prohibited, and consequently unconsidered and slavish imitation ('taqlid') became the rule. The books dealing with law making ('fiqh') were written before there was any such literature called Hadith. The cause of this was plain. Law and the treatises of law were a necessity for the public and thus were encouraged by the State. The study of traditions was on the other hand less essential and was more of a personal and private nature.

Malik ibn-Anas (d. 179 A.H.) was a forerunner of the four Sunni schools of law. Imam Malik was a lawyer who gathered traditions not for their own sake but to use them in law. Imam Abu Hanifa (d. 150 A.H.) who died earlier than Imam Malik, was more interested in developing theoretical principles which could be used as a basis for the development of law. He relied little upon tradition and preferred to take the Qur'anic texts and develop them in detail. It was two of his immediate pupils, Qadi Abu Yusuf (d. A.H. 182) and Muhammad Ibn-Hasan (d. A.H. 189), who converted his theoretical principles into codes of law. The third school is that of Imam Al-Shafi (d. A.H. 204). His system was based on four sources: the Qur'an, Traditions, analogy and 'agreement'. All the schools have practically accepted Al-Shafi's classification of the sources for legitimate thought.

The last of the four schools is that of Imam Ahmad ibn Hanbal (d. A.H. 241). He was a theologian and made no claim as a lawyer. His 'musnad' is an immense collection of 30,000 ahadith. These were not arranged for legal purposes. He suffered terribly for his orthodox faith under the Caliph Mamun. After his death his disciples drew together and established the fourth school. His school reduced the influence of agreement and analogy and tended towards literal interpretation. The four schools of thought (law) are generally classed together as 'Ahle-Fiqh'. In Muslim eyes they are all equally valid and their decisions equally sacred. The believer may belong to any one of these, but he must choose one. The liberty of variety in unity is again due to agreement. However, the conflict in the application of the law between the followers of the various schools has also caused sectarian division among the Sunnis. The Hanafi School has the largest following. The next in order of size of following are the Shafi and the Maliki schools while the smallest is the Hanbali school which is followed by the Wahabite state of Saudi Arabia.

There is another school of thought, commonly called the 'Traditionalists' ('Ahle-Hadith'). They maintain that it is not 'fiqh' but the 'sayings' of the Prophet, which should be enforced as they are, since they supposedly contain fundamental and unchangeable law. This school holds that after scrutiny, Hadith occupies the same position and authority as the Qur'an, and a denial of Hadith affects one's faith and honesty in the same manner as the denial of the Qur'an itself will do—i.e., beyond the pale of Islam. The social fabric of early Muslim societies shaped this religious dogma. Pre-Islamic tribal law and the cultural constructs internalized by the early Muslim communities discriminated against women and influenced the Sunnah of the early Muslims and the exercise of 'Ijtihad'. It is this social fabric that maintains Islamic traditionalism today and must itself be revamped in order to accommodate a revision of Islamic law and morality. The vision of Islamic law and morality that the majority of believing Muslims aspire to today is based on the opinions of jurists and often strays from the express injunctions of the text. The slate, in whole or in part, must be wiped clean.

Selective Use of the Traditions

The Qur'anic verses are strongly critical of women's low status in pre-Islamic Arabia, and bring substantial reforms in the ways in which women were viewed and treated pre-Islamic Arabia. For instance, the practice of female infanticide is condemned; aspects of marriage, divorce and inheritance practices are reformed to give women a greater say and autonomy (16:58–9). As equal, independent creations of God, the ultimate role of men and women is to serve as vicegerents on earth, to worship God and follow His commands so that we may return to Him. Both men and women share this responsibility, which constitutes our basic role in life. The Qur'an outlines the attributes believing men and women should try to live by, but in no specific way are we told in what capacity each individual man and woman should practice these: "Say: Behold, my prayer, and all my acts of worship, and my living and my dying are for God alone" (6:163). This verse, which was addressed to the Prophet but serves as an inspiration to all, reveals that our vicegerency is not only spiritual, but must be consolidated with actual service. The Qur'an does not distinguish between a man and a woman's vicegerency (2:30, 2:38). Each gender has the ability to contribute to successive generations, as implied by the term 'Caliph' in the Qur'an (vicegerent). But that doesn't limit a woman's vicegerency solely to bear or rear children.

What is commonly understood today about women's status in Islam is, by and large, the product of biased interpretation and selective acknowledgment of textual sources from which rights have been derived. The selective uses of traditions, as well as religious interpretations were used in order to structure an image of women, which conforms to their reconstructed identity. The conservative theocratic order also continues to discriminate against women by refusing to sanction such changes as raising the minimum age of marriage, abolishing men's unilateral right to divorce, and failing to provide women access to scripturally enjoined rights to divorce. The implementation and enforcement of laws based squarely upon the notion of gender equality is one of the principal means by which the widespread discrimination suffered by women in the name of Islam could be eliminated. The absence of such laws in the Muslim world is a damning indictment of the failure of many states to live up to the true ideals of Islam. Trying to incorporate 9th century Arab customs to 21st century populations is often inappropriate despite intentions to have a pure society. When looking to Islam for guidance, it's important to separate what is cultural from the essence of the religious prerogatives. If an authoritative ruling from Saudi Arabia states that women cannot drive because it would increase possible contact to freely mix with men, who can lead to sins, this logic must be judged against Islam and history. It is a fact that the Qur'an emphasizes modesty for both men and women in order so that we conduct ourselves respectfully (24:30-31). It is also a fact that men and women in the time of the Prophet did interact, so the justification of this law on Islam is bogus. It is unduly harsh and anti-Islamic. It should not serve as an example of how Islam restricts women, as much as it should serve an example of how illogical it is to cut off one's nose to spite one's face.

There are few women interpreters in the history of Islam because women are seen to be the subject of the Islamic shari'ah and not its legislators. Yet even the few interpreters who have appeared during the long history of Islam have been kept at the periphery, their views never allowed influencing Islamic legislation. Moreover, even men interpreters who were open-minded about women were marginalized and, in some cases, found their authority questioned. When one delves into the volumes of 'fiqh' concerning women's agency, one becomes acutely aware of gender differentiation and discrimination. It is the 'fiqh', which for all intents and purposes is what is commonly understood as Islamic law, that has defined relations between men and women and that has limited women's right to self-determination. This is, and has been, of great concern to Muslims and non-Muslims alike. Such concerns are met with the rhetoric of men and women being equal, but different, or the argument that the rights of men and women in Islam are complementary. Traditional jurists claim that women's agency is fettered, but that women are given privileges to protect their status in society. There is, they insist, an exchange of rights for privileges. For example, a woman is required to comply with her husband's wishes, and in return, her husband is financially responsible for her and her children. Sex differentiation is therefore central to the traditional analysis of rights and responsibilities in Islam. One of the most prominent contemporary interpreters of the Islamic position on women accounts for the ideology that discriminates against women by pointing to: physiological differences between men and women such as the size of the heart, the weight of the brain, and the size of the skull. The psychological differences are that women are affectionate and emotional and have weaker nerves. Men, however, are wise and intellectual and have strong nerves, which make them more qualified to strive, struggle and campaign against the odds of everyday life. This discriminatory ideology was and continues to be the product of social and political assumptions concerning state and family relationships that are traditionally authoritarian/patriarchal. The aggressive/

passive, strong/weak, intellectual/emotional, stable/ threatening dichotomies implicit in such cultural notions have become important assumptions in many exegeses on the Islamic, and therefore the ideal, position on women in society. These assumptions lie in stark contrast to the life experiences of women at the time of the Prophet Muhammad, including the experiences of his wives, who were active participants in politics, commerce, religion, and war. These assumptions also open the gates to an onslaught of criticism from those who argue that Islam denies women's self-determination. Unfortunately, however, in the formative years of Islamic law, these social norms were assimilated into Islamic jurisprudence through a set of theological, legal and social theories and assumptions. They claim that these texts by the great theologians and jurists of centuries past have perfected the understanding of Islam and the doors of 'Ijtihad' should therefore remain closed. As Sachedina notes: 'It is remarkable that even when women transmitters of hadith were admitted in the 'ilm al-rijal' ("Science dealing with the scrutiny of the reports"), and even when their narratives were recognized as valid documentation for deducing various rulings, they were not participants in the intellectual process that produced the prejudicial rulings encroaching upon the personal status of women. More importantly, the revelatory text, regardless of its being extracted from the Qur'an or the Sunnah, was casuistically extrapolated in order to disprove a woman's intellectual and emotional capacities to formulate independent decisions that would have been sensitive and more accurate in estimating her radically different life experience.'[1]

The Qur'anic verses addressing women and unambiguously declaring their spiritual equality to men did not sink well in the religious community decades after the Prophet's death. Abu Hamid al-Ghazali, an eminent 8th century theologian, shares sentiments similar to Aristotle's argument that women are innately inferior to men. Al-Ghazali gives this advise to his followers: "Consider the women who have struggled in the path of God and say, 'O my soul, be not content to be less than a woman, for it is despicable for a man to be less than a woman in matters of religion or of this world.' "[2] How was it that such a negative sentiment could be made, despite its clear contradiction to the Qur'an? Leila Ahmed explains that it was the conquests that Islam made in other territories, such as the Iran-Iraq region of al-Ghazali and also the Mediterranean Middle East, which kept their cultural attitudes to women, despite their acceptance of Islam. [The pronouncements and broad recommendations of the Qur'an would be heard one way in Arabia [during the time of the Prophet] and quite another way in the societies to which it was transposed. Arab mores themselves, moreover, changed as the Arabs adopted the ways of the conquered peoples and were assimilated into their new environments.[3]

In their understanding of sacred texts, their outlook guided these jurists, and in discerning the terms of the shari'ah, they were constrained by a set of legal and gender assumptions and theories that reflected the state of knowledge and normative values of their time. These theories, which are the product of either juristic speculations or social norms, continued to be treated by subsequent generation of jurists as though they were immutable, and part of the shari'ah. What is often missing in these narratives is a recognition that gender inequality in the Ancient World was assumed, and that perceptions of women in Christian and Jewish texts are not that different from those of Islamic texts. What transformed women's situation in the Christian West were new social conditions that were shaped by and in turn shaped new political and socio economic discourses—and new understandings of religion. By both uncovering a hidden history and rereading textual sources, they are proving that the inequalities embedded in Islamic law are neither manifestations of divine will, nor cornerstones of an irredeemably backward social system, but human constructions. They are also showing how such unequal constructions go contrary to the very essence of divine justice as revealed in the Koran, and how Islam's sacred texts have been tainted by the ideology of their interpreters. For example, men's unilateral rights to divorce ('talaq') and to polygyny were not granted them by God, they show, but by Muslim jurists. They are juristic constructs that follow from the way that early Muslim jurists conceptualized and defined marriage: as a contract of exchange patterned after the contract of sale, which, by the way, served as a model for most contracts in Islamic law. The genesis of gender inequality in Islamic law, these scholars tell us, lies in an inner contradiction between the ideals of Islam and the social norms of the early Muslim cultures.

Once we recognize that Islam had to be introduced to the world within a cultural context—which of the Arabs in Arabia—how does we then sort through what is strictly cultural and what is the essence of the religious teachings? Through time, two schools of interpretation on Islam's teachings and how they take into account cultural context prevailed: the dissenting, non-traditional view is that Islam's teachings are broad fundamentals, and the specific practices and regulations Prophet Muhammad put into use was intended for their immediate social context, as not necessarily binding to Muslim societies at all times; the more traditional view of Islam's teachings emphasizes the practices and regulations and paid little attention on Islam's fundamental teachings of spiritual equality of men and women and the fair treatment of women. "Had the ethical voice of Islam been heard, I here suggest, it would have significantly tempered the extreme androcentric bias of the law, and we might today have a far more humane and egalitarian law regarding women," argued Leila Ahmed.[4]

The ethical and moral qualities outlined in Islam may be universal, but the practice will be affected by time and space. Through time, it became clear that cultural, historical and political contexts directly affected the status of women, despite the Qur'an's clear guidelines, as explained by Noel J. Coulson and Doreen Hinchcliffe.[5] The small amount of Qur'anic rulings was naturally observed, but outside this the tendency was to interpret the Qur'anic provisions in the light of the prevailing standards. In particular, the general ethical injunctions of the Qur'an were rarely transformed into legally enforceable rules, but were recognized as binding on the individual conscience. Thus, for example, a husband was never required to show that he had any reasonable or proper motive before exercising his power to repudiate his wife. And while the Qur'an might insist upon impartial treatment of co-wives in polygamous unions, classical Islamic law did not elevate this requirement into any kind of legal restriction upon the husband's entrenched right to have four wives. The result was that the Qur'anic provisions concerning women's status and position in the family were dissipated and largely lost.

In many cases, the Qur'an only sets down principles and they should not be, merely, taken literally. Indeed, they can and should be interpreted by each successive generation to fit circumstance and culture. But they often seem to have been progressively forgotten in favour of a traditional, androcentric Islam, based as much on self-interest as on myth, and on a partial and biased reading of what, nevertheless, remains potentially a radical document and tradition, precisely because of its egalitarian ethos. However, we find that Islamic Shari'ah, prevalent in the Muslim world, has equated the blood money of both men and women. The point that must be emphasized is that the modern Shari'ah laws are basically laws derived from the Hadith literature, and frequently on weak ahadith. Not all of the hadith (the statements, actions, and approvals of Prophet Muhammad) can be taken as a valid reference. There are hadith, which are 'sahih' (authentic), 'mutawatir' (agreed upon by the scholars), 'hasan' (good), and 'daif' (weak or forged). In order to apply them, we must first study the hadith that are used in the book. In the case of blood money there is not any single hadith, which discriminates, in the whole corpus of six authentic collection of hadith literature ('sihahu-ssitha') between man and woman.[6] Prophet Muhammad taught: 'All people are equal, as equal as the tooth of a comb. There is no claim of merit of an Arab over a non-Arab, or a white over a black person, or a male over a female. Only God-fearing people merit a preference with God' (*Bukhari*). "The vanishing of the Earthly life is lighter in the sight of God than the killing of a single Muslim soul" (*Tirmithi*). "O people, O your Lord is one, your ancestor is one, O there is no preference to an Arab over a non-Arab, or a non-Arab over an Arab, or a red-skinned over a black-skinned, or a black-skinned over a red-skinned except by the level of piety" (Narrated by Ahmed 411/5). This oft-quoted hadith is considered a definitive statement of the ideology of equality espoused in the Qur'an and thus in Islam. It is an important instruction to humankind to treat fellow human beings with dignity and respect, without discrimination or prejudice based on any ground. The only distinction that can be made between human beings is a distinction based on their fear of God, which is mentioned in Qur'an 49:13.

The Qur'an proclaims: "Therein We decreed for them a life for a life, an eye for an eye, a nose for a nose, an ear for an ear, a tooth for a tooth, and a wound for a wound" (5:45). God—the Just, the Merciful and the Wise—has ordained and enforced the principles of equality among all Muslims, making no distinction between males and females under law. As per the verse, a man is sentenced to death if he kills a woman, and other wits are treated in the same manner. Since blood money comes as compensation in the case of killing by mistake, hence, the sex should not determine the size of the blood money. Some scholars do not accept the usage of this verse as a justification for equality in punishment and blood money based on the argument that this story was initially narrated on the Sons of Israel in the Torah and that it does not relate to Muslims. However, this argument is not well founded since whatever was ordained on previous generations was ordained on us unless otherwise indicated in the Qur'an and the Sunnah, for or against it. This is the approach that the "verifiers" took from among Islamic scholars. The Islamic Shari'ah has set equal blood money for both men and women. The view that says that the blood money of a woman is less than that of a man is tantamount to saying that her life is less important than that of a man. Therefore, this view is contradictory to the Islamic Shari'ah by default and the idea does not have any supporting evidence, and even the ahadith that were mentioned in support of this argument were verified and identified by a number of Hadith jurists as weak in authenticity. In Islam, no person has preference over another except by the criteria of the levels of faith, piety and good deeds. The Scripture says: "O people! We have created you from a male and a female, and made you into nations and tribes so that you may know one another. The noblest of you in God's sight is the most pious amongst you" (49:13). It further informs: "A believing bondwomen is better than an idolatress, though the latter may please you. Nor shall you wed idolaters, unless they embrace the Faith. A believing slave is better than an idolater, though the latter may please you. These call you to Hellfire, but God calls you, by His will, to Paradise and to forgiveness. He makes plain his revelations to mankind, so that they may take heed" (2:221). "Claim not purity unto yourselves, He knows best those who guard themselves against evil" (53:32). The Muslim blood of both men and women is equally forbidden, regardless of their age, as evidenced in the Qur'an and Sunnah. The Qur'an says: "Whoever kills a believer by design shall burn in the Hellfire for ever. He shall incur the wrath of God, who will lay His curse on him and prepare for him a mighty scourge" (4:93). "It is unlawful for a believer to kill another believer, accidents excepted" (4:92). "Do not kill yourselves, God is merciful upon you" (4:29). Women's inferior social status has nothing to do with their mind or religion just as the inequality that prevailed between the serf and the master the result of the former's shortcomings. There is not a single verse that grants men a degree over women in either mind or religion: 'If any one do deeds of righteousness, be the male for female and have faith, they will enter Heaven, and not the least injustice will be done to them' (4:24). We find that Qur'anic statement is general and does not privilege the man with any special status: "And whosoever kills a believer by mistake (it is ordained that) he must set free a believing slave and a compensation (blood money, i.e., 'Diya') be given to the deceased's family" (4:92). While the Qur'an is replete with commandments that man and woman are equal in God's eyes, it is prudent to reflect on the following verse, 'The true believers, men and women are friends to each other. They enjoin what is just and forbid what is evil' (9:71).

Let me quote Sheikh Yusuf Al-Qaradawi, the eminent Islamic scholar, in this context: 'There is neither a single well-authenticated statement by the Prophet Muhammad nor any consensus of religious authorities ('Ijma') to establish that the blood money paid for the killing of a woman is half the sum paid for the killing of a man. There are two ahadith, which are not perfectly authenticated, that address the question. The best one on terms of authentication is that narrated Al-Nisai and Al-Daraqatni, which still suffers a time gap in the chain of transmitters up to the Prophet, as was pointed out by Statements related to the Companions suffer in the same manner. What remains then is the only well-authenticated tradition on the subject "for a soul, a hundred camels."

"The general agreement of authorities that make the value of the blood money paid for the killing of a woman half that for the killing of a man falls short of a consensus. Ibn 'Ulayya and Al-Asam, two scholars from the high order of jurisprudents (fuquh, as-salaf) make the value of the blood money the same for both men and women. This opinion is in agreement with the generality of reference to "believer" and "soul" in the Qur'an and the Hadith. If we opt for this opinion today, we are not to blame since, in addition to the previous reason, the legal opinion ('fatwa') could change with the age and environment but the new legal opinion is neither in conflict with the relevant textual statements nor with the general objectives of Islamic Teachings. Under the subtitle of "Blood Money, the Same for Men and Women," Sheikh Shaltut writes: "Woman's humanity stemming from the same origin as that of the man, her blood is the same as his, he being from her and she from him and equal retaliation in kind being the rule common to both cases of homicide and hell and damnation being the other worldly punishment for the killing of either man or woman, so the rule of the verse applies to the accidental homicide of either a man or a woman'.

"It is true that the scholars have differed over the amount of blood money, whether it is the same or double in the man's case. Al-Razi tells us in his 'Tafsr al-Kabir' that the majority of jurisprudents double the sum in cases of male homicide. He adds that Al-Asam and Ibn Ulayya make the sum paid the same. The majority cite the ruling of the Companions 'Ali, Umar and Ibn Mas'ud ruling on this matter, as well as the rules of inheritance and legal testimony in which the woman's inheritance and testimony equals only half those of the man. Al-Asam, however, cites the verse:

'and whosoever kills a believer by mistake' (4:92). All agree this verse addresses both men and women; therefore the ruling on the sum paid is the same. They cite as evidence for this the following hadith: Mu'adh ibn Jabal reported that God's Messenger said: "The woman's blood money is half the man's." Researchers of the Qur'an and the authentic Sunnah would conclude rather naturally that women's blood money in Islamic Shari'ah is equated to that of men, and that there is no solid evidence that proves otherwise."

Syed Qutb wrote in his 'Fi Zilal Al-Qur'an' (In the Shades of the Qur'an): "The first thing that was ascribed by the Islamic Shari'ah in the capital punishment is equality of blood and in all other punishments. This great principle of Islam is the first true and universal declaration of human rights in which all people are equal before the law."[7]

If Islam is to be dragged into an interpretation which is precisely in conflict with the welfare of mankind or even oppresses the human race, then that kind of Islam will have become a fossil religion that is no long useful to humanity. Islamic law has been regarded as the embodiment of Divine Justice (5:8, 4:135). In order for Muslims to attain that divine scale of justice they must implement these norms of justice in their everyday life. Ironically, the tension felt by the Muslims in the fulfillment of this obligation is the consequence of elevating the historical development of Islamic law to the plane of restricted historicity of juridical prescriptions. All people, men and women, are equal in the sight of God. In fact, what makes one person better than the other is righteousness.

Women's contribution to Islamic sciences dates back to early Islam, and has not ceased through the centuries, with interruptions here and there in history due to different reasons in each case. Male scholars themselves in books of history of Islamic sciences recorded this history of women's involvement in 'Ilm' and 'fiqh'. The issue is not initiated by contemporary Western feminism but has its roots in our culture. This is important to clarify that the liberating potential of Islam is inherent in Islam itself and its history and is not a result of forces outside the culture and civilization of Islam or a result of the contact with the West in the colonial era. The issue is not necessarily "feminist" and other terminology can—and sometimes should be used instead of the confusion and the enforcement of the concept "feminist" on the Islamic concepts and their semantic field as a key concept.

From the start, the West has depicted Islam as restricting women's rights, with Muslim women suffering as passive and subjugated victims under a succession of repressive Islamic regimes. Classical Islam contains a de-conceptualized application of those verses of the Qur'an, which, on a literal reading, appear to discriminate against women. This, in turn, has resulted in the biased scriptural interpretations that are so deeply embedded in Islamic legal and theological literature. Associated with this is the belief that classical Shari'ah has become fossilized in such a way that the 'ethical voice' of Islam—an egalitarian impulse which points clearly to equality between the sexes—has been lost in favour of a pragmatism based on political expediency. This pragmatism has given rise to Shari'ah, which contains legal dictates that are explicitly discriminatory against women and the creation of equal legal rights. The 'new epistemology' movement aims to address this inequality by advocating that a radical reform of Qur'anic interpretive methodologies is needed and that the use of such methodologies will yield new interpretations of canonical Islam. The creation of such new egalitarian interpretations of Qur'anic verses will then form the basis for a new, revitalized Shari'ah, incorporating the concept of gender equality.

The guiding principle of Islam's social ideal strives for freedom, justice and social unity. The Qur'an describes the mandate of monotheist prophets as inspiring humankind to rise up and establish 'Qist', the ultimate stage of social freedom, justice and unity the Qur'an says: "We sent aforetime, our apostles with Clear Signs and set down with them The Book and the Balance (of right and wrong), that peoples may stand forth in justice" (57:25). In such a society, the oppressed and the talented—whose talents have been suppressed—will be free and, at the zenith of their development, will occupy positions of leadership, and the community will flourish. Indeed, in a society where women are second-class citizens, deprived of their genuine rights, how can any man claim to be free and not suspect his own humanity? If justice and fairness are indisputable objectives of the shari'ah, should they not be reflected in laws regulating relations between, and the respective rights of, men and women?

Shari'ah, which represents the moral and ethical values of Islam, from which Islamic law can be distilled, is aimed at establishing a just society. But how can Islam be credible as a force for social justice, how can it proclaim itself as egalitarian, when Islamic law has come to enshrine gender injustice, which explicitly denies women real, tangible equality? How do we explain this seeming contradiction at the heart of Islam? Is this a reflection of Divine Will? Or could it be that masculinist ideology with its own interpretive slant has become institutionalized into the very heart of Islam and has found ways to subvert Divine Will, with its core message of justice, equality and compassion? The latter is certainly possible if we consider that over the centuries, distilling Islamic law from the Shari'ah has become the exclusive preserve of men, to the point where many now appear to believe that only men, and then only a select group of men—the 'ulema', have the divine right to interpret holy texts. Hence the balance that women's contribution would have given to Islamic law was never achieved.

Reform and traditionalism are not homogeneous entities; they are constantly engaged in an overlapping movement of interaction. We must rid ourselves of the Western modernist reverence for the new, of its glorification as a value immanent in itself. Renovation is a socio-historical need, one that expresses the demands and interests of a society as a whole. Only if it takes this crucial point into consideration can any project of 'tajdeed' aspire at success. An elitist agenda of reform carries within its folds the seeds of its own destruction, inevitably turning into a deep hole of despotism and repression.

End Notes

1. Abdulaziz Sachedina, *Woman, Half the Man? Crisis in Male Epistemology in Islamic Jurisprudence*. In 'Perspectives on Islamic Law, Justice and Society', (Ed. R.S. Khare), Rowman and Little World: New York, 1999, p. 149.
2. Laila Ahmed, *Women and Gender in Islam: Historical Roots of a Modern Debate*, Yale University Press: New Haven, 1992, p. 68.
3. Laila Ahmed, *ibid*, p. 68.
4. Laila Ahmed, *ibid*, p. 88.
5. Noel J. Coulson and Doreen Hinchcliffe, "Women and Law Reform in Contemporary Islam," in *Women in the Muslim World*, ed. Lois Beck and Nikki Keddie Harvard University Press: Cambridge, 1978, pp. 37-38, quoted in Laila Ahmed, *ibid*, p. 92.
6. For the firm defense of discrimination in the payment of blood money, please see: Abdulrahman Al-Sheha, *Women in the Shade of Islam*, Tr: Mohammed Said Dabas (available online at: http://www.cocg.org/books1/cocg/woman/woman_misco.htm#sub14), Safir Press: Riyadh, 2000. ISBN: 9960-800-23—See Chapter 4) and Islamonline English Fatwa section dated 1 Dec. 2004, given by Sheikh Mustafa Az-Zarqa (www.islamoline.org). The two sources deliberately ignore the fact that there is no difference had

the victim been minor and they assume that such discrimination is the absolute verdict of Islam. Founded on weak evidence they argue that being breadwinners, it is legitimate to allow a double share, than the female, to the relatives of the male victim, ignoring the cases, where female partners are breadwinners.

7. Sheikh Yusuf Al-Qaradawi, '*The Status of Women in Islam*' (available at: http://www.jannah.org/sisters/qaradawistatus.html).

8

Beyond the Patriarchal Interpretation

The issue of women has been dealt with repeatedly through history, by both secular and religious thinkers. At one time, many Dark Ages thinkers argued that the women's soul was something animalistic, and completely distinct from that of the superior male soul. Medieval European literature generally portrayed women as second-class citizens. But then, Western thinkers switched gears, shifting from these backwards conceptions to the opposite extreme. They then began to argue extensively for the most liberal standpoints, which are now being firmly criticized by some feminist activists. All of this wavering has occurred, while Islamic ideology has continuously put emphasis on the neutral nature of the human soul, and maintained that any form of androcentric position is to be rejected, and argued that any sort of unfounded gender-based favoritism was futile.

Misogyny, termed as men's hatred of women, denotes the belief that women are not only morally and intellectually inferior to men, but also the source of evil in the world. Such misogynistic views of women date from the time of the ancient Athenians who linked women to what was dark and "unspeakable" in human nature, viewed their bodies as evil, polluting, and open to demonic possession, and believed that they threatened male order, life, and sanity. Images of

Women in Antiquity, for centuries, also have been associated with sex, thought of as "an overpowering force which the social/moral/medical has to control."[1] Men therefore sought to control women by veiling and secluding them and routinely committing horrendous acts of violence against them. Eve was considered less intellectual than Adam, and therefore closer to nature than to rationality. As such, she was more vulnerable than Adam. Hence, the devil tempted Eve, who then tempted Adam. With this model, woman is perceived as the seducer who lures man into sin. Since sin is the result of lust, and lust is most evident in the way that sexual desires can override the intellect, sexuality is also associated with sin and women

Such views have percolated down into Jewish, Christian, and Muslim representations of women as "unclean, sinful, and debilitating" as well.[2] Among early Christians, for example, women were veiled in order to protect men's sexual virtue, which was seen to lie in sexual renunciation and abstinence even though many Christians also had a "grossly male view of sexuality" that justified male sexual abuse of women as a way to obtain sexual release.[3]

Islam and Patriarchy

Patriarchy, according to Zillah Eisenstein, is a politics of sexual differentiation that privileges males by 'transforming biological sex into politicized gender, which prioritizes the male while making the woman different (unequal), less than, or the 'Other.'[4]

The Qur'an does recognize that in historically existing patriarchies, men are the locus of authority and it does address patriarchies, but addressing a patriarchy is not the same as condone or advocating one and indeed, the Qur'an repeatedly says that "following the ways of the father" has prevented people from the path of God Specifically, we may ask whether the Qur'an privileges men over women in their biological capacity as males, or treats man as the Self and woman as the Other, or views women and men as opposites, as modern patriarchal theories of sexual differentiation and inequality do. In a nutshell, the Qur'an does not advocate traditional patriarchy because, to begin with, it does not represent God as 'Father' or male and in fact it explicitly forbids sacralizing God as 'Father' or using any sort of similitude for God (6:19,13:16). It also does not render fathers or fatherhood sacred. In fact, its teachings suggest that there is a natural conflict between patriarchy and monotheism inasmuch as patriarchy treats men as sovereign whereas monotheism treats God as the only sovereign (6:164, 26:28, 31:9). The Qur'an repeatedly warns that "following the ways of the father" has prevented people from the path of God (2:170-171, 7:173, 12:49, 21:44, 43:24). There is no clearer way to define patriarchy than by referring to the 'ways of the father', which we can interpret narrowly as 'rule by the father' or more broadly as 'tradition'.

A man came to Prophet Muhammad and said: 'O messenger of God! Who from amongst mankind warrants the best companionship from me?' He replied: "Your mother". The man asked: 'then who?' So he replied: "Your mother". The man then asked: 'Then who?' So the Prophet replied again: "Your mother". The man then asked: 'then who?' So he replied: "then your father" (Bukhari, No. 5971). So from this Hadith, we can clearly ascertain that it is the mother who holds the most elevated position within the family, three times greater than the patriarch / father. The Qur'an also doesn't teach that men are ontologically superior to women or are entitled to rule over them or even to be heads of the household in the sense in which they were in traditional patriarchies. To the contrary, it designates women and men as each other's "guides" ('awliya') and establishes love and mutuality ('sukun') as the basis of marriage (30:21, 9:71). Islamic sexual equality is ontological in that the Qur'an (4:1) teaches that God created humans from a single 'self' ('nafs'); there is no mention that God created the 'nafs' of the man before that of the woman. In other words, the Qur'an does not prioritize man's creation over women. This concept is a marked departure from the Judaeo-Christian tradition, which teaches that God first created man, and only afterward created woman as his companion. The image of creating Eve from one of Adam's ribs reinforces the concept of women as inferior or as an appendage to men. The Qur'an also does not advocate any forms of patriarchy because it does not associate sex with gender. It is very incredible that the Scripture does not link women and men to any specific division of labor (or gender roles).

Mary has been depicted by the Qur'an as a woman possessing a strong personality with attractive and charismatic attributes, namely, decision-making power, and perseverance, capable of accepting responsibility, among other attributes that constitute a strong character (see Qur'an 19:16-34). Umm Salama's question and the consequent Qur'anic revelation, reveals that much before the advent of modernity, feminism, and forms of human subjectivity, some pre-modern, illiterate, Muslim women were thinking critically about the role of language in shaping their sense of 'self' (see Qur'an 33:35). If that were not so, Umm Salama would probably not have asked her question, and if her question was not important, presumably God would not have heeded it. From this fact one infer that for divine discourse to speak to us, we must also continue asking questions of it. Prophet Muhammad washed his own clothes and darned his own socks, and often served meals to his wife Ayesha. Ayesha, herself, played a visible and active role in the political, legal, and scholastic activities of the early Muslim community. The Prophet chose her as one of the people who would pass on knowledge of the Qur'an and his practices to later generations of Muslims. Ayesha herself taught famous scholars about the Qur'an and Hadith, and discussed complex problems of jurisprudence and commentary with them. Her knowledge and intellect were such that her critique of some of the legal decisions of eminent jurists caused them to change their minds and instead adopt her views. In addition, she narrated 2210 *ahadith* of the Prophet, and scholars have noted that one-fourth of the norms of *shari'ah* law were also narrated by her. In almost every respect, Ayesha appears to have been an exceptional genius. Other women also played prominent roles in the growth and enrichment of Islamic civilization. Imam Nawawi stated that Hafsa, another wife of the Prophet, "was one of the intellectual and intelligent persons." He also spoke about Umm Sulaim, as one of the learned and knowledgeable companions of the Prophet. Islam did not prevent women from participating in armed revolutionary resistance or legal decision-making. Zaynab, Ali's daughter, was a revolutionary, and Umm Atiyah, Hafsa, Asma' bint Abi Bakr, and Sahla bint Suhail were all jurists. Women also participated in the bay'ah (expression of political opinion) and, thus, were integral part of the political process. In fact, through the bay'ah, they contributed later on to the election of the third Caliph. In short, women were equal participants in the growth of the early Islamic state.

Historically, the Qur'an was revealed in seventh-century Arabia. It was a mark of dishonor, at that time, for any man to have a daughter and many preferred to bury their female children alive rather than face social opprobrium (16:58-59, 91: 8-9). The well-known saying of Umar Ibn al-Khattab, the second Rightly-Guided Caliph, expressed the tremendous change in the status of women which had occurred with the advent of Islam: "By God, we did not pay attention to women in *jahiliyyah* (pre-Islamic) until God said about them in the Qur'an what is said, and gave them their share in matters." However, after the schism in Islam that occurred when Ali died at the hands of the Kharijites, women in Islam began to lose their influence to the forces of patriarchy and despotism. It was through a biased interpretation of the *shari'ah*, along with the rigid cultural tendencies of male jurists, that women became confined to a secluded life and subordinate existence to men. Traditional clerics have generally supported monarchs, sultans, generals and emperors throughout history, bowing to the reality of power. They argued that Muslims should not rebel against the unjust ruler, that injustice is better than chaos or anarchy. Partly under the influence of Western political philosophy, many Islamists have now turned this concept on its head, stating that when governance is not just, there is a positive obligation for Muslims to condemn it and replace it. This thinking leads to confrontation with most contemporary regimes in the Middle East.

Louise Marlow argues that as early as the second Islamic century, Muslim religious scholars (*ulema*) had begun to dilute the egalitarian impulse in various parts of tradition, by justifying hierarchical "models of kingship" in a society whose Scripture extolled the virtues of egalitarianism. Thus, the *ulema* who had "gained incontestable possession of the moral high ground [refused to] translate the anti-hierarchical and antiauthoritarian moral at the heart of their scholarly tradition into an active social and political opposition." Instead, they sought to justify not only hierarchies, but quietism as well, even though some of them "felt obliged to defend their quietism, since it was activism that had been suggested most strongly by early Muslim experience." By the third Islamic century, even Qur'anic exegesis showed that the egalitarianism once associated with the Qur'an had lost its "subversive connotation."[5] On its part, the early Muslim state also became involved in promoting certain interpretive practices and certain readings of Islam that were oppressive to women. Several scholars, including Leila Ahmed, who also points out those different readings of the same texts yield, "fundamentally different Islams" for women.[6]

Tawhid is usually understood to refer to God's absolute unicity. However, a number of scholars are increasingly reflecting on the implications of that unicity for humankind in particular and for creation in general. For those committed to progressive values it has also come to mean a principle of holism that permeates all of creation and a struggle to repair the wholeness of creation destroyed by racism, environmental mismanagement, economic exploitation and sexism. A belief in the unity of God can only become meaningful if we display a concern for the way in which manifestations of it are being damaged. Sexism and the discrimination against women fly in the face of the holism of *Tawhid*, which is in direct contrast to the misogynist worldview where man replaces God for a woman and where a male-female relationship is expected to mirror that between males and God. There is thus no place for alleged sayings of the Prophet such as "if prostration were permitted for any of God's creation then women would have been ordered to prostrate to their husbands."

According to *Tawhid*, there can't be any similitude (i.e., similarity) to describe God. Secondly, God is just and God's justice lies in never doing 'zulm' to human beings, the Qur'anic meaning of 'zulm' being to transgress against their rights. Thus, even divine justice is based in recognition of the right of human beings to be protected against transgression. In fact, the Qur'an suggests that there is a natural conflict between monotheism and patriarchy inasmuch as the former is based on God's sovereignty and the latter on men. We can see that the so called misogynistic verses-dealing with "wife beating," divorce, and polygyny-can be read in different or alternative ways and that even if we are not happy with some of the Qur'anic provisions today, none of the verses establish men as being ontologically superior to women or entitled to their submission. Since gender is not a meaningful determinant of moral personality in the Qur'an, we also cannot ascribe sexual inequality to the Qur'an (16:97, 3:195). On this basis, the Qur'an also does not support any modern forms of patriarchy. Qur'an treats women and men differently with respect to some issues but while Muslims interpret this as a sign of inequality, the Qur'an itself does not tie its different treatment to the claim that men and women are unequal or opposites, or that women are like lesser or defective men or that the sexes are irreconcilable, incommensurable, or disproportionate. Moreover, difference does not always signify inequality as many feminists themselves now argue who initially theorized women's liberation in terms of the identical treatment of women and men.

Men not only coerce women into submitting to them, but also by claiming that they are entitled to women's submission, set themselves up as rivals to God on earth. Additionally, they demean God by projecting a sexual identity and sexual bias onto God by claiming that God "Himself" is partial to men who have a special affinity with God. They also read 'zulm' into God's speech by reading the Qur'an as an oppressive text and they themselves commit 'zulm' against women by denying their right to dignity and equality as articulated in the Qur'an. Dominant readings of the so-called misogynistic verses ignore the totality of these teachings and, indeed, undermine them by making it seem that in religious matters, the Qur'an grants women and those who read male supremacy and sexual equality into the Qur'an ignore that male authority as it is structured in Muslim patriarchies violates each and every one of these teachings and leads to 'shirk', the heinous sin (Associationism).

The Qur'an does not advocate gender differentiation, dualisms, or inequality on the basis of biological differences between women and men. It neither privilege men over women in their biological capacity as males or treat man as the 'Self' and woman as the 'Other' or view women and men as binary opposites, as modern patriarchal theories of sexual differentiation and inequality do. Thus, contrary to what many Muslims claim, the Qur'an does not establish men as ontologically superior to women or as rulers over them; rather, it designates women and men as each other's "guides" ('awliya') and establishes love and mutuality as the basis of marriage (9:71). Moreover, in Islam sexual equality is ontological in that the Qur'an (4:1) teaches that God created humans from a single self ('nafs'). It does not privilege the man's creation or endow him with attributes or faculties not given to the woman. Rather, humans "manifest the whole."[7]

According to the Qur'an (27:62, 7:69), all human beings, male and female, are the vicegerents of God (the word for vicegerent in Arabic is a grammatically feminized one). The Qur'an also does not define men and women as opposites, or portray women as lesser or defective men, or the two sexes as ill-assorted, incommensurable, or unequal. In fact, it does not even associate sex with gender; thus, while the Qur'an recognizes biological differences, it does not assign them any gender symbolism making it difficult to derive a theory of sexual and gender inequality from its teachings. The Qur'an also does not link women and men to specific gender roles. There is not a single verse that suggests that men's gender roles are a function of their biology, or that biological differences between men and women make them unequal.

Misinterpretations

Muslims consider the Qur'an the revealed word of God. No Muslim can adopt a point of view contrary to that of the Qur'an. The Qur'anic teachings about God as well as about human creation, ontology, sexuality, and marital relationships challenge sexual inequality and patriarchy. 'Ijitihad' (reasoning from the Qur'an and *Sunnah*) was abandoned in the 10th century by human edict and not by divine will. And whilst those who today challenge the male hierarchy that dispenses Islamic law are often accused of challenging divine will, yet the men who discarded 'Ijtihad' with so little concern for the future consequences of their action are not condemned for going a step too far against divine will. So who decides and on what basis do they decide, that 'Ijtihad' must remain forever a no go zone?

The Qur'an, seen as the eternal and inimitable text, provides for Muslims both the foundational basis and the point of convergence for many different, human interpretations in light of specific socioeconomic and political situations. Theoretically these texts are beyond negotiation because they emanated from divine. Practically, however, the Divine Writ has to be translated, taught, and made understandable to the faithful, especially to illiterate and semiliterate people who cannot read original Arabic texts. This means it has to be interpreted. Interpretation is a political process: the selection of texts from among a great many that potentially give widely divergent messages, and their exegesis are unavoidably influenced, if not out rightly motivated, by the political programs and interests of those who control the formulation and dissemination of religious power.

The Qur'an, despite its inner coherence, was never formulated as a connected whole, but was revealed in response to the demands of concrete situations. The picture, which the Qur'an portrays of the Transcendent, is one of God actively engaged in the affairs of this world and of humankind. One of the ways in which this constant concern for all of creation is shown is the sending of Prophets as instruments of His progressive revelation (10:47, 35:24, 16:36). The socio-historical and linguistic milieu of the Qur'anic revelation is reflected in the contents, style, objectives and language of the Qur'an. This contextuality is also evident from the distinction made between the Meccan and Medinan verses and from the way its supposedly miraculous nature is located in the 'purity of its Arabic', its 'eloquence' and its 'unique rhetorical style' (12:2, 72:1). Even a casual perusal of the Qur'an will indicate that, notwithstanding its claim to be "a guide for humankind" (2:175) revealed by "the Sustainer of the universe" (1:1), it was primarily addressed to the people of the Arabian Peninsula who lived during the period of its revelation.

Verses such as 15: 89-93, 6:91, 5:14, and 5:44 suggest that the Qur'an is a textual and hermeneutic unity and that we should not read it in a piecemeal, selective, and de-contextualized way since doing so distorts its real meanings. So does the failure to distinguish between its foundational and allegorical verse. Thus, the Qur'an also criticizes those who ignore its "basic or fundamental" verse of "established meaning" in order to focus on the "allegorical, [verse] seeking discord, and searching for its hidden meanings" (3:6-7). Although allegory has a clear edifying function in the Qur'an, it is not meant to obscure its meanings, which the Qur'an says, are clear. In fact, if it is read holistically and intra-textually, it is easy to see its internal coherence. Unhappily, however, Muslims have fallen into the immoral and opportunistic habit of reading the Qur'an selectively, piecemeal, and in a de-contextualized and misogynistic way. Otherwise, which verse do they read as allowing men to circumscribe what women should wear or hear while letting their own dress and behaviors go unregulated?

The fact that the Qur'an is clear and consistent does not mean that our own readings of it also are always clear or consistent or that all readings are equally legitimate. The Qur'an itself acknowledges this fact when it asks us to read it for its best meanings. This is clear when it praises "those who listen to the Word and follow the best (meaning) in it" (39:18). Finally, no matter how scrupulous a work of interpretation is, we should not confuse it with the Qur'an. In fact, the Qur'an clearly distinguishes between itself and its exegesis by condemning those "who write The Book with their own hands, and then say: 'This is from God'" (2:79) It is a warning to us not to confuse Divine Discourse with its interpretations, or perceptions. In this context, the Qur'an is clear that "those who are bent on denying the truth attribute their own lying inventions to God. And most of them never use their reason" (5:105). It makes the idea clearer when it says: 'Who is more unjust than those who suppress the testimony they received from God, and God is not oblivious as to what they do' (2:40). 'These folks, the cult they are in, is destined to ruin, and false is what they practice' (7:139). Not only do people fabricate false meanings, but they also project their own base desires into the Qur'an; as one verse makes it clear, "And there are among them illiterates, who know not the Book but (see therein their own) desires, and they do nothing but conjecture" (2:78).

We as a society must debate and discuss in a rational and informed manner which interpretation will serve the best interest of our multi-ethnic, multi-religious, industrializing and modernizing society. The reason Muslims historically have failed to read the Qur'an as an anti-patriarchal text has to do with who has read it (basically men), the contexts in which they have read it (basically patriarchal), and the method by which they have read it (basically one that ignores the hermeneutic and theological principles that the Qur'an suggests for its own reading). This way of framing the question allows us to distinguish between the Qur'an and its exegesis on the one hand, and between religious texts, cultures, and histories on the other, both of which we must learn to do in order to challenge oppressive readings of Islam.

While Muslims are the first to point out that Islam gave women certain rights in the seventh century that European women would not win until fairly recently, they do not believe that equality was one of the rights. Indeed, Muslims read three or four words in the Qur'an to our abiding shame; most Muslim societies are hindered in discriminatory and patriarchal cultures that have the weight of history, tradition, and hegemonic readings of the Qur'an behind them. In the mainstream view, sexual differentiation mean that God has made men ontologically superior to women even if only by a single degree ('darajah'), preferred ('faddala') them to women, put them in charge ('qawwamun') of women, and given them a license to beat ('daraba') disobedient wives. In addition, most Muslims interpret the Qur'anic provisions on polygyny as an unqualified right for all men and as a sign of male privilege, while they read one of the Qur'anic provisions about testimony as equating two women with one man, hence as confirming their inequality. Such readings, which are amplified by the secondary religious and literary texts, have led Muslims to conclude that inequality and patriarchy are scripturally mandated in Islamic readings which show that the much vaunted degree that men have over women is a reference to the husband's rights in a divorce and not a proclamation about male ontology or privilege. In most Muslim societies in which women are excluded from knowledge-production and public life, citizens are denied basic civil and political rights and liberties, and religious knowledge is the preserve of a professional class of male interpreters that considers itself the final arbiter of religious dogma. The most eloquent testimony of our moral and hermeneutic failure to read the Qur'an in the light of its own teaching that those who listen to the Word and follow the best (meaning) in it: are the ones whom God has guided, and those are the ones endued with understanding (39:18).

It is imperative to analyze the historical circumstances in which specific Qur'anic ethical norms were negotiated. Many of the institutions referenced in the Qur'an-such as the poll tax or the formation of alliances with non-Muslims-can be understood only if the reader is aware of the historical practices surrounding the revelation of the text. By emptying the Qur'an both of its historical and moral context, the puritan trend ends up transforming the text into a long list of morally non-committal legal commands. Radical Muslim thinkers, through their scrupulous interpretations of the Qur'an, demonstrate how verses have been erroneously read to indicate male superiority and domination of women. For example, the often cited verse 4:34. The new exegetes cogently demonstrate how patriarchal interpreters have attached misleading meanings to key words, taken verses out of context, and made normative that which is specific and contingent. While fundamentally equal, humans have been created biologically different in order to perpetuate the species. Only in particular contexts and circumstances will males and females assume different contingent roles and functions. Woman alone can give birth and nurse, and thus, in this particular circumstance, a husband is enjoined by the Qur'an to provide material support as indicated in 4:34.

The Qur'an does not distinguish between male and female testimonies and in the case of adultery; it privileges the woman's testimony. If a man accuses his wife of adultery and cannot produce four male witnesses to corroborate his testimony, the Qur'an allows the wife to be her own witness; if she swears her innocence, it gives her husband no further legal recourse against her (65:2). But the *shari'ah* clearly does not see the Qur'anic privilege given to women in this instance as proof that women's evidence isn't automatically half that of a man's.

Like all other texts, the Qur'an also is polysemic (has more than one meaning) and one reading cannot wear out its meanings. As such, it becomes necessary to ask why

Muslims have tended to embrace only some readings of the Qur'an and why different readings of the scripture and of law have not resulted in more flexibility on women's issues. Muslims generally tend to view men as being ontologically superior to women and to believe that a woman is duty-bound to submit to the man in his capacity as her husband, father or brother. This ideology of male supremacy infuses Muslim cultures and consciousness to such an extent that it has given rise to representations of Islam as a religious patriarchy that professes models of hierarchical relationships and sexual inequality and puts a sacred stamp onto female subservience and degradation. A reading of the Qur'an that challenges oppressive interpretations and demonstrates the egalitarian nature of the Qur'anic teachings can help to challenge sexual discrimination among Muslims. Historically, patriarchy was a form of rule by the father that derived its legitimacy from re-presenting God. So long as men continue to oppress women in God's name, neither can hope to encounter God as full human beings inasmuch as the dialectic of oppression reduces the humanity of both the oppressor and the oppressed. Few Muslims would deny that justice, or 'adl', is a central concern in Islam, and while not everyone may agree on the nature or degree of the overlap between Islam and democracy, many are willing to extend the Islamic concept of consultation, or 'shura', to include the principle of accountable and representative, hence to some extent, democratic governance. However, few Muslims like to apply the concept of 'adl' or 'shura' to gender relationships or to incorporate gender equality into their definitions of democracy and justice. To the contrary, most Muslims stubbornly insist that Islam is concerned with justice and not with equality, thus counterpoising them to one another. The majority also holds that, within the context of the family, 'shura' does not imply a dialogue of equals or even a mutuality of dialogue. Rather, it is the man's prerogative as head of the family and the woman must simply submit to him in his capacity as her 'husband', 'father' or 'brother'.

Conservative Muslims view women as morally lax, corrupting and unclean and this is the basis on which they demand that women cover their heads, and even their faces, hands, and feet and remain in their homes, even though the Qur'an does not describe women as morally or sexually corrupting, or dangerous, or unclean or explicitly mandate covering their head, face, hands, and feet, or advocate domestic seclusion. Alongside this debased view of women, many Muslims have an equally debased view of male sexuality which they regard as out of control and in need of free outlet even though the Qur'an repeatedly counsels modesty and restraint on the part of both the sexes (24:30).

Qur'anic verses have been misinterpreted and distorted for the perpetuation of patriarchy. According to traditional *shari'ah* interpretations of 4:34, men as a group are superior to women as a group, and the men of a particular family are superior to the women of that family. This notion of general and specific 'qawama' has had far reaching consequences for the status and rights of women in both the private and public domains. For example, this interpretation provides that women are disqualified from holding general public office, which involves the exercise of authority over men, because, in keeping with verse 4:34 of the Qur'an men are entitled to exercise authority over women and not the reverse. The fact that men are generally physically stronger than most women is no longer relevant in modern times where the rule of law prevails over physical might. Moreover, modern circumstances are making the economic independence of women from men more readily realized and appreciated. The fundamental position of the modern human rights movement is that all human beings are equal in worth and dignity, regardless of gender, religion, or race. The Qur'an can substantiate this position. For example, in numerous verses the Qur'an speaks of honor and dignity for "humankind" and "children of Adam", without distinction as to race, color, gender, or religion (17:70, 49:13). By drawing on these verses and being willing to set aside archaic and dated interpretations of other sources, we can provide Islamic legitimacy for the full range of human rights for women.

Conservative 'ulema' continue to resist new readings of the Qur'an on the ground that they destroy its integrity by forcing Western feminist ideas onto it. While such a critique may be true in some cases, this line of reasoning suggests problematically that the Qur'an is a historically specific text whose meanings could best be understood by male scholars in the seventh and eighth centuries, most of whom read patriarchy and inequality into it. As such, claims about defending the Qur'anic integrity cannot be taken at face value so long as this defense protects the status quo in Muslim societies. Although the Qur'an (4:11-12, 2:181-183) gave women the right to receive an inheritance not only on the death of a close relative, but also to receive other bequests or gifts during the lifetime of a benevolent caretaker, the idea of giving wealth to a woman in preference to a man, even when her need or circumstances warrant it, is repugnant to many Muslims.

A case in point was the introduction of segments of Muslim law, the *shari'ah,* into the country by its previous military ruler, Ziaul Haq. The *shari'ah*, unfortunately, legalizes sexual inequality by equating the testimony of two women to that of one man and it also fails to distinguish between rape, adultery, and extramarital sex. Such laws naturally had devastating consequences for women. One particularly notorious case involved the rape of a blind woman who became pregnant. The court took this as evidence that she was guilty of extramarital sex and sentenced her to be stoned, though the sentence was later stayed. Meanwhile, the rapist went free because, being blind, she couldn't identify him. However, even if she had been able to see him, the court would still have discounted her testimony because another woman didn't corroborate it. This, however, is a gross misreading of the Qur'an since in only one out of several instances of evidence-giving does the Qur'an say that two women can serve as witnesses to a financial transaction if a man is not available (see Qur'an 4:6, 4:15, 5:106-109).

The Intrusion of Cultural Practices

Many conversions to Islam, in many areas, all over the world, occurred far from centers of Muslim education, through the influence of Muslims not themselves well versed in the law of Islam. In family and property relationships, old attitudes and customs died hard if at all: thus in many circles of Muslim society, widow re-marriage was not permitted, divorcé frowned upon. In parts of the Punjab and in Uttar Pradesh (in India), Muslim women were denied the rights of inheritance, while among the Mappilas of Malabar (in Kerala, India) matrilineal rules of succession were followed. In Muslim societies, just like many others, female children are discriminated against from the moment of birth, for it is customary in Muslim societies, including Pakistan, to regard a son as a gift, and a daughter as a trial, from God. Therefore, the birth of a son is an occasion for celebration while the birth of a daughter calls for commiseration if not lamentation. Many girls are married when they are still minors, even though marriage in Islam is a contract and presupposes that the contracting parties are both consenting adults. Marriage in Islam cannot be contracted without the willingness and consent of both parties but a large number of Muslim girls and women are prohibited from exercising the right of free choice given to them by God. In Pakistan it is commonplace to refer to the husband as "majazi khuda" (god in earthly form) and regard him as his wife's gateway to heaven or hell and the arbiter of her final destiny. That such an idea can exist within the framework of a strictly monotheistic Islam which does not tolerate the attribution of divinity to any human being and which puts a strong emphasis on the moral accountability of each person represents both a profound irony and a great tragedy. Although the purpose of the Qur'anic legislation dealing with women's dress and conduct, was to make it safe for women to go about their daily business (since they have the right to engage in gainful activity as witnessed in 4:32 without fear of sexual harassment or molestation, a large number of Muslim girls and women, in most societies, are confined to the four walls of the house. Here it may be pointed out that according to the Qur'an, confinement to their homes was not a normal way of life for Muslim women but a punishment for "unchastity" (4:15-16).

In Saudi Arabia, women cannot vote, drive, or show their faces or talk with male non-relatives in public. While Islam at a normative level encourages women to be educated and guarantees their rights, the empirical reality is that the overwhelming majority of women in Pakistan have nothing more to look forward to other than the proverbial domesticated housewife. Barring a small elite cross-section in the upper echelons of society, most women do not have the luxury of even realizing that there is an alternative. The status of women throughout Muslim-majority countries remains a most disturbing fact. Cultural influence masked as religious authority constantly deems women second-class citizens. Female members of all class groups become part of a second-class constituency categorically denied their rights due to the male patriarchy. Patriarchal structures and values have been modernized in "neo-patriarchal" forms, and male domination of the family and state remains firmly ingrained. The neo-patriarchal state, using Islam as an ideology, has reintroduced restrictions by enforcing aspects of Muslim family law. Where does it say in the Qur'an that women cannot drive cars, as in Saudi Arabia? Or those women's faces must be covered or that they may not work? Muslim women are boldly challenging these traditions in many parts of the Muslim world, provoking a split between Islamic modernists and traditionalists on their place in society.

There is no term in the Qur'an, which indicates that childbearing is 'primary' to a woman. No indication is given that mothering is her exclusive role, in spite of the fact that, the capacity is essential to the continuation of human existence. This function becomes the primary only with regard to women since they are the only ones capable of doing so. This responsibility is neither biological nor inherent, but it is valuable. Such a perspective on 'qiwama,' as referred to in Qur'an 4:34, will allow men to truly fulfill their Caliph (trusteeship) on earth, as ordained by God upon human creation. Such an attitude will overcome the competitive and hierarchical thinking which destroys rather than nurtures.

The diversity of Muslim societies shows that Islam does not have a static or monolithic tradition. Islam has absorbed not only the practices and traditions of the two other monotheistic religions-Judaism and Christianity-from the region of its birth, but also other pre-Islamic practices and traditions from the geographic location in which it strove to survive and gain power as a cultural and political system. There is a strong correlation between the subordination of women in the Muslim world and the traditional and cultural understandings of Islam. There needs to be a strong distinction between religion and culture. Unfortunately, however, many Muslim countries have intertwined the two and have tied Islam to the corruption of its culture. Several customary practices that constitute violations of women's human rights in the region-honor crimes, stoning, female genital cutting, or virginity tests-have no Qur'anic basis, as experts and activists in the region point out. Moreover, the prevalence of such practices varies greatly among the countries in the region. The Qur'an does not mention female genital mutilation (FGM). Yet, it is a customary practice primarily found in Africa and those countries influenced by African culture. They have taken the religion to their own convenience and integrated their cultural practices with Islam to make it "Islamic". Although the practice was prevalent before Islam in African communities, and although the practice has continued in some Christian, Jewish and Muslim communities in Africa after the advent of Islam, it is often strongly associated with Islam because some African Muslim communities cite *hadith* as the basis for performing it, and because Westerners have mistakenly related FGM to Islam. In the Middle East, FGM is common in Egypt and Sudan; in the majority of Muslim communities, the practice was unheard of until it became a topic of media attention through the advocacy efforts of women's groups.

The flexibility of Islamic law is not accidental. It is an essential part of Qur'anic philosophy, because Islam was revealed for all people and for all times. Consequently, its jurisprudence must be capable of responding to widely diverse needs and problems. Furthermore, Islam was revealed gradually. This fact (as well as certain verses in the Qur'an) illustrates the divine recognition of the human difficulty in adjusting to sudden change. Hence, flexibility and evolution are inherent characteristics of the religion. It must be noted, however, that this flexibility has its limitations. It does not extend to the most fundamental tenets of Islam, such as the belief in the unity of God. Islam has been designed to be flexible enough to be interpreted in a variety of ways to cover a variety of cultures, times, contexts, individual personalities etc. however it can safely be said that there appears in the Qur'an, a concept that both men and women should dress (in public) in a manner that will de-accentuate their sexuality. In order to achieve equity of results, (both men and women wearing de-sexualized dress) women cover more, but this is merely a functional matter, it does not reflect on the value or status or ability to move freely in public society (24:30-31).

First, while the Qur'an distinguishes between the dress of women' and men, it does not suggest that modesty lies only in how women dress or behave. Rather, one half of its injunctions on modesty have to do with male dress and behavior and the other half with female; the two are mutually defining and inseparable (24:30-31). Secondly, neither in these verses nor in any others, does the Qur'an tie modesty of dress on the part of women to the idea that women are weak, unclean, sinful, or evil temptresses from whom men have to be protected. Nor does the Qur'an suggest that men have been endowed with an out of control libido that they can indulge in whatever way they want, a view that also puts the onus on women to veil and seclude themselves in order to protect themselves from barbaric and un-Islamic conduct on the part of men. In a truly Islamic society, men would not assume that morality lies in how women dress and not in how they themselves view women or behave towards them.

In the notes to the verse 24:30-31, Muhammad Asad writes in his 'The Message of the Qur'an': "Although the traditional exponents of Islamic law have for centuries been inclined to restrict the definition of "what may (decently) be apparent" to a woman's face, hands and feet-and sometimes even less than that-we may safely assume that the meaning of 'illa ma zahara minha' is much wider, and that the deliberate vagueness of this phrase is meant to allow for all the time-bound changes that are necessary for man's moral and social growth. The pivotal clause in the above injunction is the demand, addressed in identical terms to men as well as to women, to "lower their gaze and be mindful of their chastity": and this determines the extent of what, at any given time, may legitimately-i.e., in consonance with the Qur'anic principles of social morality-be considered "decent" or "indecent" in a person's outward appearance."[8]

Varying on the condition of the climate, heat, wind and dust, women however do cover their face in different regions. Eminent thinker and intellectual and former German diplomat Murad Wilfried Hofmann pointed out that veiling women totally is "a custom that is not Arab but Byzantine and Iranian in origin. Women of leisure and high social standing had obviously found out that they could underline their class by taking to the veil. Making them seem slightly remote, this device would make them appear more rare and precious. And of course, cultivating the veil simultaneously enhanced the Oriental proclivity for jealously. At any rate, it is a fact that at the time of Prophet and immediately afterwards, Muslim women were not totally veiled (and Bedouin women in Saudi Arabia are still not). Indeed, women pilgrims to Makkah must not be veiled because their predecessors, contemporaries of the Prophet, were not when they went out on pilgrimage"[9] Modern psychologists and public relations experts study face to ascertain the character and mental makeup of the individual. Face is the reflection of personality. Forcing women to totally veil or cover their face in fact tantamount to destruction of the personality of the women.

It must be said that the specific commands about seclusion (33:32-33) apply only to the Prophet's wives as the Qur'an says they are not like any other women, and the historical context of the verse demonstrates that the wives and in turn the Prophet were vulnerable from the attacks of his enemies and the hypocrites which entailed the extra-ordinary measures of protection applied to the wives of the Prophet: this does not apply to ordinary Muslim women. This passage then goes on to suggest that believing women should draw their veils over their bosom. The message of the verse is primarily concerned with covering the breast area ("juyubihinna"). If it were as fundamental for women to cover their face, forehand etc. this would have been specified in the verse, as comparatively, the Qur'an is extremely detailed in narrating which categories of people a woman can 'relax' and with whom she can maintain private dress.

'Purdah' system is neither of Islamic nor Arabian origin. It is of Zoroastrian Persian, and Christian Byzantine origin. It has nothing to do with the religion of Islam, and, for practical reasons, the great majority of Muslim women has never adopted it. So long as it was applied only to the women of great houses, who had plenty of space for exercise within their palaces and had varied interests in life. So long as it did not involve cruelty and did no harm to women, it could be regarded as unobjectionable from the standpoint as a custom of a period. But the moment it involved cruelty to women and did harm to them, it became manifestly objectionable, from the point of view of the *shari'ah,* which enjoins kindness and fair treatment towards women, and aims at the improvement of their status. It was never applicable to every class of society and when applied to every class, as now in India, it is a positive evil, which the Sacred Law can never sanction. The veiling of the face by women was not originally an Islamic custom. It was prevalent in many cities of the East before the coming of Islam, but not in the cities of Arabia. The 'purdah' system, as it now exists in India, was quite undreamt of by the Muslims in the early centuries, who had adopted the face-veil and some other fashions for their women when they entered the cities of Syria, Mesopotamia, Persia and Egypt. It was once a concession to the prevailing custom and was a protection to their women from misunderstanding by peoples accustomed to associate unveiled faces with loose character. Later on it was adopted even in the cities of Arabia as a mark of ('tamaddun') a word generally translated as 'civilization', but which in Arabic still retains a stronger flavor of its root meaning 'townsmanship' that is carried by the English word. It has never been a universal custom for Muslim women, the great majority of whom have never used it, since the majority of the Muslim women in the world are peasants who work with their husbands and brothers in the fields. For them the face-veil would be an absurd encumbrance.

Islam has set consent of both the woman and the man as a pre-condition of marriage. In the main classical schools of legal jurisprudence of Islam (*Hanafi* or *Shi'a* law, for example), a girl who has attained majority age is free to contract marriage without the consent of her father or any other relative and cannot be forced into a marriage by her male relatives. Accordingly, the practice of "forced marriages" in Muslim societies constitutes a clear violation of the basic premise of marriage as specified in the Qur'an. The temporary marriage, one of the various forms of marriage practiced in pre-Islamic Arabia, was incorporated into the Islamic legal school of Shi'a jurisprudence in Iran after the arrival of Islam. Yet, after the Iranian President, Ali Akbar Hashemi Rafsanjani, revived this extinct practice in 1990, Islamic religious right groups declared it "Islamic" and imported it to other Maliki or Sunni Muslim communities. In Sudan, where the majority of the population is *Sunni*, temporary marriage was introduced in the 1990s and even legalized in 1992.

Intellectual Interventions

The present day social stagnation; economic underdevelopment; scientific, technological, and industrial backwardness; political despotism; military weakness; cultural incompetence; and psychological demoralization of Muslims are all directly traceable and attributable to the frustration, obstruction, and holding back of the evolution and progress of society under the dead weight of what organized religion in alliance with the state imposed upon society under the guardianship of orthodox, traditionalist, and fundamentalist religion. Especially in denying women opportunities for personal growth and development and to play a social role in society and a measure of equality with men, the orthodoxy denied the whole society to evolve and grow. Inequality, inequity, and oppression in the home translated themselves into inequality, inequity, and oppression in society at large. As the husband and father denied freedom and dignity to wives and children, so the ruler and his ministers denied freedom and dignity to citizens and subjects. What is called 'Zulm' in Islam, meaning injustice, inequity, oppression, and more, became the most outstanding feature of Muslim society in history. Justice simply meant carrying out the punishments of the Shari'ah without any real concern for social, economic, and political justice. Our main concern is with the situation that resulted from the doctrinal and sociological genderization in Islam and the Muslim family and society.

The intellectual is an individual with a specific role in society that cannot be reduced simply to being a faceless professional, a competent member of class just going about her/his business. He is an individual endowed with a faculty for representing, embodying, articulating a message, a view, an attitude, philosophy or opinion to, as well as for, the public.[10] Edward W. Said clearly beseeches intellectuals to avoid the assimilated traps of "subaltern functionaries" and give their active consent to counter-hegemonic movements by representing the "weak and unrepresented"[11] This "art of representing" in a critical manner is crucial for the emancipation of Muslim women. As stated by Edward Said, "the purpose of the intellectual's activity is to advance human freedom and knowledge."[12]

The rereading of the Qur'an is a central project of some Muslim scholars, whose own religious convictions are spurring, renewed inquiries regarding women's role in the Islamic discourse. Fully aware of the high stakes in combating male dominated readings of the Qur'an, without any sanctioned interpretive authority, they are bravely attempting to break the monopoly on religious knowledge, traditionally assigned as a male epistemic privilege in Islam. While it seems inconclusive and controversial if Muslim women share the interpretive space with men, such a dialogue has never been more urgent, although it remains largely one-sided. Nevertheless, a concerted effort to provide fresh interpretations of the Qur'an in order to present a balanced, nuanced and ultimately more accurate rendition that illuminates its hidden depths and enhances the full relevance of the text is currently under way. The fundamental premise is to challenge laws and policies that are based on orthodox, literalist or misogynist interpretations and in doing so, allow women to seek liberation within an Islamic framework. Primarily, it is a matter of Muslim women seeking to exercise their God given rights within Islam, to use their full intellectual capacity (*aql*), and to remove the male bias of an inherently gender neutral faith. In her well-acclaimed book, 'Qur'an and Woman', Amina Wadud through the utilization of a hermeneutic methodology argues for a "holistic" interpretation as an alternative approach for interpreting Islamic teachings on the role of women in society and gender equality. Reflecting Fazlur Rahman's idea of a Qur'anic Weltanschauung, holistic interpretation "reconsiders the whole method of Qur'anic exegesis with regard to various modern social, moral, economic, and political concerns"[13] In addition to Wadud's hermeneutical model based on a continuous aspiration to understand "the whole-text", she concentrates on historical context as well as grammatical composition and syntactical analysis. In historical *shari'ah*, Muslim women are simply appendages to their men, first their fathers and brothers, later their husbands (and possibly, at the end of a long life, finally their sons). Within historical *shari'ah*, the situation is one where Muslim men exercise domination over women and enjoy a monopoly of political power and force cannot now be appropriately implemented because of its ability to accommodate modern understandings of gender relations and the status of women. Because it is male biased, a new interpretation needs to be arrived at-which it readily can-through a new methodology of Qur'anic interpretation.[14]

It is important to understand how the Qur'an focuses on woman as an individual because it treats the individual, whether male of female, in exactly the same manner: that is, whatever the Qur'an says about the relationship between God and the individual is not in gender terms. God does not distinguish on the basis of wealth, nationality, sex, or historical context, but on the basis of 'taqwa'. It is from this perspective then that all distinctions between woman and woman, between man and man, and between woman and man, must be analyzed.[15] Through her analysis of 'taqwa', Wadud builds her argument against the traditional delineation of roles between men and women and the hierarchal, pre-ordained patriarchal intellectual system. She demonstrates that emphasis should be placed on "human dignity, equal rights before the law and before God, mutual responsibility and equitable relations between humans" rather than on the complementarity of men and women, which can be easily misconstrued.[16] In advocating an "effective history" methodology, Wadud emphasizes the importance of reflexivity in advancing knowledge claims. In particular, she challenges the tendency to exalt past interpretations of Holy texts, and notes, "tafsir (historical and contemporary commentary) is man-made and, therefore, subject to human nuances, peculiarities, and limitations."[17] She then goes a step further by advancing a dynamic rather than static concept of the divine principle, stating that, 'divine will is always in the process of becoming, humankind can only hope to gain direction toward that will by likewise being in process, never complete.'[18] Therefore, Wadud not only challenges the methodological underpinnings of traditionalist Islam but also the ontological and epistemological foundations.

However, in order for reformists to achieve such intellectual empowerment, they need to procure what Michael Walzer characterizes as a "critical distance" from the dominating, gender-hegemonic Muslim *'ulema* (the learned, religious male leaders), who support and uphold a variety of traditional interpretations of religious texts and play a central role in determining social norms.[19] This intellectual distancing instigates and allows for what Gramsci framed as a process of differentiation and ideological transformation.[20]

Fazlur Rahman boldly poses his life-long question: "How does Islam as a religious, cultural, political, and ethical heritage deal with a modernizing and rapidly changing world?"[21] Through this process of reinterpretation, Rahman advocates a renewal of Islamic intellectualism as it relates to the moral improvement of humankind. Since, Muslims have long lacked a well-developed "Qur'anic Weltanschauung" that might help them differentiate that which is essential and relevant to the demands of a situation from that which is not. For Rahman, it was the intellectual ossification and replacement and replacement of scholarship based on original thought by one based on commentaries and super-commentaries, the closing of the gate of 'ijtihad', and basing of Islamic method solely on 'taqlid' (blind imitation) which led to the decline. He stresses the importance of knowing our pre-determinations and questioning our self-awareness of historical influences. However he also questions the reliability of "whose" effective history is being asserted: This means that the process of questioning and changing traditions-in the interests of preserving or restoring its normative quality in the case of its normative elements-can continue indefinitely and that there is no fixed or privileged point at which the predetermining effective history is immune from such questioning and then being consciously confirmed or consciously changed. This is what is required for an adequate hermeneutical method of the Qur'an.[22] By pointing out the impermanent, ever-changing, nature of reality, Rahman challenges traditional, static tendencies and stresses the need for the development of an Islamic dynamism or an Islamic theory of social evolution. Such a theory would be based in his "double" reform movement of historical context analysis and social and moral context analysis. The concept of 'Ijitihad' ("the effort to understand the meaning of a relevant text or precedent in the past, containing a rule, and to alter that rule by extending or restricting or otherwise modifying it in such a manner that a new situation can be subsumed under it by a new solution"), independent juristic interpretation, provides a notable example.[23] Due to its potentially boundless, individualistic nature, 'Ijitihad' could have been impossible to regulate. It contradicted the "absolute authority" of the consensus of learned male elders, 'ijma'. Rather than give free rein to individual interpretive efforts, jurists sought to restrict them and eventually proclaimed that the "doors of 'Ijitihad'" had been closed. Rahman notes that, ironically, closing the doors of 'Ijitihad' implied closing the doors of intellectual 'jihad' (striving) for both men and women. Ultimately, historical reflection and open debate were sacrificed to the fear of abandoning historical authenticity.

At the very outset of her monumental study on the patriarchal interpretation of the Qur'an and its possible alternatives, 'Believing Women', Asma Barlas, poses this question: "I am asking whether its teachings about God as well as about human creation, ontology, sexuality, and marital relationships challenge sexual inequality and patriarchy. Alternatively, do the teachings of the Qur'an allow us to theorize the equality, sameness, similarity, or equivalence, as the context demands, of women and men?"[24] She venture to show that it is possible "to answer the first set of questions-is the Qur'an a patriarchal or misogynistic text-in the negative, while [answering...] the second-can the Qur'an be a source for women's liberation-in the affirmative"[25] She convincingly argues that if "patriarchy is a continuum at one end of which are misrepresentations of God as Father, and of fathers as rulers over wives and children, and at the other end, the notion of sexual differentiation which is used to privilege males while Otherizing women, then the Qur'an's teachings are antipatriarchal."[26]

She goes on to analyze the difference between patriarchy and Tawhid thus: "The principle of Tawhid has the most far-reaching implications for how we understand God and God's Speech. Here, I wish to note only its implications for a theory of male rule/ privilege that underpins traditional patriarchies. In its simplest form, Tawhid symbolizes the idea of God's Indivisibility, hence also the indivisibility of God's Sovereignty; thus, no theory of male (or popular) sovereignty that pretends to be an extension of God's Rule/ Sovereignty, or comes into conflict with it, can be considered compatible with the doctrine of Tawhid; in fact, this is the axiomatic meaning of the term: that God is Absolute Sovereign and no one cam partake in God's Sovereignty. To the extent that theories of male rule over women and children amount to asserting sovereignty over both, and also misrepresent males as intermediaries between women and God, they do come into conflict with the essential tenets of the doctrine of Tawhid and must be rejected as theologically unsound. A reading of the Qur'an that suggests even subtle parallels between God and males, in their capacity as fathers or husbands must then be rejected as an insufferable heresy."[27] A reading that projects oppression, inequality, and patriarchy into the Qur'an must be viewed as a "failure in reading, since it attributes *zulm* against women to God" and we must be willing to re-examine an oppressive exegesis "in light of a more ecumenical definition of *zulm* which coheres with the totality of the Qur'an's teachings" about sexual equality.[28] Third, the Qur'an forbids us from using similitude (comparisons) for God because "God is Incomparable, hence

Unrepresentable, specially in anthropomorphic terms. The Qur'an's tireless and emphatic rejections of God's sexualization / engenderment as Father (male) confirm that God is not a male, or like one. However, if God is not male or like one, there also is no reason to hold that God has any special affinity with males" (by positing such an affinity, men claim God as their own and project onto God sexual partisanship).[29] Asma Barlas' discourse reflects in essence the basic idea that Islam if rightly understood reflects a philosophy of enlightenment and egalitarianism, that unsavory practices relegating women to second-class citizenship are not intrinsic to true Islamic values or to the *shari'ah* and never where Islamists diverge from this stance and reflect an apologetic approach to the status qua of women in Muslim societies today. Asma Barlas returns again to her central argument, i.e., not only that the Qur'an is not patriarchal, but also that "the teachings of the Qur'an are radically egalitarian and even anti-patriarchal"[30] Abraham leads to the conclusion that "Abraham begins by rejecting his father's *gods*, and then his father's *authority*, calling on his father to follow him instead, challenging the very core of father-right as it is structured in patriarchies."[31] Likewise, Abraham's submission to God's will (not association with God's authority), his designation as a prophet/*imam* (a gender-neutral term etymologically related to the words for community and mother), and the near sacrifice of his unnamed son (who himself accedes to God's will), all emphasize the authority of God and the rejection of patriarchy, in the sense of father-rule. The author finds that "both women and men have the same capacity for moral agency, choice, and individuality," arguing that the Qur'an "does not sexualize moral agency" and that it "appoints women and men each other's guides and protectors."[32]

Abou El-Fadl analyzes how patriarchal, authoritative voices of Islam (e.g. *ulema*) are "co-opted and reconstructed" to create an authoritarian discourse that in turn results in the co-optation of the Muslim populous.[33] This perpetuates a vicious cycle of consent and coercion until, as Abou El-

Fadl points out, there is a questioning in the patriarchal authoritativeness itself.

Towards Equity

A fundamental Qur'anic idea is that God vested all of humanity with a kind of divinity by making all human beings the viceroys of God on this earth (2:30). In particular, human beings are responsible, as God's vicegerents, for making the world more just. By assigning equal political rights to all adults, democracy expresses that special status of human beings in God's creation and enables them to discharge that responsibility. Three values are of particular importance: pursuing justice through social cooperation and mutual assistance (Qur'an 49:13, 11:119); establishing a non-autocratic, consultative method of governance; and institutionalizing mercy and compassion in social interactions (6:12, 54, 21:107, 27:77, 29:51, 45.20). So Muslims are duty bound to endorse the form of government that is most effective in helping them promote these values.

God gave human beings fundamental human rights so that they could actualize the destiny envisioned for them by their Creator. These fundamental human rights are so deeply rooted in our humanness that their denial or violation is tantamount to a negation or degradation of that which makes us human. Religion has been, and is being, used to legitimize all kinds of crimes and evils against women, not only in Pakistan or other Muslim countries, but globally. However, if one can separate the normative teachings of Islam from patriarchal interpretations, which reflect negative cultural assumptions, ideas and attitudes regarding women, Islam can become a most powerful means of women's empowerment.

Islam does not endorse the oppression of women and denial of their basic rights of equality and human dignity. We are saddened that religion has been used to justify cultural practices and values that regard women as inferior and subordinate to men and we believe that this has been made possible because men have had exclusive control over the interpretation of the text of the Qur'an. It is a tragedy for Muslims that we find no problems today with projecting our own ignorance, misogyny, obscurantism, and hatred onto the Qur'an, and thus onto God. Women are indeed persecuted in Muslim societies, as they are in other societies. The world community has a duty to ensure that women in all countries are granted the same human dignity. This must be done, however, from within a framework of respect and especially understanding of the religion that plays such a large role in Muslim culture and society. Islam must be understood as it truly is, not as it has been depicted in the press. Indeed, Muslim scholars must, also, share the blame for this distortion, for many have interpreted the religion through a patriarchal prism, which has resulted in practices that deny women the rights they were granted by Islam. Patriarchies are a form of 'zulm' because they transgress against women's rights by oppressing them. We should therefore be willing to re-examine those readings of the Qur'an that are oppressive to women.

Women's rights in Islam must be preserved by the world community and not simply brushed aside because of ignorance concerning how Islam, as a religion, treats women. Islam has been presented to the West in a negative fashion, both by governments in the Muslim world that deny fundamental rights to women, as well as by the Western press, which is quick to pin the blame on the religion itself rather than on the misogynists who use it as a pretext for persecution. These zealots in Muslim society have failed to understand the role of Islamic gradualism in ameliorating the status of women. Islam is supposed to adjust to all times, places, and circumstances, but this cannot occur without an embrace of the concerns of Muslim women. Unfortunately, negative stereotypes reinforced by distortions caused by a lack of understanding in the West-do not help the women who are harmed. The first step in helping Muslim women lies in identifying what forces actually govern their treatment. Islam, as a religion, is not the problem, and may in fact be part of the solution. Critics of the arguments raised here are gladly invited to refute the major points of the thesis outlined. What the Muslim world needs now is not conservatives who want to maintain the status quo, who wish to keep the unjust order intact, but radical intellectuals who can advance an egalitarian and equitable socio-political and economic order. Take this baton from here and run with it!

End Notes

1. Jeffrey Weeks, *Sexuality and its Discontents: Meanings, Myths and Modern Sexualities*, Routledge & Kegan Paul: London, 1985, p. 8.
2. Kate Millett, *Sexual Politics,* Doubleday: New York, 1970, p. 51.
3. Geoffrey Parrinder, *Sexual Morality in the World's Religions*, One World: Oxford, 1996, p. 226.
4. Zillah Eisenstein, *Feminism and Sexual Equality: Crisis in Liberal America*, New York: Monthly Review Press, 1984, p. 90.
5. Louise Marlow, *Hierarchy and Egalitarianism in Islamic Thought*, Cambridge University Press: Cambridge, 1977, pp. 93; 66.
6. Leila Ahmed, *Women and Gender in Islam, Historical Roots of a Modern Debate*, Yale University Press: New Haven, 1992.
7. Sachiko Murata, *The Tao of Islam: A Sourcebook on Gender Relationships in Islamic Thought*, State University of New York Press: Albany, 1992, p. 43.
8. Muhammad Asad, *The Message of the Qur'an*, Dar al-Andalus: Gibraltar, 1984, p. 538.
9. Murad Wilfried Hofmann, Journey to Islam, The Islamic Foundation: London, 1998, pp. 78-79.
10. Edward W. Said, *Representations of the Intellectual*, Pantheon Books: New York, 1994. p. 11.
11. Edward W. Said, *Ibid*, p. 22.
12. Edward W. Said, *Ibid*, p. 17.
13. Amina Wadud, *Qur'an and Woman*, Penerbit Fajar Bakti Sdn. Bhd: Kuala Lumpur, 1992, p. 3.
14. Amina Wadud, *Muslim Women as Citizens*, In "The Many Faces of Islam: Perspectives on a Resurgent Civilization", (Ed. Nissim Rejwan), University Press of Florida: Gainesville, 2000, p. 206-209.
15. Amina Wadud, *Ibid*, pp. 34, 37.

16. Amina Wadud, *Ibid*, p. 63.
17. Amina Wadud, *Ibid*, 2000, p. 11.
18. Amina Wadud, *Ibid*, 2000, p. 11.
19. Michael.Walzer, *Interpretation and Social Criticism*, Harvard University Press: Cambridge, 1987, p. 38.
20. Antonio.Gramscii, *Selections from the Prison Notebooks*, (Eds: Quintin Hoare and Geoffrey Nowell Smith), International Publishers: New York, 1971, p. 195.
21. Fazlur Rahman, *Islam and Modernity: Transformation of an Intellectual Tradition*, University of Chicago Press: Chicago, 1982, p. 4.
22. Fazlur Rahman, *Ibid*, p. 11.
23. Fazlur Rahman, *Ibid*, p. 8.
24. Asma Barlas, *Believing Women*, University of Texas Press: Austin, 2002, p. 1.
25. Asma Barlas, *Ibid*, p. 2.
26. Asma Barlas, *Ibid*, p. 204.
27. Asma Asma, *Ibid*, pp. 13-14.
28. Asma Barlas, *Ibid*, p. 14.
28. Asma Barlas, *Ibid*, pp. 14-15.
30. Asma Barlas, *Ibid*, p. 93.
31. Asma Barlas, *Ibid*, p. 111.
32. Asma Barlas, *Ibid*, p. 140.
33. Khaled Abou El-Fadl, *And God Knows His Soldiers: The Authoritative and Authoritarian in Islamic Discourses*, University Press of America: Lanham, 2001, p. 34.

Glossary

Abbasids: A major Muslim dynasty that flourished in Baghdad from 1258 CE.

Ablution Purification ritual every Muslim performs prior to the start of each daily prayer or voluntary prayer.

Adl: Justice, equilibrium.

Adam: Name given to the first created male (with Eve as female) in the creation story in the Jewish and Islamic scriptures. He has been interpreted over the centuries both literally (as an actual historical person) and symbolically (as generic humankind).

Adat: Custom

A.H: After Hijra; the zero point of the Islamic calendar corresponding to the Muslim Hijra (migration) from Makkah to Medina in July of the year 622 CE. Subsequent dates were calculated according to the lunar calendar, which differs from the Julian calendar by roughly 10 days each year.

Ahadith: Plural of hadith

Al-Hakam: Judge

Al-Halim: The Mild

Allah: The Arabic name of the Supreme Being, God. (Arab Christians use the same term to refer to God)

Al-Qawi: Powerful

Al-Rahman:: All Compassionate

Al-Wadud: The Loving-Kind

Andocentric: Dominated by or emphasizing masculine interests or a masculine point of view

Arab: A person whose origins may be traced to an Arab cultural, ethnic or linguistic heritage. Countries such as Saudi Arabia, Iraq, Syria, and Jordan have predominantly Arab populations. There are some countries in the Middle East, such as Iran or Turkey, whose populations are not predominantly Arab. Other countries such as Egypt, Libya, and Morocco have mixed Arab and North African populations. Arabs belong to many different religions. Throughout the Middle East, millions of Arab Christians and Arab Jews live peacefully with their Arab Muslim neighbors.

Arranged Marriage. A good thing if all parties are happy with the match. It is not permissible in Islam for a woman to be married against her will (see Qur'an 4:19, 4:21). Arranged marriage is more of a society's culture. Neither does Islam recommend it, nor is it nullified. However, there are several distortions and misperceptions in this regard. Any prospective bride or groom of legal age (Islam does not provide any specific definition of legal age; society has to establish it, if necessary) can initiate the marriage proposal for his or her own marriage. Islam neither requires nor idealizes that marriage proposal has to be initiated by someone other than the prospective bride/groom. If anyone (parents, guardians, relatives) thinks that it is his or her right to initiate the proposal, such right simply does not exist. Another related problem is bride/grooms not knowing or seeing each other. There are some cases when bride/grooms either haven't seen or don't see each other at all before their marriage. It is done for them. This is certainly against the Islamic guidance.

Asbâbun nuzûl: Reasons and events related to the revelation of Qur'anic verses

Ayesha: Daughter of Abu Bakr and one of the wives of Prophet Muhammad. Ayesha transmitted a large number of the Prophet's hadith, which were compiled by scholars in early Islamic history.

Azl: Coitus Interruptus (the male withdrawing from the female just short of climax) as a form of birth control. It is very unreliable. Prophet Muhammad allowed it as a method of contraception, but only with the permission of the wife.

Bay'ah: Oath of allegiance; an expression of political position.

Bukhari: The great scholar (810-870 CE.) who has collected about 7,275 ahadith (3,000 to 4,000 independent sayings) almost universally recognized as "next only to the Qur'an in authority".

Burqa: A particular form of dressing that covers women from head to toe

Caliph: Successor; vicegerent; the Imâm or the Muslim ruler

C.E: Common Era

Da'if: Weak; used for a faulty hadith

Darajah: Degree

Day of Judgment: Belief in the Day of Judgment is a basic article of faith in Islam. After God ends the present world and order of creation, a day will follow on which He will judge every person according to his or her intentions, deeds, and circumstances. Judgment by God is followed by punishment in Hell or eternal reward in Paradise.

Dhat: Divine essence

Dhimmi: A person belonging to the category of "protected people" within the Islamic state. Historically, Jews and Christians traditionally received this status due to their belief in One God, but others such as Zoroastrians, Buddhists and Hindus were also included. Dhimmis had full rights to practice their faith and implement their own religious laws within their communities. In exchange for a guarantee of protection and exemption from military service, 'dhimmis' paid a specific tax to the state, just as their fellow Muslim citizens did.

Diya: Blood-money (for wounds, killing etc.); compensation paid by the killer to the relatives of the victim (in unintentional cases).

Dowry: In the Indian Subcontinent, the practice of giving dowries to the bridegroom or his family is on the increase among Muslims, but this habit is hardly known elsewhere in the Muslim world, and is almost certainly a borrowing from other culture. According to the Qur'an (4:24-5), it is the man who has to give a wedding-gift, not the other way around, the idea being to make him take the marriage seriously, and to provide her with some financial security.

Empowerment: Empowerment is about people-both women and men-taking control over their lives: setting their own agendas, gaining skills, building self-confidence, solving problems and developing self-reliance. For women, it involves becoming aware of unequal power relationships and acquiring a greater voice in which to speak out against the inequality found in the home, workplace and community. It is only the individual that can empower her-or himself to make choices or to speak out.

Faskh: The dissolution of a contractual bond; annulment of a marriage open to the wife or her relatives, adjudicated by a third party

Fatwa: An opinion by a religious-legal scholar, mufti, on a point of law. Linguistically, 'fatwa' means an answer to a question; the question may be rhetorical or actual. The answer represents only the opinion of the person who offered it. In Islamic jurisprudence, 'fatwa' means the opinion of a scholar based on that scholar's understanding and interpretation of the intent of the sources of Islam, that scholar's knowledge of the subject in question, and the social milieu that produced the issue or question. The scholar's answer or 'fatwa' is not a binding rule; rather, it is a recommendation. The answer ('fatwa') may be opposed, criticized, accepted, or rejected. In addition, the answer ('fatwa') may itself become the subject of debate or questions. To consider a 'fatwa' issued by anyone as binding on all Muslims is a dangerous contemporary trend that merely stifles Islam's rich history of debate and dissent. Moreover, it would allow individuals to claim authority over others by virtue of their supposed knowledge of God's will. The purpose of a 'fatwa' is to offer an opinion, not to silence discourse.

Feminism: It is a theoretical perspective and a practice that criticizes social and gender inequalities, seeks to transform knowledge, and aims at women's empowerment. Feminists are scholars and activists challenging gender bias and working towards gender equality. Feminism holds the belief in what is usually referred to as sex equality, but what might be more clearly expressed in the negative, as opposition to sex hierarchy. Equality is such a difficult quantity to apply to human beings (because it is colloquially taken to mean sameness) that the point is served better by expression in terms of opposition to ranking one sex inferior or superior, or opposition to is one sex's categorical control of the rights and opportunities of the other.

Fiqh: Jurisprudence, the understanding and application of shari'ah

Fitrah: Pure nature; an Arabic term designating the innate, original spiritual orientation of every human being towards God the Creator. Muslims believe that God endowed everything in Creation with a tendency towards goodness, piety and God-consciousness, and that one's environment, upbringing, and circumstances serve to enhance or obscure this tendency.

Five Pillars of Islam: A term referring to the five core religious practices incumbent upon all Muslims, and which demonstrate a Muslim's commitment to God in word and in deed. They are as follows: Shahadah (declaration of faith), Salah (formal worship), Zakah (mandatory alms-giving tax), Sawm (fasting during Ramadan), and Hajj (pilgrimage to Makkah).

Gender: Refers to the social, biological and cultural codes used to distinguish between what a particular society considers 'masculine' or 'feminine' qualities, characteristics, attributes or behaviors. The definition of gender varies widely and is often the subject of exhaustive debates, although most agree that gender is largely socially and culturally determined. People are attributed a social and cultural gender that usually corresponds to their (assumed) biological sex and they are then expected to behave in accordance with gender roles as defined by their social and cultural context. Gender can be expressed in physical appearance, dress, mannerisms, speech patterns, and social behaviors and interactions.

Gender Analysis: Men and women both perform different roles. This leads to both genders having different experiences, knowledge, talents and needs. Gender analysis explores these differences so that policies, programs and projects can identify and meet the different needs of men and women. It studies the linkages between these and other factors in a larger cultural, economic, environmental, political and social context. Gender analysis entails the collection and analysis of sex-disaggregated data and gender-sensitive information about the population concerned. Sex-Disaggregated Data is data that is collected and presented separately on men and women and constitutes the first step in gender-sensitive planning for the overall promotion of gender equality. This information is necessary because the needs of women and girls are often overlooked within society and therefore warrant specific attention and analysis.

Gender Equality: Refers to people receiving equal opportunities to realize their full human potential, irrespective of gender. This can for example include equality in opportunities to take part in social, economic, cultural and political developments and benefiting equally from the results. It can also refer to the equality in protection of (human) rights. Gender equality does not necessarily mean 'identical conditions' or 'identical rights' as these conditions and rights may in themselves already be gendered. To achieve gender equality, recognition is needed that current social, economic, cultural, and political systems are gendered (i.e., constructed according to some preconceived 'gender roles') which lead to women being disadvantaged in all areas of life (gender bias). This pattern is further affected by other factors of oppression and inequality such as race, ethnicity, culture, immigration status, class, age, disability, sexuality, and gender identity. Gender equity requires the empowerment of women in their particular contexts, and taking their experiences and perspectives into account.

Gender Roles: Gender affects how people perceive themselves and others and how they expect themselves and others to behave, that is, either in a 'masculine' or 'feminine' manner. These gender roles are, mostly, learned and culturally and socially determined. They are also affected by factors such as education and economics. Therefore, gender roles can evolve over time. Gender roles and expectations are often identified as factors hindering gender equality. In practice gender roles usually affect women adversely in relation to many aspects of their life, such as family, socio-economic status, health, life expectation, independence, freedom and rights (gender bias).

Ghusl: Complete ablution

Hadd: A fixed punishment for certain crimes stipulated in the Qur'an

Hadith: A saying or tradition of the Prophet Muhammad. Bukhari and Muslim are the major collectors and compilers of Islamic traditions; and their collections are named after them.

Hanbali School: Fiqh School founded by Ahmad ibn Muhammad ibn Hanbal (780-855 C.E)

Hanifite School: Fiqh School founded by an-Numan ibn Thabit Abu Hanifa (700-67 C.E)

Haraj: Adversity

Hijrah: Migration; the act of leaving a place seeking sanctuary of freedom or worship in another or for any other purpose. Specifically, the 'hijrah' refers to the Prophet's journey from Makkah to Madinah in the twelfth year of his mission, corresponding to June 622 AC. The Islamic calendar begins from this event (A.H). The word hijrah means to leave a place to seek sanctuary or freedom from persecution or freedom of religion or any other purpose. Hijrah can also mean to leave a bad way of life for a good or more righteous way.

Honor killing: This may be defined as acts of murder in which a woman is killed for her actual or perceived immoral behavior. Such "immoral behavior" may take the form of marital infidelity, refusing to submit to an arranged marriage, demanding a divorce, flirting with or receiving phone calls from men, failing to serve a meal on time, or-grotesquely-"allowing herself' to be raped. The problem of "honor killings" is not a problem of morality or of ensuring that women maintain their own personal virtue; rather, it is a problem of domination, power and hatred of women who, in these instances, are viewed as nothing more than servants to the family, both physically and symbolically thousands of girls and women across the globe (although mostly centered in the Middle East) are murdered by male family members each year in the name of family honor. Honor killings are executed for instances of rape, infidelity, flirting or any other instance perceived as disgracing the family's honor, and the woman is then killed by a male relative to restore the family's name in the community. The allegation alone is enough to defile a man's or family's honor and is therefore enough to justify the killing of the woman. The men who commit the murder typically go unpunished or receive reduced sentences. Honor killings have been reported in Bangladesh, Brazil, Ecuador, Egypt, India, Israel, Italy, Jordan, Morocco, Pakistan, Sweden, Turkey, Uganda and the United Kingdom. It is actually a pre-Islamic, tribal custom stemming from the patriarchal and patrilineal society's interest in keeping strict control over familial power structures. This practice is deadly against Islam. Qur'an upholds the sanctity of human life, as it declares that killing one innocent human being is akin to killing the entire human race (see Qur'an 5:32, 6:151, 17:33).

Haram: Forbidden, prohibited. It is necessary to abstain from the acts, which are 'haram'.

Hawwa: Arabic name for Eve

Hijab: The Islamic dress code and related attitudes. Although the word "Hijab" is often used by English-speaking Muslims to refer specifically to the head covering, it in fact refers to the whole dress code.

Homosexuality: Every human being is a mixture of male and female traits, and sometimes a person is born with an inner balance unsuited to his or her physical characteristics. Nowadays, when the distinction between male and female character is being increasingly blurred in the population at large, homosexuality is becoming more socially acceptable to the secular mind. This is no justification, of course, for committing what is the most unnatural of all human acts; but Muslims have to recognize that a person struggling for self-control deserves approval. The increasing recognition of this tendency as a genetic rather than a purely moral problem holds out hope of medical treatment, as technology advances; and the day may not be far off when all human beings can benefit from the delights and responsibilities of parenthood (see Qur'an 26:165-6, 27:54-5).

Hudud Ordinance of Pakistan: The Ordinance states the maximum punishments for adultery (stoning), false accusation of adultery (80 lashes of the whip), theft (cutting off the right hand), drinking alcohol (80 lashes) and apostasy (death). The military ruler Muhammad Zia ul-Haq, under pressure from Islamic parties, imposed the ordinance on Pakistan in 1979. It makes no distinction between rape and adultery; thus women who are raped often end up being whipped while the rapists are exonerated. Girls who have reached the age of puberty are treated as adults. Worse, women are not allowed to give evidence on their own behalf. Among the high-profile injustices was the case in 1983 of 15-year-old Jehan Mina, raped by an uncle and his son. She was sentenced to ten years in prison and 100 lashes, reduced to three years and 15 lashes in view of her age. In 1985, a blind maidservant, Safia Bibi, was sentenced to a similar punishment. In both cases, the girl's pregnancy was used as proof that the sex act had been committed but the men were acquitted on the benefit of the doubt. Several women have been sentenced to death by stoning, the most recent being Zafran Bibi in Kohat in 2002, although that sentence was quickly overturned on appeal.

Ibn: Son; used before a proper name with the meaning: 'son of'

Ibadah: An act of religious devotion; all activities in obedience to God

Iddah: "Waiting period," usually three menstrual cycles, which a divorced woman must observe before she is free to remarry. The purpose is to establish whether she is pregnant with her ex-husband's child (if she were to remarry immediately, there is the possibility of doubt regarding the paternity of a child conceived immediately). If she is pregnant, her 'iddah lasts until the baby is born.

Ijtihad: The process of understanding and formulating legal and religious opinions from the Qur'an and hadith is known as interpretation ('Ijtihad'). It is believed by traditional Muslim scholars that somewhere between the tenth and the fourteenth century 'the gate of Ijtihad' was closed, preventing new interpretations of the Qur'an being recognized as shari'ah. Ijitihad was then replaced by the doctrine of 'taqlid' or imitation of the rules, norms and laws that already existed. The idea of 'taqlid' has made it difficult for reformists to challenge the shari'ah and formulate new interpretations of the Qur'an.

Ijma: An assembly of scholars held to formulate a consensus on a point of Islamic jurisprudence.

Ilm: Knowledge

Ilm al-rijal: Science of Hadith evaluation dealing with the scrutiny of the reporters.

Imam: Leader

Insa-n Al Kamil:" The perfect man"; in Sufism, it denotes the highest type of humanity.

Irshad: Instructional

Islam: In a general sense, submission to the Will of God and the religion propagated by all the Prophets of God; in the specific sense, the final statement of God's guidance to mankind revealed through Prophet Muhammad.

Isnad: The chain of transmitters of a hadith or other historical narration

Jahiliyyah: Ignorance; the time preceding the revelation of Islam

Jalbab: This is a long loose fitting garment worn by the Arabs.

Ja'iz: Lawful acts

Jalal: Majesty

Jamal. Beauty

Jihad: Literally, "struggle" or "striving". Although this word is often translated as "holy war," it has a broader meaning than warfare on the battlefield. Other meanings include endeavor, strain, effort, diligence, and struggle. Any act of striving to please God may be described as jihad.

Khadija: The first wife of Prophet Muhammad, and during her lifetime, the only one. Khadija was a successful businesswoman in Makkah who employed Muhammad as a merchant/trader because of his well-known reputation for honesty and trustworthiness. The Prophet was márried to her for 25 years until her death at the age of 65 in 619 C.E. They had two sons [both died in infancy] and four daughters together.

Khula: A method of dissolution of marriage initiated by woman by giving up some of her property to her husband.

Khutba: Speech

Madhhab: This Arabic word has a range of meanings including 'ideology', 'doctrine', 'creed', and 'movement'. In 'fiqh' it indicates one of the four major Schools of Law

Mahr: Bridal gift, bride-wealth, nuptial gift

Mahram: A man whom a woman may never marry because of the degree of closeness of the blood-relationship, i.e., father, brother, son, uncle, etc.

Maliki School: Fiqh School founded by Abd-Allah Malik ibn Anas (715-795 C.E)

The Marriage Contract: The marriage contract is a necessary component in the marital process. Marriage itself is actually considered to be a contract agreed upon by the two parties. It is a binding, permanent agreement that can only be broken through the process of divorce. It is the most important contract that most people execute throughout their lives. Since the marriage contract has such great significance, it should be chalked out with great care and diligence. The female partner can, naturally, make some legitimate demands to safeguard her interests.

Ma'ruf: Kindness, equity

Matn: Body part or substance of the hadith

Mihrab: Niche in the wall of a mosque, indicating the 'qiblah', the direction of Mecca.

Misogyny: Hatred of women

Mufti: Religious scholars who are capable of issuing 'fatwas'

Mulla: A religious scholar, who is generally ignorant of the world-affairs.

Muhammad: The Prophet and righteous person believed by Muslims to be the final messenger of God, whose predecessors are believed to include the Prophets Adam, Noah, Abraham, Moses, David, Jesus and others. Born in 570 C.E., Muhammad grew up to become a well-respected member of Makkan society. In 610 C.E., he received the first of many revelations that would eventually form the content of the Qur'an. Soon after this initial event, he was conferred prophethood and began calling people to righteousness and belief in One God. Muhammad died in 632 C.E., after successfully reestablishing the religion known as 'Islam' and providing Muslims with a model for ideal human behavior.

Muslim: Muslim in a general sense, anyone who submits to God (Allah). The term includes all Prophets of all times and their true followers. In the more specific sense, one who submits to God by following the religion of Islam.

Mutawatir: Literally meaning 'successive' and used as a technical term in hadith criticism to characterize a tradition with a very large number of reliable transmitters.

Mut'a: Temporary marriage. This is permitted by the law of the Ithna 'Asharis but not sanctioned elsewhere in Islam.

Nafs: Soul; Muslims believe that humans are ultimately spiritual beings, housed temporarily in a physical body. The nafs represents that core of each individual which exhibits an innate orientation towards God, called fitrah, and which passes into a different unknown realm upon a person's physical death in the present world. Natural instinctive knowledge has been given to each creature according to its characteristics (30:30, 87:2-3).

Nushuz: Desertion; when one deserts his/her spouse

P.B.U.H: These letters are abbreviations for the words: Peace Be Upon Him.

Quist: Justice. It is the real goal of Islam. It was the mission of every Prophet. It is the message of every Scripture. Qur'an abounds in references to justice. Its importance is emphasized in a whole variety of human situations, in inter-personal relationships, within the family, within the community, in the interaction between communities and nations, in the interface between the human being and nature (see for instance 4:58, 65, 105, 135; 7:29; 16:90 and 7:25). If any further proof is needed of the singular significance of justice in Islam it is provided by that well-known Qur'anic call, "Be just; that is next to piety" (5:8). Qur'an not only gives us an indication of what justice is, it also emphasizes over and over again our responsibility as human beings to strive relentlessly for justice. Upholding justice is undoubtedly one of the primary duties of human beings. It is a duty that he / she must perform as the bearer of God's trust, as the vicegerent of God, the Caliph of Allah.

Qur'an: The word Qur'an means "the recitation" or "the reading," and refers to the divinely revealed scripture of Islam. It consists of 114 chapters revealed by God to Muhammad over a period of twenty-three years. The Qur'an continues to be recited by Muslims throughout the world in the language of its revelation, Arabic, exactly as it was recited by Prophet Muhammad nearly fourteen hundred years ago. The Qur'an is viewed as the authoritative guide for human beings, along with the Sunnah of Muhammad. Translations of the Qur'an are considered explanations of the meaning of the Qur'an, but not the Qur'an itself.

Qiyas: Analogy; using analogies for the purpose of applying laws derived from the Qur'an and Sunnah to situations not explicitly covered by these two sources. Qiyas is one of the most important tools for interpreting and implementing the Shari'ah (Islamic Law).

Rawi: Transmitter of a report from Prophet Muhammad.

Sahabah: Companion or disciple of Prophet Muhammad.

Sahih: With reference to ahadith, sound, authentic.

Sahih Muslim: Recorded by Imam Muslim (817-875 C.E) is the second most authoritative collection, with 7,190 ahadith (4,000 independent sayings).

Seerah: Biographical sketch or study of Prophet Muhammad

Shafi'ite School: Fiqh School founded by Muhammad ibn Idris ash-Shafii (767-820 C.E)

Shari'ah: It is a system of Islamic law based on four main sources: the Qur'an (God's revelation to the Prophet Muhammad); the Sunnah, or actions of the Prophet, described in the Hadith; the 'Qiyas' or process of analogical reasoning based on understanding of the principles of the Qur'an or the Hadith; and the 'Ijma', or consensus of opinion among Islamic scholars.

Shi'a: Doctrine of the legitimacy, which holds that Ali ibn Abi Talib, the fourth of the Orthodox Caliphs, was the true spiritual and political heir of the Prophet Muhammad.

Shiite School: The most important Shiite school of law is the school of the Jafarites or Imamites. According to Shiite belief it goes back to the Sixth Imam Hazrat Ja'far As-Sadiq (700-765 C.E).

Shirk: Associating others with God's divinity; polytheism, or idolatry; literally, "association," this term is commonly used to mean association of something other than God with God. For Muslims, God is Absolute, Complete, and Self-Sufficient. To set anything alongside or in place of God, as Reality is to commit the sin of association, which is the only sin, that God does not forgive, according to the Qur'an. Thus, paganism, or even atheism, is viewed as expressions of shirk.

Shura: Consultation; consultative assembly

Sufi: One who endeavors to achieve direct inward knowledge of God through adherence to various spiritual doctrines and methods. These include repeatedly invoking the Divine Names and reciting other religious expressions, living an austere lifestyle, and participating in various spiritual gatherings usually formed around a spiritual master with the title shaykh. Historically, sufis have been grouped into organizations known as tariqahs.

Sunnah: A path, a way of life, all the traditions and practices of the Prophet Muhammad that have become models to be followed by Muslims. The Qur'an (word of God) and Sunnah of the Prophet (his traditions) are the fountainhead of Islam.

Sunni: Short for 'Ahl al-Sunnah wa al-Jama'ah', the people of the Sunnah and the community; the majority of Muslims belongs to this section.

Tabi'een: Peoples who have inherited the knowledge of the 'sahabah'

Tafsir: Exegetic interpretation; commentary on the Qur'an

Tajdeed: Renovation.

Tahkim: Arbitration. In cases where the spouses seem unable to resolve a dispute, it is useful to put it to arbitration. The Qur'an explains how this is to be done (4:35).

Talaq: Pronouncement of divorce by husband.

Taqlid: The blind acceptance of recognized scholars

Taqwa: Piety, God-consciousness

The Rightly Guided Caliphs: Those Caliphs who truly followed in the Prophet's footsteps are called 'The Rightly-Guided Caliphs' ('Al-Khulafa-ur Rashidun' in Arabic). They are the first four Caliphs: Abu Bakr (632-634 C.E), Umar (634-644 C.E), Uthman (644-656 C.E), and Ali (656-661 C.E). All four were among the earliest and closest companions of the Prophet. They lived simple and righteous lives and strove hard for the religion of God. Their justice was impartial, their treatment of others was kind and merciful, and they were one with the people-the first among equals. After these four, the later Caliphs assumed the manners of kings and emperors and the true spirit of equality of ruler and ruled diminished to a considerable extent in the political life of Muslims.

Tawhid: Monotheism, the Unity of God—the basic creed of Islam

Triple Talaq: A method of divorce, which gives a man the absolute right to divorce his wife by uttering, "I divorce thee" three times. He can do it by letter, telegram, telephone, fax, even by e-mail message. Quite apart from denying women's rights, the law has inherent absurdities. For example, the moment a Muslim male utters 'talaq, talaq, talaq', his wife becomes unlawful to him, even if he has uttered those words under coercion, in a fit of rage or a drunken state, and regrets his utterance the very next moment. Such a method of divorce is entirely against the method prescribed by the Qur'an (6:21, 4:34-35, 65:1, 2:231-232, 2:236-241). Unfortunately, however, this is being practiced by many Muslims and is, even, sanctioned by the Muslim Personal Law prevalent in India.

Ulema: Scholars, or learned men, especially applied to religious scholars, but often used also for those learned in other branches of knowledge

Umma: Community or nation, the body of Muslims as a distinct and integrated entity

Unisex: The Prophet had a great respect for natural gender distinctions. He did not like men who try to resemble women, and women who try to resemble men (Bukhari).

Usul: The sources of law, viz., the Qur'an, the Sunnah, consensus, and analogical reasoning; principles, origins.

Usul al fiqh: Principles of Islamic jurisprudence, philosophy of law; the methodology of deriving laws from the sources of Islam and of establishing their juristic and constitutional validity.

Urf: Custom. In the absence of anything to the contrary, derivation of the law from the common and approved mores of a people is acceptable to Islam

Wahy: Revelation

Wajib: Obligatory

Wali: Legal guardian

Yin and yang: According to traditional Chinese philosophy, yin and yang are the two primal cosmic principles of the universe. Yin is the passive, female principle. Yang is the active, masculine principle. According to legend, the Chinese emperor Fu Hsi claimed that the best state for everything in the universe is a state of harmony represented by a balance of yin and yang. Unsurprisingly, legend has it that, according to Fu Hsi, true harmony requires yang to be dominant. It's just the nature of things. In classical Chinese, yin and yang refer to the shady and sunny sides of a hill or valley.

Zawj: Husband or wife; couple or mate

Zina: Adultery, unlawful sexual intercourse

Zulm: Oppression, wrongdoing, and negation of legitimate rights.

Appendix

Qur'anic References on Woman

This is a compilation of the verses of the Qur'an that have the word "woman" in them:

2:49. And when We delivered you from Pharaoh's people, who subjected you to severe torment, killing your sons and sparing your women, and in this there was a great trial from your Lord.

2:221. And do not marry the idolatresses until they believe, and certainly a believing maid is better than an idolatress woman, even though she should please you; and do not give (believing women) in marriage to idolaters until they believe, and certainly a believing servant is better than an idolater, even though he should please you; these invite to the fire, and God invites to the garden and to forgiveness by His will, and makes clear His communications to men, that they may be mindful.

2:222. And they will ask thee about [woman's] monthly courses. Say: "It is a vulnerable condition. Keep, therefore, aloof from women during their monthly courses, and do not draw near unto them until they are cleansed; and when they are cleansed, go in unto them as God has bidden you to do. Verily, God loves those who turn unto Him in repentance and He loves those who keep themselves pure.

2:228. And the divorced women should keep themselves in waiting for three courses; and it is not lawful for them that they should conceal what God has created in their wombs, if they believe in God and the last day; and their husbands have a better right to take them back in the meanwhile if they wish for reconciliation; and they have rights similar to those against them in a just manner, and the men are a degree above them, and God is Mighty, Wise.

2:231. And when you divorce women and they reach their prescribed time, then either retain them in good fellowship or set them free with liberality, and do not retain them for injury, so that you exceed the limits, and whoever does this, he indeed is unjust to his own soul; and do not take God's communications for a mockery, and remember the favour of God upon you, and that which He has revealed to you of the Book and the Wisdom, admonishing you thereby; and be careful (of your duty to) God, and know that God is the Knower of all things.

2:232. And when you have divorced women and they have ended—their term (of waiting), then do not prevent them from marrying their husbands when they agree among themselves in a lawful manner; with this is admonished he among you who believes in God and the last day, this is more profitable and purer for you; and God knows while you do not know.

2:235. And there is no blame on you respecting that which you speak indirectly in the asking of (such) women in marriage or keep (the proposal) concealed within your minds; God knows that you win mention them, but do not give them a promise in secret unless you speak in a lawful manner, and do not confirm the marriage tie until the writing is fulfilled, and know that God knows what is in your minds, therefore beware of Him, and know that God is Forgiving, Forbearing.

2:236. There is no blame on you if you divorce women when you have not touched them or appointed for them a portion, and make provision for them, the wealthy according to his means and the straitened in circumstances according to his means, a provision according to usage; (this is) a duty on the doers of good (to others).

2:241. And for the divorced women (too) provision (must be made) according to usage; (this is) a duty on those who guard (against evil).

2:282. O you who believe! When you deal with each other in contracting a debt for a fixed time, then write it down; and let a scribe write it down between you with fairness; and the scribe should not refuse to write as God has taught him, so he should write; and let him who owes the debt dictate, and he should be careful of (his duty to) God, his Lord, and not diminish anything from it; but if he who owes the debt is unsound in understanding, or weak, or (if) he is not able to dictate himself, let his guardian dictate with fairness; and call in to witness from among your men two witnesses; but if there are not two men, then one man and two women from among those whom you choose to be witnesses, so that if one of the two errs, the second of the two may remind the other; and the witnesses should not refuse when they are summoned; and be not averse to writing it (whether it is) small or large, with the time of its falling due; this is more equitable in the sight of God and assures greater accuracy in testimony, and the nearest (way) that you may not entertain doubts (afterwards), except when it is ready merchandise which you give and take among yourselves from hand to hand, then there is no blame on you in not writing it down; and have witnesses when you barter with one another, and let no harm be done to the scribe or to the witness; and if you do (it) then surely it will be a transgression in you, and be careful of (your duty) to God, God teaches you, and God knows all things.

3:14. The love of desires, of women and sons and hoarded treasures of gold and silver and well bred horses and cattle and tilth, is made to seem fair to men; this is the provision of the life of this world; and God is He with Whom is the good goal (of life).

3:41. He said: My Lord! Appoint a sign for me. Said He: Your sign is that you should not speak to men for three days except by signs; and remember your Lord much and glorify Him in the evening and the morning.

3:42. And when the angels said: O Mary! Surely God has chosen you and purified you and chosen you above the women of the world.

3:61. But whoever disputes with you in this matter after what has come to you of knowledge, then say: Come let us call our sons and your sons and our women and your women and our near people and your near people, then let us be earnest in prayer, and pray for the curse of God on the liars.

4:1 O people! be careful of (your duty to) your Lord, Who created you from a single being and created its mate of the same (kind) and spread from these two, many men and women; and be careful of (your duty to) God, by Whom you demand one of another (your rights), and (to) the ties of relationship; surely God ever watches over you.

4:3 And if you fear that you cannot act equitably towards orphans, then marry such women as seem good to you, two and three and four; but if you fear that you will not do justice (between them), then (marry) only one or what your right hands possess; this is more proper, that you may not deviate from the right course.

4:4 And give women their dowries as a free gift, but if they of themselves were pleased to give up to you a portion of it, then eat it with enjoyment and with wholesome result.

4:7 Men shall have a portion of what the parents and the near relatives leave, and women shall have a portion of what the parents and the near relatives leave, whether there is little or much of it; a stated portion.

4:15 And as for those who are guilty of an indecency from among your women, call to witnesses against them four (witnesses) from among you; then if they bear witness confine them to the houses until death takes them away or God opens some way for them.

4:19 O you who believe! It is not lawful for you that you should take women as heritage against (their) will, and do not straiten them order that you may take part of what you have given them, unless they are guilty of manifest indecency, and treat them kindly; then if you hate them, it may be that you dislike a thing while God has placed abundant good in it.

4:24 Also (prohibited are) women already married, except those whom your right hands possess: Thus hath God ordained (Prohibitions) against you: Except for these, all others are lawful, provided ye seek (them in marriage) with gifts from your property, desiring chastity, not lust, seeing that ye derive benefit from them, give them their dowers (at least) as prescribed; but if, after a dower is prescribed, agree Mutually (to vary it), there is no blame on you, and God is All-knowing, All-wise.

4:25 And whoever among you has not within his power ampleness of means to marry free believing women, then (he may marry) of those whom your right hands possess from among your believing maidens; and God knows best your faith: you are (sprung) the one from the other; so marry them with the permission of their masters, and give them their dowries justly, they being chaste, not fornicating, nor receiving paramours; and when they are taken in marriage, then if they are guilty of indecency, they shall suffer half the punishment which is (inflicted) upon free women. This is for him among you who fears falling into evil; and that you abstain is better for you, and God is Forgiving, Merciful.

4:32 And do not covet that by which God has made some of you excel others; men shall have the benefit of what they earn and women shall have the benefit of what they earn; and ask God of His grace; surely God knows all things.

4:34 The men are to support the women by what God has gifted them over one another and for what they spend of their money. The upright women who are attentive, and keep private the personal matters for what God keeps watch over. As for those women from whom you fear a desertion, then you shall advise them, and abandon them in the bedchamber, and separate from them; if they obey you, then do not seek a way over them; God is High, Great.

4:43 O you who believe! Do not go near prayer when you are Intoxicated until you know (well) what you say, nor when you are under an obligation to perform a bath—unless (you are) travelling on the road—until you have washed yourselves; and if you are sick, or on a journey, or one of you come from the privy or you have touched the women, and you cannot find water, betake yourselves to pure earth, then wipe your faces and your hands; surely God is Pardoning, Forgiving.

4:75 And what reason have you that you should not fight in the way of God and of the weak among the men and the women and the children, (of) those who say: Our Lord! Cause us to go forth from this town, whose people are oppressors, and give us from Thee a guardian and give us from Thee a helper.

4:127 And they ask you a decision about women. Say: God makes known to you His decision concerning them, and that which is recited to you in the Book concerning female orphans whom you do not give what is appointed for them while you desire to marry them, and concerning the weak among children, and that you should deal towards orphans with equity; and whatever good you do, God surely knows it.

4:178 They ask you for a decision of the law. Say: God gives you a decision concerning the person who has neither parents nor offspring; if a man dies (and) he has no son and he has a sister, she shall have half of what he leaves, and he shall be her heir she has no son; but if there be two (sisters), they shall have two-thirds of what he leaves; and if there are brethren, men and women, then the male shall have the like of the portion of two females; God makes clear to you, lest you err; and God knows all things.

5:5. This day are (all) good things made lawful for you. The food of those who have received the Scripture is lawful for you, and your food is lawful for them. And so are the virtuous women of the believers and the virtuous women of those who received the Scripture before you (lawful for you) when ye give them their marriage portions and live with them in honour, not in fornication, nor taking them as secret concubines. Whoso denieth the faith, his work is vain and he will be among the losers in the Hereafter.

5:6. O ye who believe! When ye rise up for prayer, wash you faces, and your hands up to the elbows, and lightly rub your heads and (wash) your feet up to the ankles. And if ye are unclean, purify yourselves. And if ye are sick or on a journey, or one of you cometh from the closet, or ye have had contact with women, and ye find not water, then go to clean, high ground and rub your faces and your hands with some of it. Allah would not place a burden on you, but He would purify you and would perfect His grace upon you, that ye may give thanks.

7:127. And the chiefs of Pharaoh's people said: Do you leave Moses and his people to make mischief in the land and to forsake you and your gods? He said: We will slay their sons and spare their women, and surely we are masters over them.

7:141. And when We delivered you from Pharaoh's people who subjected you to severe torment, killing your sons and sparing your women, and in this there was a great trial from your Lord.

9:67. The hypocritical men and the hypocritical women are all alike; they enjoin evil and forbid good and withhold their hands; they have forsaken God, so He has forsaken them; surely the hypocrites are the transgressors.

9:68. God has promised the hypocritical men and the hypocritical women and the unbelievers the fire of hell to abide therein; it is enough for them; and God has cursed them and they shall have lasting punishment.

9:71. And (as for) the believing men and the believing women, they are guardians of each other; they enjoin good and forbid evil and keep up prayer and pay the poor-rate, and obey God and His Apostle; (as for) these, God will show mercy to them; surely God is Mighty, Wise.

9:72. God has promised to the believing men and the believing women gardens, beneath which rivers flow, to abide in them, and goodly dwellings in gardens of perpetual abode; and best of all is God's goodly pleasure; that is the grand achievement.

12:28. So when he saw his shirt rent from behind, he said: Surely it is a guile of you women; surely your guile is great:

12:30. And women in the city said: The chiefs wife seeks her slave to yield himself (to her), surely he has affected her deeply with (his) love; most surely we see her in manifest error.

12:50. And the king said: Bring him to me. So when the messenger came to him, he said: Go back to your lord and ask him, what is the case of the women who cut their hands; surely my Lord knows their guile.

14:6. And when Moses said to his people: Call to mind God's favour to you when He delivered you from Pharaoh's people, who subjected you to severe torment, and slew your sons and spared your women; and in this there was a great trial from your Lord.

24:4 And those who accuse free women then do not bring four witnesses, flog them, (giving) eighty stripes, and do not admit any evidence from them ever; and these it is that are the transgressors,

24:12. Why did not the believing men and the believing women, when you heard it, think well of their own people, and say: This is an evident falsehood?

24:23. Surely those who accuse chaste believing women, unaware (of the evil), are cursed in this world and the hereafter, and they shall have a grievous chastisement.

24:26. Bad women are for bad men and bad men are for bad women. Good women are for good men and good men are for good women

24:31. And say to the believing women that they cast down their looks and guard their private parts and do not display their ornaments except what appears thereof, and let them wear their head-coverings over their bosoms, and not display their ornaments except to their husbands or their fathers, or the fathers of their husbands, or their sons, or the sons of their husbands, or their brothers, or their brothers' sons, or their sisters' sons, or their women, or those whom their right hands possess, or the male servants not having need (of women), or the children who have not attained knowledge of what is hidden of women; and let them not strike their feet so that what they hide of their ornaments may be known; and turn to God all of you, O believers! so that you may be successful.

24:60. And (as for) women advanced in years who do not hope for a marriage, it is no sin for them if they put off their clothes without displaying their ornaments; and if they restrain themselves it is better for them; and God is Hearing, Knowing.

27:55. What! Do you indeed approach men lustfully rather than women? Nay, you are a people who act ignorantly.

28:4. Surely, Pharaoh exalted himself in the land and made its people into parties, weakening one party from among them; he slaughtered their sons and let their women live; surely he was one of the mischief-makers.

28:23. And when he came to the water of Madyan, he found on it a group of men watering, and he found besides them two women keeping back (their flocks). He said: What is the matter with you? They said: We cannot water until the shepherds take away (their sheep) from the water, and our father is a very old man.

28:25. Then one of the two women came to him walking bashfully. She said: My father invites you that he may give you the reward of your having watered for us. So when he came to him and gave to him the account, he said: Fear not, you are secure from the unjust people.

33:32. O wives of the Prophet! You are not like any other of the women; If you will be on your guard, then be not soft in (your) speech, lest he in whose heart is a disease yearn; and speak a good word.

33:35. Surely the men who submit and the women who submit, and the believing men and the believing women, and the obeying men and the obeying women, and the truthful men and the truthful women, and the patient men and the patient women and the humble men and the humble women, and the almsgiving men and the almsgiving women, and the fasting men and the fasting women, and the men who guard their private parts and the women who guard, and the men who remember God much and the women who remember—God has prepared for them forgiveness and a mighty reward.

33:49. O you who believe! When you marry the believing women, then divorce them before you touch them, you have in their case no term which you should reckon; so make some provision for them and send them forth a goodly sending forth.

33:52. It is not allowed to you to take women afterwards, nor that you should change them for other wives, though their beauty be pleasing to you, except what your right hand possesses and God is Watchful over all things.

33:55. There is no blame on them in respect of their fathers, nor their brothers, nor their brothers' sons, nor their sisters' sons nor their own women, nor of what their right hands possess; and be careful of (your duty to) God; surely God is a witness of all things.

33:58. And those who speak evil things of the believing men and the believing women without their having earned (it), they are guilty indeed of a false accusation and a manifest sin.

33:59. O Prophet! Say to your wives and your daughters and the women of the believers that they let down upon them their over-garments; this will be more proper, that they may be known, and thus they will not be given trouble; and God is Forgiving, Merciful.

33:73. So God will chastise the hypocritical men and the hypocritical women and the polytheistic men and the polytheistic women, and God will turn (mercifully) to the believing women, and God is Forgiving, Merciful.

40:25. So when he brought to them the truth from Us, they said: Slay the sons of those who believe with him and keep their women alive; and the struggle of the unbelievers will only come to a state of perdition.

47:19. So know that there is no god but God, and, ask protection for your fault and for the believing men and the believing women; and God knows the place of your returning and the place of your abiding.

48:5. That He may cause the believing men and the believing women to enter gardens beneath which rivers flow to abide therein and remove from them their evil; and that is a grand achievement with God

48:6. And (that) He may punish the hypocritical men and the hypocritical women, and the polytheistic men and the polytheistic women, the entertainers of evil thoughts about God. On them is the evil turn, and God is wroth with them and has cursed them and prepared hell for them, and evil is the resort.

48:25. It is they who disbelieved and turned you away from the Sacred Mosque and (turned off) the offering withheld from arriving at its destined place; and were it not for the believing men and the believing women, whom, not having known, you might have trodden down, and thus something hateful might have afflicted you on their account without knowledge—so that God may cause to enter into His mercy whomsoever He pleases; had they been widely separated one from another, We would surely have punished those who disbelieved from among them with a painful punishment.

57:12. On that day you will see the faithful men and the faithful women—their light running before them and on their right hand—good news for you today: gardens beneath which rivers flow, to abide therein, that is the grand achievement.

57:13. On the day when the hypocritical men and the hypocritical women will say to those who believe: Wait for us, that we may have light from your light; it shall be said: Turn back and seek a light. Then separation would be brought about between them, with a wall having a door in it; (as for) the inside of it, there shall be mercy in it, and (as for) the outside of it, before it there shall be punishment.

57:18. Surely (as for) the charitable men and the charitable women and (those who) set apart for God a goodly portion, it shall be doubled for them and they shall have a noble reward.

60:10. O you who have attained to faith! Whenever believing women come unto you, forsaking the domain of evil, examine them, [although only] God is fully aware of their faith; and if you have thus ascertained that they are believers, do not send them back to the deniers of the truth, [since] they are [no longer] lawful to their erstwhile husbands, and these are [no longer] lawful to them. Nonetheless, you shall return to them whatever they have spent [on their wives by way of dower]; and [then, O believers,] you will be committing no sin if you marry them after giving them their dowers. On the other hand, hold not to the marriage-tie with women who [continue to] deny the truth, and ask but for [the return of] whatever you have spent [by way of dower] just as they [whose wives have gone over to you] have the right to demand [the return of] whatever they have spent. Such is God's judgment: He judges between you [in equity] for God is all-knowing, wise.

60:12. O Prophet! When believing women come to you giving you a pledge that they will not associate aught with God, and will not steal, and will not commit fornication, and will not kill their children, and will not bring a calumny which they have forged of themselves, and will not disobey you in what is good, accept their pledge, and ask forgiveness for them from God; surely God is Forgiving, Merciful.

65:1. O Prophet! When you divorce women, divorce them for their prescribed time, and calculate the number of the days prescribed, and be careful of (your duty to) God, your Lord. Do not drive them out of their houses, nor should they themselves go forth, unless they commit an open indecency; and these are the limits of God, and whoever goes beyond the limits of God, he indeed does injustice to his own soul. You do not know that God may after that brings about reunion.

65:4. And (as for) those of your women who have despaired of menstruation, if you have a doubt, their prescribed time shall be three months, and of those too who have not had their courses; and (as for) the pregnant women, their prescribed time is that they lay down their burden; and whoever is careful of (his duty to) God He will make easy for him his affair.

71:28. My Lord! Forgive me and my parents and him who enters my house believing, and the believing men and the believing women; and do not increase the unjust in aught but destruction!

85:10. Surely (as for) those who persecute the believing men and the believing women, then do not repent, they shall have the chastisement of hell, and they shall have the chastisement of burning.

End Notes

1. These verses are excerpted from the following English translations of the Qur'an:
   (A) The Holy Qur'an, Translator: Shakir, M.H.; Tahrike Tarsile Qur'an, Inc New York, 1998.
   (B) The Holy Qur'an: English Translation of the Meaning and Commentary, Translator: Yusuf Ali; Complex for printing of the Holy Qur'an: Madinah, 1992.
   (C) The Message of the Qur'an, Translator: Muhammad Asad: Dar al-Andalus: Gibraltar, 1984.
   (D) The Meaning of the Glorious Qur'an, Translator: Marmaduke Pickthall: Taj Co: Lahore, 1974.

For Further Study

Abdel Rahim Omran, Family Planning in the Legacy of Islam, Routledge: London, 1992.

Abdu Rahman I. Doi, Woman in Shariah (Islamic Law), Islamic Book Center: Lahore, 1996.

Abdul Hamid A. AbuSulayman, Chastising Wives: Qur'anic Verse Re-Interpreted, IIIT: Herndon, 2002.

Abu'l A'la Mawdudi, Purdah and the Status of Woman in Islam, Islamic Publications: Lahore, 1979.

Abul Fadl Mohsin Ebrahim, Abortion, Birth Control and Surrogate Parenting, American Trust Publications: Indiana, 1989.

Abedlwahab Bouhdiba, Sexuality in Islam, Routledge & Kegan Paul: London, 1985.

Afkhami, M & Friedl, E (Eds.), Muslim Women & The Politics Of Participation Syracuse University Press: Syracuse, 1997.

Aftab Hussain, Status of Women in Islam, Law Publishing Company: Lahore, 1987.

Afzal-ur-Rahman, Role of Muslim Woman in Society, Seerah Foundation: London, 1986.

Aisha B.Lemu, Fatima Heeren, Woman in Islam, The Islamic Foundation: London, 1976.

Aisha Bewley, Islam: the Empowering of Women, Ta-Ha Publishers: London, 1999.

Al-Ghazali, Marriage and Sexuality in Islam, University of Utah Press: Salt Lake City, 1984.

Aliah Schleifer, Motherhood in Islam, Islamic Academy: Cambridge, 1986.

Al-Mughni, H., Women in Kuwait: The Politics of Gender, Al Saqi Books: London, 1993.

Ameer Ali, The Legal Position of Women in Islam, University of London Press London, 1912.

Amina Wadud, Qur'an and Woman: Rereading the Sacred Text from a Woman's Perspective, Oxford University Press: New York, 1999.

Amira El Azhary Sonbol (ed.), Women, the Family, and Divorce Laws in Islamic History, Syracuse University Press: Syracuse, 1984.

Anis Ahmed, Women and Social Justice: An Islamic Paradigm, Islamabad Institute of Policy Studies: Leicester, 1996.

Anne Sofie Roald, Women in Islam, The Western Experience, Routledge: New York, 2001.

Annemarie Schimmel, My Soul Is a Woman: the Feminine in Islam, Continuum: New York, 1997.

Anwar Hekmat, Women and the Koran, Prometheus Books: Amherst, N.Y., 1999.

Arvind Sharma (Ed.), Feminism and World Religions, State University of New York Press: Albany, 1998.

Arvind Sharma (Ed.), Women in World Religions, State University of New York Press: Albany, 1987.

Asghar Ali Engineer, The Qur'an, Women, and Modern Society, Sterling Publishers: New Delhi: 1999.

Asghar Ali Engineer, The Rights of Women in Islam, Sterling Publishers: New Delhi, 1992.

Asma Barlas, Believing Women: Sex/Gender, Patriarchy and the Qur'an, University of Texas Press: Austin, 2002.

Ava Muhammad, The Myths and Misconceptions of The Role of Women in Islam, Uprising Communications: Atlanta, 1996.

Azizah al-Hibri (Ed.), Women and Islam, Pergamon Press: New York, 1982.

Azza M. Karam, Women, Islamism and the State: Contemporary Feminisms in Egypt, Macmillan Press: London, 1998.

Barbara Aswad, and Barbara Bilge, Family and Gender among American Muslims. Temple University Press: Philadelphia, 1996.

Barbara Freyer Stowasser, Women in the Qur'an, Traditions, and Interpretation, Oxford University Press: Oxford, 1994.

Basim Musallam, Sex and Society in Islam: Birth Control Before The Nineteenth Century. Cambridge University Press: Cambridge, 1983.

Bingham, M. W., & Gross, S. H., Women in Islam, Glenhurst Publications: St. Louis, 1980.

Brooks G., Nine Parts of Desire: The Hidden World of Islamic Women, Hamish Hamiliton: London, 1995.

Carol Tarvis, The Mismeasure of Woman, Simon and Schuster: New York, 1992.

Denise Spellberg, Politics, Gender, and the Islamic Past: The Legacy of A'isha Bint Abi Bakr, Columbia University Press: New York, 1994.

Deniz Kandiyoti (Ed.), Women, Islam, and the State, Temple University Press: Philadelphia, 1991.

Dr. Kaukab Siddique, Liberation of Women thru Islam, American Society for Education and Religion: Maryland, 1990.

El Alami & Hinchcliffe, Islamic Marriage and Divorce Laws of the Arab World, Kluwer Law International: London, 1996.

Elizabeth Warnock Fernea, In Search Of Islamic Feminism: One Woman's Global Journey, Doubleday: New York, 1998.

Fadwa. El Guindi, Veil: Modesty, Privacy, and Resistance, Oxford University Press: New York, 1999.

Fakhro, M. A., Women at Work in the Gulf: A Case Study of Bahrain, Kegan Paul International: London, 1990.

Fathi Osman, Muslim Women in the Family and the Society, Minaret Publications: New York, 1998.

Fathi Osman, Sharia in Contemporary Society: The Dynamics of Change in the Islamic Law, Multimedia Vera International: Los Angeles, 1994.

Fatima Mernissi, Beyond the Veil: Male-Female Dynamics in Muslim Society, Al Saqi Books: London, 1985.

Fatima Mernissi, Can We Women Head A Muslim State? Women's Resource and Publications Centre: Lahore, 1991.

Fatima Mernissi, Islam and Democracy: Fear of the Modern World, Addison-Wesley Publishing Company Mass, 1992.

Fatima Mernissi, The Forgotten Queens of Islam, Univesity of Minnesota Press: Minneapolis, 1997.

Fatima Mernissi, The Veil and the Male Elite: A Feminist Interpretation of Women's Rights in Islam. Addison-Wesley: New York, 1991.

Fatima Mernissi, Women and Islam: An Historical and Theological Enquiry, (Trans. Mary Jo Lakeland), Basil Blackwell: Oxford, 1991.

Fatima Mernissi, Women in Moslem Paradise, Kali for Women: New Delhi, 1986.

Fatima Mernissi, Women's Rebellion and Islamic Memory, Zed Books: London, 1996.

Fatima Mernissi, Women's Rebellion and Islamic Memory, Zed Books: N.J, 1996.

Fazlur Rahman, Islam and Modernity: Transformation of an Intellectual Tradition, The University of Chicago Press: Chicago, 1982.

Freda Hussain (ed.), Muslim Women, Croom Helm: London, 1984.

Geraldine Brooks, Nine Parts of Desire: The Hidden World of Islamic Women, Anchor Books/ Doubleday: New York, 1994.

Haifaa Jawad, The Rights of Women in Islam: An Authentic Approach MacMillan Press: London, 1998.

Haleh Afshar (Ed.), Women in the Middle East: Perceptions, Realities and Struggles for Liberation, St. Martin's Press: New York, 1993.

Hallaq, W, A History of Islamic Legal Theories: An Introduction to Sunni Usul al-fiqh, Cambridge University Press: Cambridge, 1997.

Hammuda 'Abd al Ati, The Family Structure in Islam, A.T.P: Indianapolis, 1977.

Hasan Turabi, Women in Islam and Muslim Society, Milestones Publications: London, 1991.

Hassan Hathout, Islamic Perspectives in Obstetrics & Gynecology, University of Kuwait: Safat, 1986.

Herbert L. Bodman, and Nayereh Tohidi, Women in Muslim Societies: Diversity within Unity, Lynee Rienner Publishers: London, 1998.

Huda Al-Khattab, Bent Rib: A Journey Through Women's Issues In Islam, Ta-Ha: London, 1997.

Ibn Sa'd Christi, Muhammad, The Women of Madina, Ta Ha Publishers: London, 1997.

Jamal Badawi, Status of Women in Islam, A.T.P: Indianapolis, 1992.

Jan Goodwin, Price of Honor: Muslim Women Lift the Veil of Silence on the Islamic World, Little Brown & Co: London, 1994.

Jean Holm, John Bowker (Eds.), Women in Religion. Pinter Publishers: London, 1994.

John L. Esposito, Women in Muslim Family Law, Syracuse University Press, 1982.

John Stratton Hawley (Ed), Fundamentalism and Gender, Oxford University Press: New York, 1994.

Judith E. Tucker, In the House of the Law: Gender and Islamic Law in Ottoman Syria and Palestine, University of California Press: Berkeley, 1998.

Kabbani,H & Bakhtiar L, Encyclopaedia Of Muhammad's Women Companions & The Traditions They Related. ABC International Group: Chicago 1998.

Karin Ask, and Marit Tjomsland (Ed.), Women and Islamization:, Contemporary Dimensions of Discourse on Gender Relations, Berg: New York, 1998.

Leila Ahmed, Women and Gender in Islam: Historical Roots of a Modern Debate, Yale University Press: New Haven, 1992.

Leonard Grob, Riffat Hassan and Haim Gordon, (Eds.), Women's and Men's Liberation: Testimonies of Spirit, Greenwood Press: New York, 1991.

Lila. Abu-Lughod (Ed.), Remaking Women: Feminism and Modernity In The Middle East, Princeton University Press: New Jersey, 1998.

Louis Lamya' al Faruqi, Women, Muslim Society and Islam, A.T.P: Indianapolis, 1988.

Mahnaz Afkami (Ed.), Faith and Freedom: Women's Human Rights in the Muslim World, Syracuse University Press: Syracuse, 1995.

Mahnaz Afkhami, Erika Friedl (Eds.), Muslim Women and the Politics of Participation, Syracuse University Press: Syracuse, 1997.

Mai Yamani (Ed.), Feminism and Islam: Legal and Literary Perspectives, Ithaca Press: Berkshire, 1996.

Margot Badran, Feminists, Islam, and Nation: Gender and the Making of Modern Egypt, Princeton University Press: Princeton, 1995.

Metcalf, B. D. (Trans), Perfecting Women: Maulana Ashraf 'Ali Thanawi's 'Bihisti Zewar', University of California Press: California, 1992.

Miriam Cooke, Women Claim Islam: Creating Islamic Feminism Through Literature, Routledge: New York, 2001.

Moghissi, H: Feminsim & Islamic Fundamentalism: The Limits Of Postmodern Analysis. Zed Press: London, 2002.

Mona AlMunajjid, Women in Saudi Arabia Today, Macmillan Press Basingstoke, 1997.

Murtada Mutahhari, The Rights of Women in Islam, World Organization for Islamic Services: Tehran, 1981.

Musallam, B.F, 'Sex and Society in Islam, Cambridge University Press: Cambridge, 1983.

Naila Minai, Women In Islam: Tradition and Transition in the Middle East, Seaview Books: New York, 1981.

Nawal El Saadawi, The Hidden Face of Eve: Women in the Arab World Beacon Press: Boston: 1980.

Nicholas Awde (Ed), Women in Islam: An Anthology from the Qur'an and Hadiths, St. Martin's Press: New York, 2000.

Patricia Jeffery, and Amrita Basu (Eds), Appropriating Gender: Women's Activism and Politicized Religion in South Asia, Routledge: New York, 1997.

Paula M Cooey, William R. Eakin, and Jay B. McDaniel (Eds.), After Patriarchy: Feminist Transformations of the World Religions, Maryknoll: New York, 1991.

Rafiq Zakaria, Women and Politics in Islam: The Trial of Benazir Bhutto, New Horizons Press: New York, 1990.

Raoul Mortley, Womanhood: The Feminine In Ancient Hellenism, Gnosticism, Christianity, And Islam, Delacroix Press: Sydney, 1981.

Ronald, A.S, Women In Islam: The Western Experience. Routledge, London, 2001.

Rosemary Radford Ruether, Sexism and God-Talk: Toward A Feminist Theology, Beacon Press: Boston, 1993.

Sachiko Murata, The Tao of Islam: A Sourcebook on Gender Relationships in Islamic Thought, State University of New York Press: Albany, 1992.

Safia Iqbal, Woman and Islamic law, Al-Asr Publications: Delhi, 1988.

Saliba, T., Allen, C. and Howard, J.A. (Eds,) Gender, Politics and Islam, Chicago: University Press: Chicago, 2002.

Serenity Young (Ed.), An Anthology of Sacred Texts by and About Women, Crossroad: New York, 1993.

Shaheen Sardar Ali, Gender and Human Rights in Islam and International Law: Equal Before Allah, Unequal Before Man? Kluwer Law International: Hague, 2000.

Sheikh Abrar Husain, Marriage Customs among Muslims in India, Sterling Publishers: Bombay, 1990.

Sheikh Nefzawi, The Perfumed Garden (tr. Richard Burton). Vermont: Park Street Press: Rochester, 1989.

Soffran, L., Women in the United Arab Emirates, Croom Helm: London, 1980

Soraya Altork, Women in Saudi Arabia: Ideology and Behavior Among the Elite, Columbia University Press: New York, 1986.

Theresa Saliba (Ed.), Gender, Politics, and Islam, Orient Longman: Hyderabad, 2005.

Wahiduddin Khan, Woman Between Islam And Western Society, Islamic Centre: New Delhi, 1995.

Welchman. L (Ed.), Women's Rights &Islamic Family Law, Zed Books: New York, 2004.

Wiebke Walther, Women in Islam: from Medieval to Modern Times, Markus Wiener: Princeton, 1993.

Yamani,M (Ed:), Feminism & Islam. New York Univ. Press: New York, 1996.

Yusuf Da Costa, The Honor of Women in Islam,: Islamic Supreme Council of America: Washington, DC, 2002.

Yvonne Yazbeck Haddad, John L. Esposito (Eds.), Islam, Gender and Social Change Oxford University Press: New York, 1998.

Zakaria Bashier, Muslim Women in the Midst of Change, Islamic Foundation: Leicester, 1980.

Zeenat Shoukat Ali, Marriage and Divorce in Islam, Jaico: Bombay, 1987.

Zeenat Shoukat Ali, The Empowerment of Women in Islam, Feffer & Simon: Mumbai, 1997.

Ziba Mir-Hosseini, Islam and Gender: The Religious Debate in Contemporary Iran, Princeton University Press: New Jersey, 1999.

Resources from the Web-world

http://www.arches.uga.edu/~godlas/Islamwomen.html

http://www.ccmw.com/

http://www.islam21.net/pages/keyissues/key2-6.htm

http://www.islamfortoday.com/women.htm

http://www.islamicgarden.com/page1050.html

http://www.kamilat.org

http://www.karamah.org/

http://www.maryams.net/index.html

http://www.muslimedia.com/archives/movement00/wom-move.htm

http://www.mwlusa.org/welcome.html

http://www.sistersinislam.org.my

http://www.wluml.org

Index

M

N

O

P

Q

R